I0113114

Toward Leader Democracy

Toward Leader Democracy

Jan Pakulski and András Körösényi

ANTHEM PRESS
LONDON · NEW YORK · DELHI

Anthem Press
An imprint of Wimbledon Publishing Company
www.anthempress.com

This edition first published in UK and USA 2013
by ANTHEM PRESS
75–76 Blackfriars Road, London SE1 8HA, UK
or PO Box 9779, London SW19 7ZG, UK
and
244 Madison Ave. #116, New York, NY 10016, USA

First published in hardback by Anthem Press in 2012

Copyright © Jan Pakulski and András Körösényi 2013

The moral right of the authors has been asserted.

Front cover image © 2012 iStockphoto.com/SaulHerrera

All rights reserved. Without limiting the rights under copyright reserved above,
no part of this publication may be reproduced, stored or introduced into
a retrieval system, or transmitted, in any form or by any means
(electronic, mechanical, photocopying, recording or otherwise),
without the prior written permission of both the copyright
owner and the above publisher of this book.

British Library Cataloguing-in-Publication Data
A catalogue record for this book is available from the British Library.

Library of Congress Cataloging-in-Publication Data
The Library of Congress has cataloged the hardcover edition as follows:
Pakulski, Jan, 1950–
Toward leader democracy / Jan Pakulski and András Körösényi.
p. cm.
Includes bibliographical references and index.
ISBN 978-0-85728-388-7 (hardback : alk. paper)
1. Democracy. 2. Political leadership. I. Körösényi, András. II. Title.
JC423.P247 2011
321.8–dc23
2011042504

ISBN-13: 978 1 78308 064 9 (Pbk)
ISBN-10: 1 78308 064 7 (Pbk)

This title is also available as an ebook.

To our families in Budapest and Hobart:
Erzsi, Orsi, Bori, Zofia, Magda and Peter

CONTENTS

LIST OF TABLES AND FIGURES

Tables

Figures

PREFACE

In a rapidly globalising world, it is perhaps not unusual that two scholars representing different disciplines and working independently might come to similar conclusions. Yet, this recently discovered similarity of diagnoses – one made from the bustling metropolis of Budapest at the heart of newly democratised Central Europe, another from small antipodean Hobart, the southernmost tip of Australia – strikes us as quite remarkable. After all, we had quite different formative experiences, embraced different disciplinary traditions, and observed the world from quite different perspectives. In spite of these differences, both of us conclude that contemporary democracy, as seen from both sides of the globe, drifts in the direction of 'leader democracy'. This joy of a shared conclusion has been translated into a book that combines the insights of a political sociologist and a political scientist-cum philosopher. While the burden of writing fell mostly on Jan Pakulski, the key ideas are shared, and we shoulder jointly the responsibility for the arguments in the book. Jan Pakulski has developed the main arguments concerning the changing shape of contemporary democracy, whilst András Körösényi can take credit for articulating the model of 'leader democracy'. Both share the view that the Weberian–Schumpeterian theoretical insights on which 'leader democracy' rests are relevant today, though these insights need some dusting and rejigging – which is quite natural considering their age.

While the book is a product of two classical and two contemporary minds, it draws on numerous other insights and sources of inspiration. Above all, we should mention our colleagues from the International Sociological Association/ International Political Science Association (ISA/IPSA) research group in political sociology and elites, especially John Higley and Heinrich Best, as well as many other members of the 'elite circle' of scholars. We acknowledge their inspiration and critical feedback. The University of Tasmania and the Hungarian Academy of Science funded our explorations, together with ANZSOG and an Australian Research Council Discovery Grant DP1096203 and a Hungarian Scientific Research Fund Grant OTKA K–72656. We are most grateful for this support. The Anthem Press editors prodded us tactfully about deadlines and gave us valuable editorial advice. And finally we would like to thank our families, who tolerated our obsessive conversations and endless reclusive periods of redrafting – we are grateful for their patience, and dedicate this book to them.

Jan Pakulski and András Körösényi
Hobart and Budapest, September 2011

Chapter 1

THE NEW 'NEW POLITICS'

Let us start with three vignettes from three key political events on three continents: the French presidential elections of 2007, the 2007 Australian federal elections, and the American presidential elections of 2008.

The May 2007 presidential elections in France broke a number of new grounds. First, both major contenders were selected – intentionally and openly – on the grounds of their popularity and mass appeal. Nicolas Sarkozy, a son of Hungarian migrants, was selected by the Gaullists for his personal appeal and his combative populist style. He was initially adored (together with his ex-model celebrity partner Carla Bruni) by the mass media. Ségolène Royal, the Socialist contender, was described as 'the sexiest political candidate' and 'conviction politician' with strong popular support, especially among women. The electoral campaign was dominated by TV debates accompanied by websites and blogs, talkbacks and ubiquitous 'hand shaking and baby kissing'. As never before, these public appearances shaped candidates' images as popular leaders. The prolonged 'American-style' personality-focused campaign attracted a record number of voters (84 per cent turnout), with Nicolas Sarkozy winning 53 per cent of votes in the second round. Sarkozy's success was widely attributed to four factors: the strength of his personality, skillfully projected through the media; the celebrity style of presentation enhanced by his flamboyant manners and glamorous wife; his capacity to transcend ideological and party divisions, combined with an emphasis on 'a new start'; and his image as a 'strong leader', 'man of action' and self-made politician who came from outside the political establishment. Sarkozy extolled the virtues of commitment, equality of opportunity and national solidarity. He overshadowed Ségolène Royal mainly by force of personality, by transcending the ideological and partisan agenda and stressing pragmatic egalitarianism. Following the election, Sarkozy enjoyed a nearly yearlong honeymoon of high popularity. But his shine started to fade in 2008. Three years on, he has lost most of the initial public support and trails in public opinion polls well behind the new opposition candidate.

In November 2007, Australian voters elected a new federal political leader – Kevin Rudd – after an 18-month-long 'marathon campaign' that focused almost entirely on the characters of the leadership contenders. His rival was a long-term incumbent and leader of the conservative Coalition, John Howard. Rudd promised a change not so much in policy directions as in leadership style. The campaign was conducted under the slogan of 'good leadership' (incumbent Howard) versus 'new leadership' (challenger Rudd), experience versus innovation, tough stance versus pragmatic flexibility. Rudd emerged as a winner by projecting an image of himself as an innovative, energetic and forceful – but also inclusive and pragmatic – technocrat. He promised to reform the Australian economy and society, promote reconciliation with indigenous Australians, and – thanks to his widely publicised expertise in Mandarin –develop Australia's regional links. John Howard was beaten badly, losing not only the majority in Parliament, but also his seat. His refusal to make space for his loyal successor (Peter Costello) made him look arrogant, and his support for the unpopular policies of American president George W. Bush was seen as out of step with the public. By contrast, Kevin Rudd enjoyed a honeymoon of popularity unparalleled in its strength, and he wrestled from his party the right to appoint all cabinet ministers. But his popularity faded rapidly and dramatically after some policy blunders and, a few months before the 2010 poll, the panic-stricken Labor Party engineered a leadership replacement by his deputy, Julia Gillard. From the very start, Gillard became the object of intense and almost exclusive media attention. She won the 2010 election by the narrowest possible margin and was forced into a coalition with independents and Greens. Her 'weak leadership' was widely criticised, and her policy initiatives were greeted with cynicism by the opposition. Gillard's approval rating subsequently declined to record lows.

The 2008 presidential campaign in the United States focused almost exclusively on the leadership contenders, Barack Obama and John McCain, and their relation to the 'Bush legacy'. After a record 22-month campaign focusing on the personalities of the main contenders, which cost a record $1.5 billion and secured near-record levels of voter turnout, Barack Obama emerged as the winner. In the final stage of the long and exhausting campaign, conducted under the shadow of the financial crisis (interpreted widely as a 'Bush legacy'), the contest moved to the digital domain, where personalised Facebook and Twitter appeals gave Obama a winning edge. In the final round, the American voters faced a choice of youthful vigour or maturity, intelligence or experience, stirring oratory or crafty argumentation, hope or fear. The image of a youthful committed reformer, a stirring orator, the first African American at the apex of political power appeared more powerful than the image of a 'safe-n-sure', 'tried but tired' heroic fighter. According to commentators, McCain's defeat resulted from his close ties to the 'Washington establishment', his age and health and, most importantly, his inability to inspire public trust. He was seen as tainted by the mistakes of the previous administration and unable to sever his links with Bush. Obama's victory was described as a triumph of a determined and charismatic leader. It generated an unprecedented sense of hope and very high, often unrealistic expectations of instantaneous change ('Yes, we can'). His political honeymoon lasted longer than the initial popularity of Sarkozy and Rudd. But three years into his first term, Obama's star has faded. A weak economy (high unemployment) and aggressive critique by the Republican opposition keep his approval ratings low. He has been accused of weakness in providing political leadership, confronting his opponents and promoting promised reforms.

* * *

These three vignettes illustrate the central theme of this book: a new and unexpected turn of 'new politics' in advanced democracies towards 'leader democracy', a type of politic, democratic regime and an elite configuration in which political leaders play a central role in providing a 'democratic linkage' between the rulers and citizenry. Leaders establish this 'linkage' by winning electoral contests in which they project a strong leadership image and prove successful in attracting mass confidence and votes. Contemporary democratic leaders win such electoral contests by appealing for support mainly through the mass media. They not only stand at the centre of public attention as personifications of democratic popular will, but also actively shape this will, mould the popular preferences, define national goals, and symbolise national aspirations. Armed with the authorisation of an electoral mandate, they also play an increasingly central role in integrating the political elite, reshaping the programmes of their parties, and redirecting national policies. If they fail to fulfil the widespread public expectation of firm leadership and determination, their popularity fades fast.

The diagnoses and anticipations of 'new politics' – variously described as 'life', 'movement', 'issue' and 'preoccupation' politics – were only partly accurate. They correctly highlighted the underlying party–voter dealignment, the waning of cleavage parties, declining ideology, and the appearance of the 'ideologically mixed categories', such as New Fiscal Populists, Progressivists, New Labourists, Neoliberals and Neoconservatives. However, they failed to identify another important 'novelty' – the ascendancy of political leaders/ reformers, celebrities and innovators as the key carriers of the new political idiom. These leaders were taking the political place of party directorates, and they declared if not a war, at least a clear dislike, towards the bureaucratic establishments.

Some elements of this trend are old and well known, some are new. Among the new is a combination of the centrality of political leaders – both as high-profile cultivators of the elite–mass linkage and as central elite figures – with a public expectation of such prominence and centrality. In order to cultivate the elite–mass linkage and to sustain public trust, successful democratic leaders have to *lead*, rather than merely *head* their governing teams. Public expectation of such firm leadership translates either into the popularity innovative leaders – those who have a strong image, 'clear vision', a reassuring plan of action and who display a will and determination to realise their plan – or popular disappointment with inadequate leadership. The latter results in a political backlash and swift withdrawal of mass support. If the elected leaders/heads start buckling under pressure, changing their minds, breaking their promises, pandering to sectional interests and following poll-driven agendas, they are dismissed as mere populists and 'weather vanes'.

When elected to the presidency in 2008, Barack Obama was hailed as a visionary reformist determined to confront the Washington 'establishment'. When his popularity waned three years later, he was accused of empty rhetoric, compromising too much and failing to fulfil the leadership expectations; as one critic put it: 'we need a good leader, not a good lawyer'. Similarly, in Australia Julia Gillard suffered a strong political backlash in 2010–11 because of what has been seen as her weak (or lacking) leadership. Her critics stress her lack of vision, lack of consistency and lack of determination.

Such disaffection is perhaps inevitable. All political leaders, especially those in democratic polities, start on a high note and end as disappointments, if not failures. Max Weber attributed this waning of mass popularity to the inevitable decline of charisma – mass devotion to leaders based on recognition of their 'gift of grace', their exceptional and highly cherished qualities. Charismatic domination is fickle and difficult to sustain. The modern 'oratory charisma' is no exception to this rule as it does not last long. Weber blamed the need for continuous 'proving' of the 'gift of grace' as the main reason for this fragility. Joseph Schumpeter attributed it to the very nature of entrepreneurial innovation – it soon 'self-exhausts' by becoming a standard expectation and 'routine'. This is why mass confidence, charismatic legitimacy and the accompanied broad support acquired during the electoral contest inevitably weaken.

This inevitable decline of public trust in leaders afflicts both democratic and nondemocratic leadership. Both are vulnerable to decline and both fall victims of opportunism, patronage and corruption. But democracy allows for regular renewals in the form of competitive electoral tests. Such tests allow for a prompt removal of leaders whose performance weakens and whose charisma wanes. Failing leaders are 'recalled' and replaced by more trusted ones, thus replenishing mass confidence and consent.[1] This is why both Weber and Schumpeter placed their faith not only in able leaders, but also in electoral selection and in competitive pressures inherent in modern democratic procedures. This is also why they feared 'leaderless' democracy – a democracy that is 'administered' or 'headed', rather than 'led'.

This fact alone should place the 'leadership proper' firmly within the democratic theory. Yet, as we note throughout, it seldom does. Leaders – including democratically elected and 'mandated' leaders – are looked at with suspicion by most contemporary democratic theorists and many political commentators. While good leaders are highly praised, leadership is looked upon with suspicion (as a threat to democracy, rather than its essential ingredient) and is considered as a 'blind spot' in democratic theory (Kane and Patapan 2008; Kane et al. 2009), in spite of the old tradition of democratic leadership studies (Weber 1919; Bryce 1921; Schumpeter 1943; Blondel 1987).

There seems to be some good and bad reasoning behind this suspicion. The good – or at least understandable – reasons have to do with a residual fear of autocratic leaders, such as Mussolini, Hitler and Stalin, who presided over the destruction of democratic (or democratising) regimes in the first half of the twentieth century. Such antidemocratic leadership left a deep legacy of fear and suspicion among theorists and lay public alike. This suspicion seems reinforced by two popular confusions: one between democratic and nondemocratic leadership; another between 'good' or successful leadership on the one hand, and solely prominent or strong leadership on the other. The first distinction seems more obvious: democratic leadership is based on mass trust acquired through open electoral competition and victory; nondemocratic leadership is not. Democratic leaders are subject to public critiques and electoral 'recalls'; nondemocratic leaders are not. Consequently, it is hard to confuse Mandela with Mugabe, or Sarkozy with Gaddafi. The second distinction is less obvious, and therefore more vulnerable to confusion. Prominent leaders – who, as argued here, are increasingly appearing in liberal-democratic regimes, and who are increasingly welcomed by the public – are not necessary 'good' or 'successful' in the sense of devising effective and successful policies and outcomes. They often fail to bring good governance (honest, transparent, effective etc.) and deliver the expected mass prosperity,

---

1 The autocrats, needless to add, are not placed under such competitive pressures – they gag the opposition and critics, and cannot be removed that easily; they often cling to power even when the initial public confidence withers away and they have become mere 'heads of government'.

political stability, national pride and individual dignity. For example, Silvio Berlusconi and George W. Bush were prominent but unsuccessful democratic leaders – and both faced the consequences of their leadership failures. But this does not mean that they failed to lead or that they ever ceased to act as prominent (even narcissistic) media performers and top executives of the state. By contrast, Franklin D. Roosevelt, Charles de Gaulle, Gerhard Schröder, Nelson Mandela, Bob Hawke and Lee Kuan Yew are widely regarded as examples of both prominent *and* successful leaders, who not only maintained a strong elite–mass linkage, but also performed well. Their policies left their nations more prosperous, stable and stronger, with enhanced senses of dignity and pride. The point we make is that 'leader democracy' can spawn prominent and successful ('good') leaders, as well as prominent and unsuccessful ('poor') leaders. It paves the way for political leadership success, as well as political leadership failures. In that respect, 'leader democracy' does not differ from other forms of democracy.[2]

Another corollary is that we focus on a descriptive-explanatory rather than a normative model of democracy. While normative approaches, like deliberative and neoclassical models, aim to set up substantive criteria for the normative justification of democracy, 'leader democracy', applying minimalist criteria and definitions of democracy, aims at improving our understanding how democratic politics actually works (Schumpeter 1942/1987, 150, 269; Przeworski 1999, 23). In other words, this model belongs to, and is deployed within, the Weberian–Schumpeterian tradition as an empirical-descriptive account of democratic politics. It does not advocate the ideal or best form of democracy, and does not even address the perfectibility of it. Unlike deliberative and neoclassical concepts, 'leader democracy' respects and accepts the forms of representative democracy that evolved historically in modern Western nation-states, and it is sceptical about the feasibility of democracy – applied at a national level – adopting direct forms, that is, operating as self-rule by the people. The model is also more realistic in its anthropological assumptions; it does not assume, for example, that citizens are autonomous and rational in their views – the assumptions shared by the deliberative and neoclassical rivals.

'Leader democracy' might be criticised for playing down the normative aspects of democracy. However, in our view, this is more a virtue than a vice. As a principally explanatory-analytical model, 'leader democracy' does not need more normative justification than Weber and Schumpeter provide, and that we reassert. As Adam Przeworski (1999, 23, 44) notes, Schumpeter's

---

2 One may add that there have been successful non-democratic leaders, such as Deng Xiaoping in China and Mikhail Gorbachev in the Soviet Union.

theory articulates, though often implicitly, a minimal normative backbone for the leader-centred competitive model of democracy by arguing that: (1) it gives a peaceful method for change in leadership; (2) it ensures a right to vote, and therefore rulers who are perceived as bad rulers can be easily ousted through competitive and open elections. In addition to these two normative elements, we highlight two other Weberian (in origin) relevant aspects: (3) the advantage of decisional rationality, due to the principle of 'small numbers'; and (4) accountability and responsibility. Thus while the rival neoclassical model aims at maximising the public responsiveness of leaders, 'leader democracy' aims at maximising the responsibility and autonomy of leaders. It highlights the importance of the trust-based electoral mandate understood as a broad authorisation to rule (see Chapters 3 and 4 for more details). However, this 'minimalist' normative backbone is played down in order to keep our arguments firmly on accurate identification of current trends. We argue that the model of 'leader democracy' should be judged, above all, in terms of how closely it 'approximates' current political configurations, or in terms of its accuracy in describing contemporary democratic politics and elite structure. It offers a description, a theoretical clarification and a defence of 'leader democracy', and not necessarily an advocacy of the leader-democratic model as superior or desirable in a normative sense. We try to steer away from premature evaluations and value judgements that are often woven into discussions of democracy (which is, after all, a dominant value and ideal).

However, we also have to tread some normative ground while defending the model against those 'normative' critics who see it as 'insufficiently democratic' and as undermining basic normative standards of modern democracy. While defending 'leader democracy' against such accusations (especially in Chapter 4), we inevitably enter the normative territory – but we have tried to do it in a spirit of dispassionate analysis rather than advocacy. The reason for this is obvious. An acceptable and informed judgement about the 'quality of democracy' cannot be passed before history passes her judgement. So what we have attempted to do is to persuade the readers that the leader-centric trends are real, that they do not threaten democratic values, and that they should not be seen as heralding the demise of democracy. In other words, 'leader democracy' belongs to the 'democratic family'; it fulfils the minimal normative and procedural criteria of democracy.

While in theory leadership and democracy still remain separated by mutual suspicion, we note some mutual *rapprochement* in public perceptions. Unlike a generation or two ago, today no democratically inclined citizen would be embarrassed to call for firm leadership, or expect such firm leadership from candidates for the top public office. These popular expectations of firm leadership are already widespread in democratic polities. Similarly, political disaffection of voters is often reflected in charges of 'weak' or 'lame' leadership. In fact, the declining 'leadership performance' and the accompanying waning of public confidence have become such dangerous political liabilities that they sometimes – as in the recent cases of the British and Australian labour parties – prompt desperate replacements of 'lame' leaders on the eve of elections. In turn, electoral appeal and 'strong' leadership performance during the term of office become essential conditions of political success. This is why election campaigns in the most established liberal democracies have become increasingly leader centred. Indeed, some campaigns have started to resemble leadership plebiscites in which party programmes, as well as ideological orientations, are either played down or ignored (Blondel 2005; Pakulski and Higley 2008; t'Hart and Uhr 2011).[3]

There are multiple reasons for this increasing public awareness and leader-centrism: the centripetal trend in power distribution, the discontent generated by 'party democracy', the rise of the mass media and celebrity cults, the personalisation of politics, and the widespread uncertainty-cum-concern generated by globalisation (leader-centrism is discussed in more detail in Chapter 3). Contemporary voters trust persons more than organisations, abstract principles or ideologies, and this personal locus of trust seems to increase under the conditions of mass elections and at times of uncertainty – a point made by both Weber and Schumpeter. Leaders are seen as more capable of promoting 'national interest' than party bureaucracies and entrenched parliamentary factions, especially when sectional interests and patronage threaten to 'corrupt' politics. In such circumstances, determined and trusted leaders are seen as the best 'fall backs', the trusted champions of 'national' or 'public' interests. Such leaders are also seen as uniquely capable of breaking gridlocks and overcoming bureaucratic inertia, and as primary agents of change, especially when public expectations of 'prompt and urgent action' are frustrated by parliamentary gridlocks and factional struggles. Leaders are also seen as innovators and carriers of new directions, especially when the old policies, programmes and strategies are discredited.

This focus and heavy reliance on leaders and the increasing public trust placed in leaders also focuses the minds of competing political parties and elite camps on the importance of selecting and grooming capable leaders. The defeat of the French Socialists in the 2007 presidential poll has been widely attributed to the 'wrong choice' of the leadership candidate, Ségolène Royal – a choice allegedly dictated more by political correctness than considerations of leadership potential. Similarly, the Republican Party in the USA suffers

---

3 This feature is often interpreted and analysed as 'personalisation of politics' – see, for example, Karvonen (2009) and McAllister (2007).

from the absence of credible leadership candidates on the eve of the 2012 presidential elections. Dangerous 'leadership vacuums' trigger desperate pursuits and often result in hit-and-miss appointments that undermine public confidence.

It is quite clear, as recently observed by Blondel (2005), that the political success of parties increasingly depends on their capacity to select, groom and 'field' an attractive political leader, whose personality is appealing, whose image fits the mass media presentation, and who is capable of capturing the public imagination during long (one is tempted to say 'permanent') election campaigns. The circumstances favour spectacular and innovative candidates – those with new ideas, new solutions, and above all with 'oratory charisma', who project an image of empathy, vigour and self-confidence. The high demand is for candidates who are celebrity-like and can inspire mass confidence.

However, such capable leadership candidates are in a very short supply. Successful leadership seems to rely on a rare combination of natural talent, grooming and training, and above all – as Weber famously said – on strong commitment, a cool head and good, balanced judgement. Therefore when good candidates for leadership are scouted and groomed, and when they prove successful in winning votes, they dominate party establishment, override party programmes, and sometimes transform the party organisations into their compliant 'leader party' (Blondel 2005). 'Leader parties', even if born independent, end as electoral committees and cheerleaders for successful political leaders.

This looks like a significant change, especially compared with the not-too-distant past (particularly in Europe), when electoral victory was attributed predominantly to well-organised parties and their convincing ideologically organised programmes. Even in the United States, where political parties were always spoils/patronage parties, electoral victory depended as much on issue-positioning and presentation as on the public appeal of leaders. In Western Europe, as argued in the next chapter, 'party democracy' was prevalent until the end of 1970s, when it started to decline. The concomitant rise of prominent leaders has been portrayed as 'personalisation' and 'presidentialisation' of politics. We suggest that this rise has been a symptom of a shift toward 'leader democracy', a shift that started with the decline of 'party democracy' and the ascendancy of popular and assertive leaders/reformers.

The emergence in advanced and new democracies of prominent, strong and popular leaders, such as Margaret Thatcher, Ronald Reagan, Bob Hawke, Helmut Kohl, Lech Wałęsa, Nelson Mandela, Gerhard Schröder, Tony Blair, Junichiro Koizumi, George W. Bush, Nicolas Sarkozy, and Barack Obama, took many observers by surprise. All these leaders have not only concentrated executive power in their own hands (and the hands of their trusted advisers) but also swiftly overshadowed party establishments and governmental bureaucracies as the public face of governmental power. They have dominated parliaments and state executives, and have shaped, at least initially, public opinion by maintaining a very high media profile.

The rising prominence of political leaders in democratic polities was initially seen as an anomaly, a temporary deviation caused by a combination of political crisis and media hype. But as the wave of leadership ascendancy continued, prominent leaders gradually became a recognised feature of the democratic political landscape. The proliferation of strong leaders helps to convince the experts and the lay publics that what we observe is more than a stylistic fashion or a mere 'presidentialisation' and 'personalisation' of politics, but part of a wider and more comprehensive syndrome of political change. To those familiar with Weberian and Schumpeterian analyses of political modernisation, such a change is neither anomalous nor surprising. It was anticipated and partly analysed by both thinkers, though in a fragmentary manner.

The Theoretical Argument

Weber and Schumpeter[4] pioneered the argument that leaders are key actors in modern democratic politics. Leaders play a central role in coordinating the exercise of authority, integrating national elites, and in securing and maintaining public trust and confidence. In the process of open electoral competition, leaders actively generate – rather than receive – democratic mandate-authorisation to rule. This is why this open electoral leadership competition forms the essential institutional backbone of modern democracy. Strong leadership, as noted by Weber (1919), also provides necessary 'checks' vis-à-vis other sections of political elites: parliamentary politicians, top bureaucrats (public/civil service administrative officials), and 'party machines'. Successful leaders balance – and if necessary, curtail – the influences of party officialdom and the governmental 'mandarinate', the key organised interests and influential 'power circles'. If effective in their leadership roles, they help in synthesising and harmonising the diverse pressures and interests into consistent national interest and policies. Effective leaders can 'craft' and stabilise political regimes by becoming the centre of elite integration. Such leaders can integrate the highly specialised and fragmented ('strategic') elites and perform the role of central political actors in modern democratic politics.

This centrality of leaders seems to be an increasingly prominent feature of contemporary national politics in advanced and new democracies. It is leaders

---

4 As argued in the next chapter, we regard Weber and Schumpeter as unacknowledged founding fathers of the idea of leader-centred democracy.

who give meaning to such politics by shaping the agendas of debates, defining the issues of concern, identifying the main challenges, establishing public trust in government and providing reassurance to anxious citizens. The executive 'courts', 'kitchen cabinets', 'core executives' and 'central circles' form around prominent leaders. Leaders maintain the public consent that is necessary for long-term stabilisation and play the central role in international negotiations, partnerships and alliances. If successful, leaders can transform elite or party political aims into widely understood national goals and aspirations. If unsuccessful, they weaken governments and trigger political fissures.

Such claims about the growing centrality of leaders, and about the increasing importance of leaders in building the democratic elite–mass 'linkages', will inevitably raise eyebrows at least in two quarters: among those who embrace the 'mass-participatory' view of democracy, and among those critics of contemporary politics who promote dark scenarios of 'post-democracy'. While we confront these alternative formulations in more detail in the final chapters, it is convenient to signal briefly our disagreements now.

The proposed model of 'leader democracy' belongs to the family of 'representative democracy'. It contradicts those models of democracy that interpret 'popular sovereignty' and 'democratic legitimacy' as principally 'mass' phenomena, and that stress 'mass participation', rather than leadership action, as the key elements of politics (e.g. Dryzek 2000). The leader-democratic perspective is quite different. It depicts the wielding of political authority as principally (though not exclusively) a 'top-down' process. In line with that, it also portrays leaders and elites as central political actors who are capable of energising and mobilising 'civil society' and interpreting, as well as imposing through persuasion, the elite-constructed visions of public and national interest. Similarly, the leader-democratic perspective is sceptical of the dark scenarios and anticipations of 'post-democracy'. The latter refers to political configurations in which power falls from the hands of elective national-political leaders into the hands of transnational 'corporate elites'. Politics is reduced to corporate hegemony, in which democratic practices, including electoral competitions, are just façades for corporate rule (e.g. Crouch 2004).

Such scenarios are not only at odds with our anticipations of leader-centric democracy, but also with broader political trends. The first and most obvious is the continuation of the world wide democratisation almost exclusively in the form of spreading representative forms of democracy. It is worth adding that successful 'third wave' democratisation has occurred in a predominantly 'top-down' fashion and depended heavily on the emergence of pro-democratic leaders and elites (Huntington 1991; Linz and Stepan 1996). The most successful democracies were crafted by strong pro-democratic leaders who negotiated largely peaceful transfers of power during 'round table' negotiations (Higley et al. 1998). The consolidation of democracy in these newly formed regimes took the form of copying Western models of representative democracy with strong leadership as its core feature.

We are also sceptical of the 'postdemocratic' visions and prognoses. The ascendancy of trans-national corporations and the growing reluctance of liberal-democratic regimes to regulate economy and society are undeniable. The question is whether these trends significantly weaken the state political leaders and elites, and whether they restrict the power of government vis-à-vis private corporations.

A number of implications follow from this argument. First, 'leader democracy' looks ascendant, especially in what we call advanced Western societies. Second, the shift towards more leader-centred elites may strengthen, rather than undermine, democratic political regimes. Leader-centeredness may enhance the consistency, coherence and therefore long-term effectiveness of political action. Politics directed from one centre and pursued in a consistent manner is often contrasted with fickle and opportunistic populism, the latter associated with the 'leaderless' condition. Finally, the shift may increase political creativity, entrepreneurship and innovation concerns, not necessarily in the substance of policies, but in the ways in which leaders generate public trust, and therefore the strong political authorisation (mandate). In other words, 'leader democracy' may have a particular appeal at the time of uncertainty and public anxiety about the future.

The Paradoxes of Democratic Theory

The portrayal of 'leader democracy' as both ascendant and 'sufficiently democratic' contrasts with the 'leader-phobia' afflicting the popular visions of democracy and contemporary democratic theory. Concerns about power concentration in the hands of leaders may be understandable as a reflection of popular fear of the destructive autocrats who wreaked havoc in European politics in the first half of the twentieth century. But, more than half a century later, such fear appears increasingly dated, unrealistic and confusing. It looks like it is time to move democratic theorising out of the dark shadow cast by Il Duce, Der Führer and Vozhd. Moreover, both the informed public and political scientists increasingly appreciate the fact (stressed frequently by Weber, Schumpeter, classical elite theorists and most contemporary democratic theorists) that modern national leaders, even the most popular and trusted ones, never rule alone. They always co-dominate and co-rule, and are politically embedded in, dependent on, and share their power with their 'staffs', close collaborators and leadership competitors – the political elites.

This is the central theme of the book, as well as the central paradox we confront. In spite of a rapid shift towards leader-centred democracy and the prominent role of leaders in the 'third' (some say fourth) wave of democratisation, most theoretical analyses of democracy shun leaders. Moreover, as shown in Chapter 5, the current programme of democratic reforms designed for the Council of Europe also ignores the role of leaders, and assumes that the popular demand is for widening participation, rather than improving representation.

We try to bring leaders back to democratic theory and reconcile the two.[5] It seems delaying such reconciliation carries a risk of progressive divorce of democratic theory and research from reality. This task of 'bringing leaders back' is to be done in five steps, as reflected in the content of the book. The first step is highlighting the central role of leaders in contemporary democratic politics and stressing the importance attached to leadership qualities and performance by mass publics. Second, we point to a long tradition of democratic theorising that acknowledges the importance of leadership, especially to the 'classical' analyses of Max Weber and Joseph Schumpeter who anticipated the leader-centric trends and explained the compatibility between these trends and mass democratisation. Third, we identify some more recent leader-centric trends and locate them in the general processes of political modernisation. Fourth, we elaborate a theoretical model of 'leader democracy', highlight its democratic features, and contrast it with rival models. Fifth, and finally, we look at the future of 'leader democracy' in the context of contemporary research and through the Weberian–Schumpeterian theoretical lens. The intended effect is not only a diagnosis of leader-centric trends, but also a theoretical reconciliation between democratic theory, leadership and elites. Such reconciliation, in turn, should help in understanding democratic processes and in anticipating the directions of change.

A Clarifying Note

Some additional clarifications and qualifications are necessary. The first concerns the meaning of 'power', 'leadership', 'leaders', 'elites' and 'democracy'. The focus of this book is mainly on power seen as authority – that is, a form of power exercised through binding commands. 'Leadership' is therefore treated principally as 'political leadership', the capacity of a social

---

5 In doing that, it is worth stressing again, we are aided by many students of political leadership, from Weber and Schumpeter, through Bryce, to Blondel, Sartori and contemporary 'elitists' (e.g. Best and Higley 2010).

actor – a person or a small group – to command others who voluntarily obey, especially out of trust and a sense of duty.

The book focuses on national political leadership and the top political executives in nation-states – that is, presidents, prime ministers, and the key opposition figures competing for these positions and co-exercising executive authority in the state – as the main segments of national political elites. Political leaders and the surrounding political elites always ally with nonpolitical segments of elites representing business, media, unions, churches, and other large and influential organisations and movements. But it is the top political leaders and elites alone that exercise highest authority and authoritative leadership.

We treat democracy as a form of political regime that affirms the 'sovereignty of the people' and respects the 'will of the governed'. These principles are seen today – by both the public at large and by the elites – as realised mainly through electoral representation, that is, through systematic, free, open and fair electoral contests for the popular vote and a ruling mandate (authorisation).[6] This means that 'leader democracy' is a subtype of a broader democratic family: a regime characterised by such a political-elite configuration in which leaders play a prominent role, especially in securing public trust and a ruling mandate. We treat it as an ideal type approximated to the actual political-elite configurations by varying degrees.

Weber and Schumpeter are the unacknowledged founding fathers of the idea and theoretical outline of competitive and leader-centred democracy. The concept of *Führerdemokratie* was largely ignored as controversial, perhaps even dangerous, because of its unfortunate semantic association with Der Führer. Similarly, Schumpeter's vision of an entrepreneur-driven economy and a competitive leader-driven democracy was popularised in a simplified form that blurs Schumpeter's original approach to the problem of leadership in democratic politics. For all these reasons we must turn now to the 'founding fathers' and their original formulations of 'leader democracy' – and look at them in a more careful and detailed manner.

---

6 Liberal democracies also respect and secure through legal safeguards a broad range of civil liberties, political rights, social entitlements and cultural freedoms. Illiberal democracies do not respect all these rights to various degrees.

Chapter 2

THEORETICAL ANTICIPATIONS

We wish to understand by politics only the leadership, or the influencing of the leadership, of a *political* association, hence today, of a *state*... 'politics' for us means striving to share power or striving to influence the distribution of power, either among states or among groups within a state....

...However, there is only the choice between leader democracy with a 'machine' and leaderless democracy, namely, the rule of professional politicians without a calling...'the rule of the clique'. For the time being, we in Germany have only the latter.
                                            —Max Weber, 'Politics as a Vocation' (1919/1972)

There are two basic assumptions of contemporary liberal and democratic political thinking. First, laws (not men) rule in a liberal or constitutional state. Second, many (not few) rule in a democracy. Both are simplifications that easily confuse hopes with reality. They may be correct in capturing the wishes and intentions of many liberal-democratic reformers. However, they also ignore the requirements of large-scale, complex and organised societies, and turn a blind eye to the actual paths of political modernisation and mass democratisation. Most critically, they neglect the indirect-representative character of modern democratic regimes, the key role of political leaders, and those leaders' charismatic (Weber) and innovative (Schumpeter) potential.

This does not mean that direct, participatory and grassroots democracy is impossible or unrealistic and that rational legalism and public responsibility are illusory. Participatory forms of ruling are applicable to small, simple and homogeneous social settings, and they fail in complex large-scale nation-states. Such nation-states inevitably develop indirect forms of democratic representation; they are highly organised and shaped by parties, professional politicians, elective leaders and elites. And this means that modern democracy on the state-national level has to reconcile itself not only with bureaucratic hierarchy, but also with leaders and elites. Leaders and elites remain the key political actors in all modern democratic regimes. By contrast, mass publics play an important but also circumscribed role – not as direct rulers, but mainly as citizens/voters who periodically 'vote in' the successful politicians and authorise them to rule. They may also, adds Weber, influence democratic governments by forming 'public opinion', but do so under the strong persuasive influence of leaders and elites. It is the leaders and elites who remain the main public 'opinion shapers' and key decision makers in modern democratic regimes. But in order to sustain their authority, the elective segments of democratic elites periodically have to solicit mass votes, successfully shape public opinion, cultivate the support of major 'social forces', and – generally – sustain a relationship of trust with their electorates.

This also means that in all modern regimes, democratic and nondemocratic, power is exerted predominantly in a 'top-down' direction and authority is exercised in an organised and systematic manner. However, only in democratic regimes is political authority legally circumscribed and legitimated, and political leaders and elites rely on periodic electoral competition and authorisation. Similarly, only democratic political leaders and elites are held accountable to mass publics through electoral cycles, freely and critically monitored by political rivals and forced to surrender power when they fail to win sufficient electoral support. Therefore, only democratic regimes are subject to regular, systematic elite competition and ascent (Schumpeter), mobility (Weber) and circulation (Pareto). However, these regular contests and intense mobility neither disperse nor weaken the power of political leaders and elites nor change the 'top-down' direction of authority. On the contrary, the electoral mandate-authorisation is seen as a most effective form of power legitimation, and therefore power centralisation and concentration.[1] The strength of electoral authorisation, in turn, makes democratic leaders and elites formidable agents of social change, to the extent that they can compete with most autocrats in this regard. This is widely known and appreciated by all modern power holders who seek electoral authorisation and public trust in order to strengthen their power and gain wider, more general and more effective authorisation-cum-consent for their rule. In contemporary democracies, such authorisation is always actively sought and won through effective campaigning, oratory, skilful image presentation, and manipulation of public opinion.

---

1 In fact, leaders' effectiveness in centralising power has led many modern political theorists, from Tocqueville to Weber, to warn about the danger of 'despotic democracy' in the form of popular but autocratic Bonapartism.

Yet in the past, few theorists of democracy and modern politics recognised and acknowledged these facts. Weber and Schumpeter were among the first to do so. They were not only the key analysts of modernisation, concerned mainly with expanding state bureaucracies, but also sober realists, who appreciated the inevitability of complex hierarchical organisation, power centralisation in the state apparata, and the growing importance of 'charisma of rhetoric'. Both were great scholars, well versed in history, philosophy and the social sciences, as well as political practitioners involved in the power games of the day. Therefore their analyses have both a wide interdisciplinary scope and a strong practical-experiential base.

Their observations on the concentration of power and central role of political leadership, one should add, were by no means new. The appreciation of the central of leaders and elites had also permeated political analyses from Machiavelli through Hobbes and Locke to classical liberals and elite theorists. All of them have stressed the key role of the 'federative power' in sustaining social and political order and the importance of political talent in securing wide public support. In these early 'pre-Weberian' accounts, though, political leaders with wide and discretionary power appeared mainly at times of crises. They resolved the crises and established order, but then inevitably transformed into 'heads' wielding more circumscribed, legalised and impersonal authority. In these accounts, leadership was largely exceptional, and it promptly evolved into legally regulated and 'routinised' headship.

Weber and Schumpeter embraced these accounts, but they also widened them to cover modern and more 'routine' forms of politics and inserted a cautionary note. They stressed that leadership had not diminished in its importance, let alone disappeared, in modernising societies. Today it may vary in its forms, intensity and quality, but it continues to energise modern economics and politics, even when authority is thoroughly 'routinised', legitimised and subject to democratic checks. Modern politics, including democratic politics, is 'any kind of independent leadership in action' (Weber 1919, 9). There are some subtle differences in their approach, though. Max Weber highlighted the ever-present tension between charisma, the 'gift of grace' attributed by followers to successful leaders, and routine, legalised and orderly bureaucratic authority. Both charisma and bureaucracy, he stressed, appear regularly on the modern political scene. Bureaucratic domination is the source of the stability, while charisma of 'great statesmen', political reformers and military heroes is a dynamic force. Great leaders are both order breakers and order makers; they are capable of destroying old social orders and consolidating new ones. It is the charisma of such leaders – especially the 'oratory charisma' – that heightens their creative capacities by securing the confidence, compliance and support of the masses.[2] Moreover, good leaders give coherence and a firm political direction to policies, unite and integrate elites and communicate with the masses. Therefore, charismatic leadership is bound to remain the main source of dynamic disruption, creative destruction, social innovation and change, even in the democratised and bureaucratic modern *Rechtsstadt* (constitutional state). The absence of leadership or weak leadership, by contrast, results in 'soulless and directionless' politics, threatens social inertia, political stagnation and bureaucratic rigidity – all of them diagnosed by Weber in Germany under the 'leaderless' Wilhelmine regimes (1978, 1410–31).

Joseph Schumpeter (1934 and 1942/1978) chose a slightly different argument. He pointed to the similarity in the importance of entrepreneurs in the modern industrial economy, and the parallel role of political leaders/ innovators as the dynamic forces in modern politics. Nowadays, both entrepreneurs and political leaders emerge through intense rivalry, political competition, and both have to sustain their power and influence through innovation, through breaking the established routines. The modern economy is as reliant on entrepreneurial talent as modern democracy is reliant on innovative leadership. In the modern economy, it is entrepreneurs who generate development by actively generating and moulding public demand, 'awakening' and reshaping consumer preferences, and introducing new products and forms of production. In politics, the same creative role is played by charismatic leaders emerging through open electoral competition. Electoral authorisation is won by such leaders through skilful and innovative oratory contests. The winners are those who actively canvass and win mass support.

To democrats who embrace the 'classical model' of democracy with its emphasis of the 'bottom-up' direction of power flow, this may sound scandalous. For them, democratic government has to be, above all, responsive to the wishes of the voting citizens. According to the 'classical model', political leaders predominantly perform a 'transmitting' role: they aggregate the wants and preferences of their constituencies and translate them into public policy. Hence such 'leaders' ('deputies' is an appropriate label) do not have an autonomous role or entrepreneurial character – they just 'mirror' or 'reflect' the attitudes of their constituencies, respond to mass demands and follow their voters. While highly respected, they are more followers than genuine leaders. Social dynamism and political initiative come from the masses rather than autonomous leaders/innovators. Elective deputies are mere political

---

2 It should be added here charismatic authority involves a relation between leaders and followers in which the latter feel a duty to obey because the leader represents values or causes that are widely cherished. In charismatic relations, the personalities of leaders may play a minor role.

aggregators, transmitters and managers of popular demands. Like in the equilibrated market guided by the 'invisible hand', so in modern democratic politics the incumbent deputies simply articulate the average ('median') voters' views, preferences and demands. Thus, unless such deputies – politicians in the classical model of politics and businessmen in classical economic theory – fail in their aggregating-transmitting role, the equilibrium prevails in both realms. In the economy, the demand of 'sovereign consumers' is identified and satisfied by responsive businessmen/producers. Similarly in politics, the externally shaped (or 'given') interests, preferences and proclivities of voters are identified by deputies and translated into public policy, thus guaranteeing social harmony and democratic equilibrium.

Weber and Schumpeter challenged such 'classical' models of both modern industrial economy and mass-democratic politics. They stressed the active role of principal 'social actors': entrepreneurs shaping and revolutionising production, and political leaders actively soliciting votes. Importantly, neither entrepreneurs nor political leaders can eliminate systemic tensions inherent in the modern social order. These tensions persist, and they are the sources of social dynamism. The notions of lasting social equilibrium – be it the socioeconomic balance between demand and supply, or a balance between voter preferences and leaders' policies in the sociopolitical realm – are illusory, mythical and utopian. It is persisting imbalance and disequilibrium that are the normal condition and 'order of the day' in modern society.

In this view, modern economy and society are inherently unbalanced, tension ridden and therefore dynamic, constantly disrupted by innovations, pushed by the 'winds of creative destruction' (Schumpeter), and 'charismatic revelation' (Weber). According to Weber, the sudden surge in economic growth that accompanied industrial modernisation coincided with the radical preaching of Protestant divines, social unrest and political reforms. This sudden acceleration of change, argued Schumpeter, reflected the appearance of a new dynamic figure, the innovative entrepreneur. Both were disruptive figures and agents of change. Modern political movements, parties, regimes – and since the eighteenth century the widening markets and the bureaucratising and militaristic state apparata – have depended on such creative destructors of social order. In the process of social modernisation, political power was periodically remobilised, concentrated and reorganised. Following each remobilisation cycle, its use was regulated and its exercise made more rational – that is more deliberate, systematic, calculative, impersonal – and therefore more effective and predictable. All these changes broadened the capacities of political leaders, especially leaders gifted with 'oratory charisma' and spectacular image.

Leadership and modern democracy, Weber and Schumpeter argued, were a couple, rather than congenital twins. They tended to coincide and thrive together, but they could also develop separately, one without the other. Weber stressed that charisma may be 'routinised' either in a democratic direction, whereby legitimacy is confirmed through victory in electoral contest, or it may evolve in a nondemocratic, autocratic direction, whereby mass endorsement of leaders become a pledge of allegiance typical of Caesarism. Strong political leadership, in other words, can be found in both democratic and autocratic regimes.

Weber and Schumpeter had jointly laid the theoretical foundations of competitive 'leader democracy' understood as a specific political elite configuration and a pattern of institutionalised practice. While their arguments are fragmented and dispersed, they nevertheless contain sufficient suggestions about leader-centric trends and elite configurations to form a foundation for a theoretical model. This is why we start our portrayal of 'leader democracy' with an overview of their theoretical legacies.

Max Weber: Mass Democratisation, Charisma and 'Leader Democracy'

Weber forged the concept of *Führerdemokratie*, but his references to the concept are dispersed and found mainly in his analyses of charismatic leadership and its routinisation (1978, 266–88), and in his critiques of contemporary German politics as 'leaderless' (1919/1978, 1381–1469). Moreover, 'leader democracy' is a label he applied to a broad historical 'family of types', with many historical forms ranging from the highly plebiscitary-autocratic (e.g. Bonapartism) to the modern elective-democratic. This modern form of 'leader democracy' appears in bureaucratised and mass-democratised states, such as the USA and Great Britain, and it is missing in Wilhelmine Germany. It is portrayed by Weber as a leader-centred elite configuration resulting from mass democratisation, in which political leaders use oratory charisma in gaining mass confidence and consent. This central role in securing mass confidence also gives the leaders a central role within the ruling minority. Leaders inject consistency to policies and they integrate the highly differentiated elites. Their success in sustaining mass trust and confidence depends not only on their ability to cultivate elite–mass linkages – typically accomplished with the assistance of bureaucratised party and governmental apparata – but also on their capacity to establish good working relations with their 'staffs', especially with professional parliamentarians and party directorates.

In this forms, modern 'leader democracy' constituted an evolutionary product of the centralistic-bureaucratic and mass-democratic trends.

These two trends, though logically incompatible, coincided and merged. Centralisation of authority in the constitutional bureaucratic state progressed together with the equalisation of political statuses, the opening up of political elites, formation of representative parliaments, the widening of political franchise and the expansion of citizenship rights, including the right to stand for public offices. Leaders always played the central role in these processes by exercising mass persuasion that generated public trust and shaped the preferences of mass voters. Competitive elections provided testing grounds to potential leaders, allowed leaders to claim strong ruling mandate-authorisation, created opportunities for broad elite alliances with the masses, and enabled the leaders to discharge public responsibility-cum-accountability through anticipated responses in subsequent competitive electoral cycles.

The central position of leaders, especially in modern mass democracies, depends on their 'oratory charisma' or 'charisma of rhetoric'. Weber portrays charisma, bureaucracy and democracy as both rivals and allies. Charisma of leaders is always a dynamic force – the source of empowerment and the propellant of change. Bureaucracy is a stabilising force. Modern mass democracy is a process of social accommodation between the two.

The theoretical and historical context

This is why the theoretical roots of 'leader democracy' are planted in Weber's sociology of politics and charismatic leadership. Charisma, Weber argues, is not restricted to the archaic forms of authority exercised by religious rulers and autocratic Caesarists.[3] It plays the key role in the processes of democratisation and modern governance. Popular leaders of democratic movements, such as Lassalle, personified popular sovereignty and won mass confidence, before such confidence and consent could evolve into a formalised democratic electoral mandate-authorisation. In other words, charismatic authority paved the way for the mass democratisation of the state, and it remains an important component of modern democratic leadership. But there was nothing natural or inevitable in such an evolution, Weber warned; charismatic leadership can evolve in either a democratic direction – that is, transform into competitive electoral mandate-authorisation – or turn in an autocratic direction, away

---

3 'As these examples show again, charismatic domination is by no means limited to primitive stages of development, and the three basic types of domination cannot be placed into a simple evolutionary line: they in fact appear together in the most diverse combinations. It is a fate of charisma, however, to recede with the development of permanent institutional structures.' (Weber 1978, 1133)

from democracy, thus giving rise to dictatorial power relying on fabricated pledges of allegiance.

These theoretical observations form a framework for Weber's critical commentaries on social and political developments in contemporary Germany.[4] Following its defeat in the First World War, Germany faced a crisis, 'a polar night of icy darkness' (Weber 1919/1972, 224). It emerged from the war economically ruined, socially polarised and politically weakened. Convinced of the need for urgent and deep reforms, Weber threw himself into the political fray writing articles, making speeches and for a short time campaigning in a presidential election as a candidate of the left-liberal German Democratic Party (DDP). This involvement generated some of his most interesting political analyses, in which he spoke as both a detached social scientist, capable of traversing the boundaries of sociology, history, philosophy, cultural anthropology, economics and law, and as a passionate political campaigner concerned about Germany's future, especially her backwardness vis-à-vis the major (and admired) powers, Great Britain and the USA. Modern British and American politics provided the most celebrated contrasts of effective modernisation and democratisation through political organisation and firm leadership. David Lloyd George, Theodore Roosevelt and Woodrow Wilson – political leaders praised by Weber – all played the central role in successful political modernisation and nation-building. They also strengthened mass democracy by cultivating public trust, confidence and support due to their leadership talent, 'oratory charisma' and organisational skills. By contrast, Weber saw Germany as a laggard in modernisation stakes. The country was left behind not only in economic development and political professionalisation, but also in mass democratisation. Above all, it was paralysed by a combination of archaic institutions, social tensions and political gridlocks resulting from the absence of good political leadership. The 'Bismarck legacies' of autocratic rule, a 'weakness and naivety' of the political strata, poor constitutional design and the political 'immaturity' (read: lack of political organisation) of the major social classes all added to the woes. The emergence of popular elective leaders representing national constituencies was blocked by the dominant stratum of militaristic and arch-conservative Prussian *Junkers* (landowners) allied with powerful central bureaucracies. Neither was capable of spawning popular social reformers or great statesmen that could reunify the German nation and modernise its politics. This state of political 'leaderlessness', especially when combined with political polarisation that followed the defeat in the First World

---

4 See, in particular, 1978, 1375–1462. This historical context is described by Bendix (1962/1977), Beetham (1974), Mitzman (1970), Mommsen (1974), and more recently by Radkau (2009).

War, bode ill for the nation's future. It made Germany vulnerable to both radical-anarchic drift and autocratic impositions.

Democracy and democratisation

As mentioned before, Weber never treated democracy as an end in itself. Democratic institutions and practices were always a means for achieving some more fundamental goals: effective ('working') government, rational and deliberative decision making, national integration, political strength, social dynamism and ultimately 'proud and dignified life' for individuals. Mass democratisation, Weber also added, was a working solution to the problem of modernisation. Popular autocracies may have been successful in unifying nations and promoting economic growth, but they could not accommodate and harness the forces of modern rationalism and nationalism to the same extent as the modern democracies. This success, however, did not blind Weber to the numerous pitfalls of mass democratisation. Unlike the starry-eyed radical democrats, who discussed ideals divorced from reality, he was a sober observer of actual democratic practices – which were quite diverse. He analysed authoritarian 'passive democratization' (1978, 985–6), erratic 'plebiscitary democracy' (1978, 241–71, 1111–55) and the chaotic 'democracy of the street' (1978, 1460). But the conclusion of these sober and critical analyses was never a rejection of democracy. In fact, he was as scathing about radical proposals for Caesarist leadership as he was about suggestions for direct democracy without parliaments, especially à la Soviet Russia. Both were criticised as incompatible with modern developments and dismissed as 'pipe dreams' of naïve radicals (e.g. 1978, 1439–52, 1460). The progressively enfranchised 'masses' could not be excluded from politics – a fact recognised and approved by Weber no less than by his Marxist rivals – but they could be constructively involved only in an indirect and organised manner, as party supporters and enfranchised voters in mass elections. This implied the ascendancy of bureaucratised party officialdoms, professional politicians and democratic leaders, the latter capable of wooing the mass vote and representing mass constituencies in an organised and systematic fashion (1978, 983–5).

This is why democratisation under the conditions of large-scale and complex modern society was inevitably 'mass', 'nationalised', 'indirect', 'organised', 'etatised', 'demagogic' and 'leader centred'. It followed the emergence of powerful mass movements and mass parties led by popular leaders, such as Lassalle or Disraeli. Such leaders combined mass-electoral appeal with organisational acumen and professional/political skills. They acknowledged the sovereignty of the people and relied on legitimacy that was derived from the 'will of the governed', but operated as electorally authorised – and therefore responsible and accountable – 'agents/ representatives' of the masses.

Weber never dismisses direct or participatory forms of democracy as impractical or utopian. In fact, the entirety of chapter 10 of his *Economy and Society* (1978, 289–92) is devoted to discussion of 'Direct Democracy and Representative Administration'. However, he always stresses the limited applicability of direct and participatory forms, especially in modern national politics. So, while some small-scale North American 'townships', Swiss cantons, collegial voluntary associations, trade unions, craft guilds, as well as sporting, scientific and academic bodies, may successfully adopt direct and participatory forms of democracy, large-scale societies and organisations inevitably evolve towards and embrace indirect, representative democracy. Such democracy 'works' in the sense of providing effective administration, generating rational and consistent governance, and satisfying popular egalitarian aspirations and expectations.[5] The modern 'working democracy', in other words, was inevitably evolving in the direction of mass (national in its scope), electoral (based on electoral contest and popular franchise), indirect (representative), and organised (dependent on parties and parliaments) democracy. 'Leader democracy' was one of many possible types, one of many possible elite configurations, such modern 'working democracy' could adopt. It presupposed both a considerable autonomy of leaders and elites, and a strong social anchoring of these 'representative' and 'responsible' leaders and elites in parties, communities, classes, status groups and organised 'social forces', or in a complex modern civil society. In order to perform their anchoring role, party leaders and professional politicians required not only an electoral mandate-authorisation – the reflection of trust and confidence of voters – but

---

5 'The political concept of democracy, deduced from the "equal rights" of the governed, includes these further [to popular sovereignty] postulates: (1) prevention of the development of a closed status group of officials in the interest of a universal accessibility of office, and (2) minimization of the authority of officialdom in the interest of expanding the sphere of influence of "public opinion" as far as practicable. Hence, wherever possible, political democracy strives to shorten the term of office through election and recall and to be relieved of a limitation to candidates with special expert qualifications. Thereby democracy inevitably comes into conflict with the bureaucratic tendencies, which have been produced by its very fight against the *notables*. The loose term "democratization" cannot be used here, in so far as it is understood to mean the minimization of the civil servants' power in favour of the greatest possible "direct" rule of the *demos*, which in practice means the respective party leaders of the *demos*. The decisive aspect here…is the *levelling of the governed* in the face of the governing and bureaucratically articulated group, which in its turn may occupy a quite autocratic position, both in fact and in form.' (1978, 985)

also considerable autonomy, insulation from immediate pressures that mass authorisation give. Such autonomy and insulation allows politicians to accept public responsibility, the latter discharged to both parliaments and mass electorates. Modern democracy, Weber stressed, rested on autonomous but publicly responsible elites, and not elites responsive to mass pressures or chasing mass popularity.

Electoral competitions play a crucial role in this process of cultivating autonomy-cum-public responsibility. By winning open electoral contests, leaders not only 'prove themselves' and acquire broad electoral authorisation and legitimation – a generalised normative approval for their rule – but also accept responsibility for the effects of their rule. This authorisation has to be sufficiently general to give them scope for exercising leadership in a way they wish – and therefore allow them to take a full responsibility (credit or blame) for the outcomes. The authority is not limitless, though. It is 'checked' and circumscribed by constitutional laws, ruling conventions, as well as routine parliamentary supervision and, increasingly, also by the scope of the claimed mandate and the influence of 'public opinion'. In other words, in modern democracy masses are sovereign and enfranchised, but they never govern in the sense of participating in governmental decisions or shaping directly governmental policies. Rather, they influence those decisions and policies indirectly, by granting votes to favoured leaders and provide the essential authorisation for ruling leaders and elites.[6]

Democracy and bureaucracy

However, the inescapable coexistence of modern democracy and bureaucracy poses some problems. After all, the bureaucratic form of organisation is inherently hierarchical, exclusive, and it relies on election, rather than appointment by merit. But bureaucracy and democracy also share certain egalitarian characteristics. Bureaucracies, for example, have a levelling effect by ignoring both aristocratic status and capitalistic property rights as criteria of hierarchical appointment. They replace these criteria with an emphasis on educational certificates and seniority thus violating the democratic egalitarian spirit. Therefore modern bureaucracy can coexist with and complement democratic governments – but it can also subvert democratic principles by spawning 'a privileged stratum in bureaus and offices' based on

---

6   'The demos itself, in the sense of shapeless mass, never "governs" larger associations, but rather is governed… "Democratization" in the sense intended here, does not necessarily mean an increasingly active share of the subjects in government. This may be a result of democratization, but it is not necessarily the case.' (Weber 1978, 985)

educational privilege and internal connection (Weber 1978, 984–5; Bendix 1962/1977, 461).

The solution to this tension, and to a danger of bureaucratic subversion of democracy, was a formal subordination of bureaucratic officials to elected politicians. 'Politicians must be the countervailing force against bureaucratic domination' Weber declared (1978, 1417), and politicians should exercise control over all state administrative machines to secure mass consent, as well as political dynamism and flexibility. Bureaucratic officials were to be neutral, dispassionate and nonpartisan, and they serve 'without scorn and bias', while politicians were to be passionate about their causes, engaged, committed to partisan goals and, above all, publicly elected – and trusted. They were to be political masters and policy decision makers. 'Policy-making is not a technical affair, and hence not a business of the professional civil servant', reminds Weber (1978, 1419). 'According to his proper vocation, the genuine official…will not engage in politics. Rather, he should engage in impartial "administration"' (1919/1972, 18). Bureaucratic officials are indispensable, but also subordinated to political masters and democratic conventions.[7] Consequently, it is not the strength of governmental and party bureaucracies, but their weakness, that threatens the stability and sustainability of modern ('working') mass democracy.[8]

This is a key element in a complex model of power relations within the political elite. The key components of this model are political leaders – the main power actors and direction setters – professional parliamentary politicians, the top party officials, and the heads of governmental bureaucracies. The patterns of relations among these four elite components determine a type

---

7 The best description of the relation between democracy and bureaucracy is found in chapter 11 of *Economy and Society*. It is worth quoting *in extenso*: 'Mass democracy... unavoidably has to put paid professional labour in place of the historically inherited "avocational" administration by notables… Democratic mass parties are bureaucratically organised under the leadership of party officials, professional party and trade union secretaries, etc.… The progress of bureaucratization within the state administration itself is a phenomenon paralleling the development of democracy, as is quite obvious in France, North America, and now in England' (1978, 984).

8 The tension between bureaucracy and democracy was also analysed by one of Weber's students, Robert Michels, in his *Political Parties* (1911/1958). Michels concluded that bureaucratisation of political parties would inevitably undermine democracy by spawning increasingly 'indispensable' bureaucratic oligarchy. Such claims, Weber pointed out, are based on two errors: (1) an assumption that the indispensability of modern bureaucratic 'officialdom' gives it political power, which is obviously incorrect, and (2) on an equally problematic assumption that bureaucratic power/influence cannot be checked within the complex modern state.

of 'democracy', a type of political configuration and regime – with 'leader democracy' as one possible configuration type.

Professional politicians and party officialdom

Politics is about the struggle for power, domination and leadership through building alliances and attracting following – 'any kind of independent leadership in action' (1919/1972, 9). In the process of modernisation, politics changes from occasional and honorific engagement to a fulltime profession, a specialised and normatively regulated occupation guided by the ethics of responsibility. Most importantly, political struggles take place within the increasingly complex framework of a modern state – 'a compulsory hierarchical association which organizes domination' – and this state is managed by professional politicians who live 'for' and 'off' politics. Struggle for power is both their vocation and a fulltime paid job. Politicians take a partisan stand tempered by a 'sense of proportion', both backed by sober calculation of social (national) interests. Good politicians develop balanced judgement, make realistic and responsible decisions, and most importantly, assume public responsibility for all (even the unintended) consequences of their actions. Because of that, they need good judgement, a realistic sense of proportion and prudent foresight.[9] Above all, political qualifications include a sense of public responsibility.[10] Such responsibility, and the accompanied accountability to public bodies (exercised at the time of elections), is coded into the ethical system that guides professional politicians, especially those with leadership ambitions.

Mass democratisation changes not only the roles of professional politicians and political leaders, but also their recruitment and career paths. Both are 'democratised'. Due to increasing openness of political offices and intensified elite mobility, modern political leaders often emerge from outside the traditional high status ruling groups or aristocracies. They no longer rely on inherited social status to enter politics, and no longer ascend to power by proving themselves in exclusive circles of *honoratiores* (aristocracies, nobilities).

---

9 'To take a stand, to be passionate – *ira et studium* – is the politician's element, and above all the element of the political leader. His conduct is subject to quite a different, indeed, exactly the opposite, principle of responsibility from that of the civil servant... The honour of the political leader, of the leading statesman, lies precisely in an exclusive personal responsibility for what he does, a responsibility he cannot and must not reject or transfer.' (1918/1972)

10 'This element alone guarantees that responsibility toward the public, which would evaporate within an assembly governing at large, rests upon clearly identifiable person. This is especially true of a democracy proper.' (1978, 1415)

Instead, they have to demonstrate their political talent and skill by early political activism and organisational involvement, success in mobilising support, and oratory skills. These virtues open access to the political elite. But the openness makes elites more diverse, and therefore weakens their integration which formerly depended on shared social origins and social proximity. This is why the ascendant democratic leaders have to assume the additional role of elite integrators. In this role, they maintain elite solidarity, direct electoral campaigns, select advisory staff, direct policies, and inject cohesion into proposed programmes.

The struggles for power, control of government and executive machinery of the state, are also exercised within organised, and increasingly bureaucratic, political parties. Parties are 'centres of mass loyalty' and 'machines for winning votes'. They cultivate the electoral support of dominant societal interests, 'woo and organise the masses', discipline politicians, select leadership candidates, manage public opinion, finance political campaigns and distribute political spoils. In Europe, political parties also usurp the role of ideological clearing houses that shape the programmes of prospective governments. Party politicians are either vote-delivering 'entrepreneurs' or party administrators, members of the expanding bureaucratic 'party machines' and their 'officialdom'. Both are the children of mass democracy with its concern for maximising popular vote (1978, 1395–99, 1443–59).

With the development of organised political parties, political elites were enlarged by absorbing into their ranks, 'party politicians', and party officials: local 'big shots', 'big wheels', factional 'bosses', 'political agents' (USA) and by the central 'party officialdom' (Europe). The European parliamentary systems promoted the development of centralised ideological-programmatic parties. The American presidential system, by contrast, favoured local 'patronage' and 'spoils' parties, run by local bosses who were adept in political wheeling and dealing. The bosses were the major patrons and clients of leadership candidates. They resourced the candidates, but also counted on political rewards for their good service. When 'their' candidate emerged successful in elections, the bosses expected prestigious and lucrative nominations to governmental jobs. This practice politicised (and corrupted) state administration, but also generated strong party executives loyal to their leaders.

In the more centralised and bureaucratised European 'ideological parties', influence concentrated in the hands of party officials and ideologists (1978, 1398). Party elites gained influence proportionately to their organisation and financial resources. Under their influence, modern politics evolved into 'party democracy', a configuration dominated by party officialdom and factional bosses. The European party directorates, preoccupied with organising interests (material and ideal) and with forging these interests into ideologically coherent party programmes and platforms, proved particularly powerful and influential. They expanded their influence, often at the expense of parliamentarians, governmental bureaucracies, and even political leaders. The latter became increasingly dependent on party directorates and factional leaders in organising their electoral campaigns and securing the loyalty of parliamentary colleagues.

In America, by contrast, the major parties were less centrally organised, less disciplined and less ideologically coherent than in Europe. They were typically opportunistic, nonideological and programmatically vague, 'unprincipled', 'patronage' or 'spoils' parties. Such parties, according to Weber, fitted well the more 'capitalistic' form of mass democracy. American party 'big wheels' acted more like political entrepreneurs than ideologists; they organised local interests, collected funds, wooed the voters, 'managed' public opinion, and increasingly acted as 'talent spotters' in identifying political candidates.

Leaders, parliaments and party machines

In Weber's view, democracies, including parliamentary democratic systems, do not, and should not prevent the ascendancy of strong and charismatic party leaders. In fact, 'working' parliaments should facilitate the rise of such talented leaders. Parties are charged with their identification while parliaments provide the principal forums for oratory contests, test the political will of candidates and their capacity to convince. They also provide opportunities for revealing governing competence during committee work. Above all, parliaments test the capacity of leaders for prudent judgement, responsible action, and good political instincts. Parliamentary professionalism and leadership charisma should be able to coexist in modern parliamentary settings – in spite of their differences.

But they seldom do, Weber observes, because professional parliamentarians resent popular leaders. This may result in parliamentarians forming coalitions with party politicians and 'castrating' the charisma of ascendant popular leaders. Such castration, however, may backfire by undermining public trust in parliaments. By contrast, when charismatic leaders acquire wide public trust, this 'rubs off' on all their parliamentary colleagues whose status and popularity is elevated. Therefore parliamentary factions are ambivalent in supporting leaders. Typically, they play it safe by endorsing strong and able leadership candidates, but 'deposing' of them at the sign of megalomania and repeated failure.

In the American presidential system, the relation is skewed to the leaders' advantage. Executive power is heavily concentrated in the White House and presidential elections are seen as the principal source of democratic mandate. Victorious presidential candidates often gain control of the Senate (through patronage) and, if successful, can easily generate a working majority in the House. But they cannot count on lasting party discipline and they constantly need the support of parliamentarians to secure the smooth passage of sponsored legislation and/or for blocking undesirable bills. This tests their prestige among their parliamentary colleagues. When popular, and when enjoying a strong electoral backing and high public profile, national leaders can acquire strong bipartisan support. Once the support is obtained, opposing or criticising them becomes politically risky. The opposite is also true. Declining mass popularity of presidents is immediately reflected in evaporating support in parliament and therefore reinforces the 'lame duck' performance.

Very few politicians can fulfil the role of effective leaders. Therefore, the selection and grooming of capable leaders requires well-organised parties that can identify and support talented candidates, as well as 'working' parliaments where future leaders are tested. Parliamentarians acquire leadership skills during apprenticeships in parliamentary debates and while working in parliamentary committees. Such tests and apprenticeships help in sorting talented orators and organisers from complacent 'party hacks' and opportunistic demagogues. In America, where the parliament has always been weaker vis-à-vis presidential executives than in Europe, some of these selective-formative functions are performed by party conventions and long election campaigns, especially the 'primaries'.[11]

Party machines play the crucial role in identifying and grooming successful leaders, but their top officials are also major competitors in the rivalry for power. Moreover, charismatic origins make all political parties vulnerable to periodic charismatic takeovers, especially 'in times of great excitements'. 'Since all emotional mass appeals have certain charismatic features, the bureaucratisation of the parties and of electioneering may at its very height suddenly be forced into the service of charismatic hero worship' notes Weber (1978, 1130). Under such conditions, party 'officials', who resent charisma, submit relatively easily to a leader's will. The officialdom

---

11 'The parties are fashioned for the election campaign that is most important for office patronage: the fight for the presidency and for the governorships of the separate states... In the primaries, the delegates are already elected in the name of the candidate for the nation's leadership. The (intended) consequence of such a system is a politicisation of the top rungs of administration, as well as administrative dilettantism caused by partisan patronage – a dangerous feature that nevertheless has a virtue of being seen as highly "democratic".' (Weber 1919/1972)

allows the leaders to alter party programmes, reshape electoral platforms, and forge new electoral alliances.[12]

But the key factor behind frequent ascendancy of charismatic leaders is electoral competition. All mass elections are plebiscitary in nature, and they are conducted through public (and mass-mediated) oratory contests. This turns them into 'oratory struggles' 'demagogic battles' and 'tests of extraordinary gift' (Weber 1918/1972, 111) won by those candidates who prove most spectacular, most convincing, and most trustworthy. Therefore, political parties – especially patronage (spoils) parties most dependent on electoral success – adjust to modern electoral politics by becoming leader-centred parties. They do it by momentarily shifting their *modus operandi* from the systematic cultivation of organised interests to mobilising mass electoral support behind 'their' charismatic candidate for leadership. Alternatively, conflicts between ambitious leaders and party directorates are settled by the latter 'castrating the charisma' of ambitious leaders and drifting towards a leaderless configuration.[13]

This is an important theoretical clue. Under 'normal' (though rare) conditions of social stability, party bureaucracies tend to control the selection and performance of political leaders and they can stifle leaders' charisma. The elites are 'headed' rather than 'led'. By contrast, victories of personal charisma over party officialdom are more likely under 'extraordinary conditions' of social turbulence and widespread mass anxieties. Yet, while labelled 'extraordinary', such conditions were increasingly frequent, one is tempted to say 'normal' in crises-afflicted European societies. This subtly altered Weber's arguments. Takeovers were seen as more and more typical simply because rapid change generated almost permanent crises and mass anxieties.

---

12 'Neither the parties' Caesarist character and mass demagogy nor their bureaucratisation and stereotyped public image are in themselves a rigid barrier to the rise of leaders. Especially the well-organised parties that really want to exercise state power must subordinate themselves to those who hold the confidence of the masses, if they are men [sic] with leadership abilities… Particularly under the contemporary conditions of [democratic] selection, a strong parliament and responsible parliamentary parties, fulfilling their function as a recruiting and proving ground of mass leaders as statesmen, are basic conditions for maintaining continuous and consistent policies.' (Weber 1978, 1459)

13 'In normal times…[the] bureaucratic [party] apparatus…controls the party's course, including the vitally important nomination of candidates. However, in times of great public excitement, charismatic leaders may emerge even in solidly bureaucratised parties, as was demonstrated by Roosevelt's campaign in 1912… Such an eruption of charisma, of course, always faces the resistance of the normally predominant professionals, especially of the bosses who control and finance the party and maintain its routine operations, and whose tools the candidates usually are.' (Weber 1978, 1132, 1453)

Weber also notes that charismatic impositions are easier when the party concerned is 'a pragmatic group of patronage seekers with an ad hoc programme for a given campaign' (1978, 1133). Parties controlled by notables, class parties, and ideological parties with clearly articulated world views, are more resistant to charismatic takeovers. Alternatively, patronage and spoils parties easily fall under the charismatic spell of leaders. In such parties, the emergence of charismatic leaders is often welcomed as an opportunity for 'strengthening' and 'renewal', a reorientation from one set of interests to another. A charismatic leader can break the stranglehold of 'established and dominant interests' and alter 'a crypto-plutocratic distribution of power' (1978, 989). New charismatic leaders can also pave the way for electoral realignment, which may improve their electoral prospects. This is why strong leaders, while resented by party officialdom, may nevertheless win the support of this officialdom.

Leader democracy

The key point highlighted by Weber was that popular leaders, professional politicians, party directorates and bureaucratic officialdoms all played important roles in modern democratic politics. They complemented each other as the 'core executives' of the state. But these functional complementarities did not reduce hierarchy, and therefore the inevitable competition for domination. Under the stable conditions, the dominant position was assumed by party directorates – thus resulting in an elite configuration described as 'party democracy'. At the time of mass anxieties, by contrast, power tended to concentrate in the hands of popular and charismatic leaders, thus heralding a shift towards 'leader democracy' – an elite configuration in which elected party leaders gain prominence, especially vis-à-vis party 'machines' and parliamentary cliques. It was leaders who played a dominant role in generating public trust, shaping political strategies, and integrating elites. The alternative to such domination, especially under the system of proportional representation, is a weak 'leaderless' democracy, where party/parliamentary coteries dominate, often backed by the bureaucratic officialdom.[14]

But even in modern 'leader democracy', Weber stresses, leaders never rule alone. They always 'co-dominate', that is operate together with 'working' parliaments, robust political parties ('machines'), and with loyal governmental bureaucracies that are indispensible for effective rule. They can cultivate

---

14 'Moreover, in its present form, proportional representation is a typical phenomenon of leaderless democracy. This is the case not only because it facilitates the horse-trading of the notables for placement on the ticket, but also because in the future it will give organized interest groups the possibility of compelling parties to include their officials in the list of candidates, thus creating an un-political Parliament in which genuine leadership finds no place.' (Weber 1919, 29)

'public opinion' only with the help of party and publicity machines, and they are always subjects to 'democratic recall' when they lose elite backing and (therefore) mass confidence. Thus, 'leader democracy' inevitably involves the entire elite. Moreover, prominent leaders do use oratory skills and a fair amount of demagogy.[15] 'Democratization and demagogy belong together…insofar as the masses can no longer be treated as purely passive object of administration, that is, insofar as their attitudes have some active import' (1978, 1450). Although the parliamentary and party machines moderate this demagogy and curb populism, leaders tend to be both imposing and 'spectacular' – a result of 'the tendency to favour the type of individual who is most spectacular, who promises the most, or who employs the most effective propaganda measures in the competition for leadership' (1978, 269).

This brings us to an important clarification, further elaborated in Chapter 5. Weber's comments on 'leader democracy' have sometimes been misinterpreted as an endorsement of the dictatorships à la Mussolini or Hitler. This is incorrect. Weber clearly distinguishes modern 'leader democracy', seen as exemplified by the British and American governments, from autocratic Caesarism and 'personality cults'. Moreover, he explicitly condemns the autocratic rule of Bismarck as incompatible with modern 'leader democracy'.[16] It is true that autocracy and 'leader democracy' share the reliance on oratory charisma. They may also have the same historical roots both evolve from more exclusive charismatic leadership – but they develop different practices and elite structures. Under an autocratic Caesarist regime, the leader becomes a sole and unquestioned authority; he imposes his will in an arbitrary manner, rather than co-dominating. Moreover, autocratic leaders betray political vocation and professionalism, reject electoral competition and ignore democratic recall, while democratic leaders have to maintain professional commitments and 'prove themselves' by winning electoral contests.[17]

---

15 'Active mass democratisation means that political leader is no longer proclaimed a candidate because he has proved himself in a circle of honoratiores, then becoming a leader because of his parliamentary accomplishments, but that he gains the trust and the faith of the masses in him and his power with the means of mass demagogy. In substance, this means a shift towards a Caesarist mode of selection. Indeed, every democracy tends in this direction.' (Weber 1978, 1451)

16 For the contrast with 'personality cults', see 1978, 961–2, 1457–60. For Weber's critical comments on the Bismarck legacy see 1978, 1385–92.

17 'The sin against the lofty spirit of political vocation, however, begins where this striving for power ceases to be objective and becomes purely personal self-intoxication, instead of exclusively entering the service of "the cause". For ultimately there are only two kinds of deadly sins in the field of politics: lack of objectivity and – often but not always identical with it – irresponsibility… His lack of objectivity tempts him to strive for the glamorous semblance of power rather than for actual power. His irresponsibility, however, suggests that he enjoys power merely for power's sake without a substantive purpose.' (Weber 1919/1972, 11)

Schumpeter's Theory of Economic and Political Development

In his seminal *Theory of Economic Development*, Schumpeter (1911/1959) challenged the static equilibrium model of neoclassical economics, the model that guided both the scholar-theoreticians and political practitioners of the day. He argued that it failed to explain the sources of economic dynamism, growth and development. This critical argument was restated three decades later in *Capitalism, Socialism and Democracy* (1942/1987), where Schumpeter explained economic progress and growth as the result of constant innovation carried out by entrepreneurs. But, he stressed, innovation and entrepreneurial activities always destroy equilibriums; they create tension and imbalance[18] that undermine perfect competition by creating temporary monopolies (1942/1987, 132). This was a revolutionary statement that scandalised most scholars who, at that time, adhered to what was described as the 'equilibrium model' and the accompanied vision of balanced or balance-seeking economic and political transactions.

Perfect competition, one of the central foundations of the equilibrium model, implies free entry of new producers into every existing industry and therefore intense and ongoing competition in production and sales. Before Schumpeter, it was thought that impediments to free entry would bring loss to the community in the form of monopolistic constraints. Yet, such constraints and closures seemed frequent and normal under conditions of rapid economic growth where:

> Free entry into a new field may make it impossible to enter it at all. The introduction of new methods of production and new commodities is hardly conceivable with perfect – and perfectly prompt – competition from the start. And this means that the bulk of what we call economic progress is incompatible with it. (1942/1987, 104–5)

Schumpeter's explanation of this paradox is as iconoclastic as it is simple. Free entry and free competition eliminate the advantages (extra profits) of entrepreneurial activity and therefore destroy the motive for innovation and incentives for progress. From the perspective of progress, Schumpeter argues, 'perfect competition is not only impossible, but also inferior' (1942/1987, 106). Although competition does bring some benefits, for example, it widens the diversity of products, perfect competition is an impediment to progress, an economically stultifying force. Therefore both extremes – perfect competition

---

18 But 'a new equilibrium always emerges, or tends to emerge, which absorbs the results of innovation carried out in the preceding periods of prosperity', Schumpeter (1989, 69) notes.

and the lack of competition – stultify economic growth. The most advantageous configuration, from the point of view of economic dynamism and progress, is somewhere between these two extremes.

Schumpeter (1989, 60) also proposes another important distinction: between qualitative development, that is the creation of a new product/ method/technology, and quantitative change, that results in a sudden increase in production. In the market model of neoclassical economics the emphasis is placed on explaining quantitative change. Such change may occur due to *none*conomic forces outside the system, such as population increase, expansion of the market, etc. and it has quantitative effects, that is, it changes the volume and speed, but not the character, of production. However, as Schumpeter observes, the major economic developments have a qualitative character. They resemble revolutionary 'qualitative leaps' that mark the replacement of old forms by new forms of production, generating new demand and products. Such qualitative changes occur due to internal innovation, that is, changes within the system. They mark the internally driven (endogenous) 'development proper' that is always accompanied by the 'winds of creative destruction' – sudden changes that destroy the old forms and 'create expansion' (1989, 63). 'By "development", therefore, we shall mean only such changes in economic life as are not forced upon it from without but arise by its own initiative, from within' (1934, 63).

Innovation, the crucial element of this qualitative change, involves creating something new, unique, untried, and therefore revolutionary in its impact. The difference between coach transport and steam-driven railroad transport illustrates well the concept of qualitative change and its revolutionary social impact.[19] While in classical equilibrium economics 'economic life is essentially passive and merely adapts to the natural and social influences which may be acting on it' (1989, 159), Schumpeterian economic development and the accompanying qualitative change are always products of entrepreneurial innovation. He draws on Karl Marx in his search for a 'vision of economic evolution as a distinct process generated by the economic system itself' (1989, 160). In contrast with this vision, neoclassical economists attempt to make sense of the market economy as a process that actually does not change due to its own dynamics and initiative, but rather

---

19 'By innovation I understand such changes of the combinations of the factors of production as cannot be effected by infinitesimal steps or variations on the margin. They consist primarily in changes in the methods of production and transportation, or in changes in industrial organization, or in the production of a new article, or in the opening up of new markets or of new source of material' (1989, 30). 'What we, unscientifically, call economic progress means essentially putting productive resources to uses *hitherto untried in practice*, and withdrawing them from the uses they have served so far. This is what we call "innovation"' (1989, 63–4).

evolves under the impact of events that are external, such as population increase, natural disaster, war, and so on.

Schumpeter offers an intriguing intellectual breakthrough and suggests a 'paradigmatic switch': 'There must be a purely economic theory of economic change which does not merely rely on external factors propelling the economic system from one equilibrium to another', he observes, and promptly offers an alternative vision of economic development attributed to continuous entrepreneurial innovations (1989, 166). Entrepreneurs are actors who are not satisfied with the application of the tested methods and experiences of the past, but they have a new vision about the future, where:

> The function of entrepreneurs is to reform or revolutionize the pattern of production by exploiting an invention or more generally, an untried technological possibility for producing a new commodity or producing an old one in a new way, by opening up a new source of supply of materials or a new outlet for products, by reorganizing an industry and so on. (1942/1987, 132)

This is quite different from the fulfilment of a mere 'business-managerial' function. While traditional business managers react to existing (identified) demand by offering their familiar products, entrepreneurial activity 'creates an expansion of demand for its own new product'. The real entrepreneurial agency is not just the invention of a new product in a technical sense. Innovation includes overcoming all the difficulties, mainly the resistance of the market used to routinise business conduct. Entrepreneurs revolutionise production by inventing new products, 'awakening' new demand, convincing buyers about its superior applicability and utility, attracting creditors and combining all these different elements of production in an appropriate way that brings to the market a new quality and configuration of supply and demand (1989, 63–6).[20]

If there are disturbances and disruptions in the market, such as recession cycles caused by outside factors, the market reacts in a predictable way, that is, through adaptation and gradual adjustment. This reaction is consistent with, and anticipated by, 'neoclassical' theory. But there is another reaction that constitutes a novelty and 'paradigmatic anomaly': 'People can also drop

---

20 In contrast, the equilibrium model narrows its focus to adaptation, a response to changes in the data (i.e. to a shift of preferences caused by exogenous factors), which drive the process back to equilibrium. Equilibrium analyses, therefore, assume full adjustment carried out by traditional businessmen and managers. Since the process of equilibration is not problematic, it leaves no room for the entrepreneur (Loasby 1984, 78).

their attitude of passive adaptation, they can react by doing new things in a new way, incompatible with the fundamental arrangements that existed before' (1989, 27). Entrepreneurship 'proper' involves this new kind of reaction. It is creative rather than adaptive, innovative rather than emulative. Entrepreneur-innovators rely on imagination and courage, rather than experience, because entrepreneurial innovations transcend the past, and therefore carry with them high risk. They are social – rather than merely economic – innovators, agents of social change, rather than mere inventors. Their appearance marks social transformation and social development, rather than merely accelerated change. This is why successful entrepreneurs are rare and exceptional figures. They are rare because 'most people find it difficult and are often unable to act in other than routine manner; those who can are rare and therefore not subject to competitive conditions, whence the phenomenon of profit' (1989, 33). Others can emulate their behaviour later, after new things have been successfully done, and innovation spreads through industries via such lower risk emulations.

The shift from equilibrium to disequilibrium, from static to dynamic model, from management to entrepreneurship, means a break with predictability in the world of economy. The Schumpeterian vision closely approximates the Weberian vision of 'qualitative' change instigated by charismatic 'switchmen of historical tracks'. Innovations occur regularly but in an unpredictable fashion, and therefore, like charismatic flare-ups in the Weberian theory – such flare-ups are sudden, contingent and largely unpredictable. Above all, entrepreneurial innovations, like charismatic mobilisations, have a disequilibrating impact. They disturb the routine flow of economic process, destroy the old forms of production, and create new forms and new patterns of relations between consumers and producers – hence the popular phrase 'winds of creative destruction'. Entrepreneurial innovation generates new demand, produces new tastes, creates new economic resources and restructures relations among the consumers. As Brian Loasby (1984, 80) notes, 'Herein lies Schumpeter's fundamental departure from the standard modern analytical method: tastes, resources and technology are themselves the product of the system, not the facts with which the system has to deal.' Consumers cease to be the masters and demand ceases to be automatic, predictable and 'given'. In the Schumpeterian model, both are the outcomes and creations of entrepreneurial action.

The theory of entrepreneurship calls for a 'paradigmatic switch' in theoretical vision. In an equilibrium economy, businessmen are seen as rational and adaptive figures using 'equilibrium routines' and drawing 'conclusions from the known circumstances' (1934, 21). To put it another way, they are habitual/rational actors who act in the way that has 'stood the test of experience' (Schumpeter, cited in Loasby 1984, 78). They act, but not as agents of change. Rather, they are routine actors following established mental templates and behavioural clichés in a calculative and predictable manner based on past experience, or guided by adaptive routines.[21]

This way of thinking also questions – and recasts – the notion of public good. In the equilibrium model, public (common) good is well defined through market procedure and perfect competition. It is the outcome of economic process tending towards equilibrium. By contrast, in the Schumpeterian model of development the economic process is dynamic and open ended. There is no direct and unambiguous relationship between institutions and outcome, and therefore no clear notion of public good. 'Progress' or development does not have any specific content or predictable direction; it means merely a 'qualitative change' that does not claim to achieve any common or higher 'good' in a normative sense, such as happiness, prosperity, and so forth. Moreover, unlike in the classical model of perfect competition, there is no invisible hand that would produce social harmony and procure public good as an outcome. The 'common good' is vague and has a contingent nature; it may be identified with progress, but progress may also create imbalance and depression ('creative destruction'). The exact nature or direction of progress is therefore unknown, as it cannot be projected from past experience or deduced from the data of a static equilibrium model. Economic process may either tend towards equilibrium or towards imbalance and tension.[22]

One of the unexpected conclusions drawn by Schumpeter is that a state of perfect competition is dangerous because it destroys the motive force for innovation and progress. Economic progress occurs under the condition of monopolistic domination or oligopolistic competition. In the case of oligopoly, innovation and progress are propelled by rivalry among a few large firms. In such cases, 'there is in fact no determinate equilibrium at all, and the possibility presents itself that there may be an endless sequence of moves and countermoves, as an indefinite state of warfare between firms' (1942/1987, 79).

Competitive elite democracy

The Schumpeterian vision of 'competitive electoral democracy' transposes his economic thinking into the political realm. But it would be incorrect to

---

21 'New methods of production, new products, new ways of making decisions, new organizational practices, are just as conjectural as new theories about the causes of cancer.' (Loasby 1984, 76)

22 Unlike in the equilibrium model of neoclassical economics, in Schumpeter's developmental model the 'market process does not lead to definitive truth; it provides an environment for testing of conjectures' of economic actors (Loasby 1984, 76–77), and reveals the ambiguity of knowledge. Habitual knowledge can be made temporary and depreciated by new innovation.

say that Schumpeter starts where Weber finishes and that the concept of 'competitive electoral democracy' (also known as 'competitive elitism' or 'competitive elitist democracy') constitutes a mere elaboration of 'leader democracy' (Held 2006, 134). Yet, there are clear parallels and, as we argue here, clear compatibility between the two visions, as well as a distinct theoretical connection linking them. Schumpeter's realistic account of contemporary democracy could easily pass as a postscript to Weber's famous 1919 lecture on 'Politics as a Vocation' and his critical essay on 'Parliament and Government in a Reconstructed Germany'. In both texts, political leaders and parties play the crucial role in binding the executive 'ruling minority' with the masses in a democratic manner. While Weber is more detailed in his historical and sociological analysis of leaders, parties and governmental bureaucracies, Schumpeter is more precise in analysing the conduct of modern democratic competition. According to him, such competition is, above all, a method of leadership selection, an open competition for executive leadership in the state. It evolves into the core democratic process and becomes the main source of political dynamics, the key propellant of political change (or 'development' in the Schumpeterian sense).

While most readers are aware of Schumpeter's desperate attempt to secure the future of democracy by reconciling it with the inevitable (in his view) 'socialist' etatisation of society, few are familiar with his other preoccupation, namely his attempts at securing the compatibility of democratic method with modern economy. This may look like an impossible or at least hopelessly ambitious task. After all, democracy, understood as electoral competition for state executive leadership, thrives only in a stable social and political climate. In comparison, modern economy is in a state of permanent revolution: inherently unbalanced, driven by entrepreneurs/innovators, and therefore undergoing cyclical and destabilising renewals through 'waves of creative destruction'. Yet, the two looked complementary to Schumpeter, in a similar way as stable bureaucracy and revolutionary charisma appeared de facto complementary to Weber. Political leaders who 'drive' the dynamic democratic process were to Schumpeter functional equivalents of entrepreneurs/innovators who 'drive' the development of capitalist economy. Political leaders have to innovate in order to secure electoral victory. Thus political 'development' and 'progress', like economic development and progress, can be seen as generated by innovations of political leaders/entrepreneurs. These leaders compete in an open manner, but like economic competition so their political competition is always imperfect, constrained by party oligopolistic, or sometimes even monopolistic, control. Perfect competition – if it were possible at all – would destroy orderly party-structured competition and result in a chaotic race of all against all.

Such argument clearly parallels Weber's argument about the disruptive-creative impact of charismatic leaders and it challenges the idea of balanced democratic politics. Charismatic leaders reappear in the Schumpeterian visions as leaders/innovators, as political entrepreneurs who pave the way for social development. Moreover, modern competitive-democratic politics appears now as a twin sister of modern economy, both sharing the same inherent disequilibrium, dynamic nature, and the similar dependency on entrepreneurs/innovators.

Leadership and innovation

Perhaps the best means of highlighting the distinctiveness of the Schumpeterian vision of 'competitive democracy' is through a comparison with a more classical and static model of 'reflective democracy' as presented by Anthony Downs in *An Economic Theory of Democracy* (1957).[23]

Downs presents a static model of political process and democracy. The model closely parallels the equilibrium model of neoclassical economics. It assumes perfect competition among the political office seekers and leadership candidates competing for voters' support – again, drawing on neoclassical economics that assumes open competition among producers and consumers. Perfect political competition encourages office seekers, that is, leadership candidates, to adapt their vote-attracting appeals to the estimated position of the average constituent or median voter. If there is a shift in voters' preferences, candidates adjust their position mechanically to the new median position. That way, the winning strategy, the most successful form of political appeal, is predictable: it consists of aiming at the median. The law of optimal appeal and policy position for candidates is thus determined by a 'political function': the relation between citizens embracing certain policy positions, the latter stretching along a left–right ideological spectrum. Those who approximate the median voter position in the fastest and most accurate manner and who shift their appeals accordingly, have the greater chance of political, especially electoral,

---

23 It was David Miller (1983) who first differentiated between Schumpeter's and Downs' models of competitive democracy. In contemporary literature there are further applications and explications of this comparison. John Medearis (2001) claims that we have to distinguish two conceptions of democracy: the well-known elite and a less known (by political scientists) transformative conception of democracy. The elite model is depicted as an equilibrium model. This is, however, at odds with chapters 22 and 23 of Schumpeter's *Capitalism, Socialism and Democracy*. We argue in line with Andrew Hindmoor (2004 and 2008) who argues that the use of the equilibrium method precludes the analysis of policy innovation.

success. In this way, according to Downs, modern democracy delivers political balance-optimum or 'common good'. There is little space in such a vision for leadership or political innovation.

Schumpeter explicitly challenges this vision of the equilibrated political market. He admits that voters/citizens embrace and constantly shift their policy preferences. However, such shifts typically follow, rather than precede, the appeals of political leaders. Moreover, politicians frequently adjust their own policy positions to the changing circumstances and conditions, in a similar way as median voters do but independently of them. In addition to these adjustments, political leaders often act like entrepreneurs by actively shaping and developing the political preferences of their constituencies. They offer new attractive visions, new goals, new directions and new strategies. By doing that, they actively create their political constituencies, rather than pursue what today we call 'structural' or 'social cleavage' vote. Such political innovation amounts to creating a new political demand and a new source/idiom of support. One side effect of such innovation is disequilibrium in the political market. In a similar way as entrepreneurs/innovators disrupt the consumer/producer market by developing new forms of production, new products and new demand, entrepreneurial political leaders disrupt and restructure politics and 'awake' a new political idiom of appeal. The disruption destroys the old political arrangements, opens new opportunities and creates new political leader/voter alliances.

What precisely does innovation mean in politics? Drawing on Schumpeter's definition of innovation in the economic realm, we can interpret 'political innovation' in the following manner as: (1) a 'qualitative', that is, substantive and significant change in policies, political strategies and policy-making methods; (2) a significant changes in political organisation; (3) the opening up of new electoral markets and alliances; (4) mobilising new political resources; (5) forming new bases of political support; and (6) providing a new ideology (a combination of political values with a concomitant vision of 'good society' and general strategies for realising this vision) or a new interpretative frame for assessing political situation.

This is the first part of the innovation story, so to speak. The second part involves the actual entrepreneurial 'product development' (to use the economic analogy) – overcoming the resistance of the old sociopolitical environment. Successful political entrepreneurs have to gain the endorsement of their parties, win parliamentary supporters, successfully realign and harmonise dominant interests, and find new campaign funders. They also have to swing the key opinion makers and media behind them. Finally, the ultimate test of their entrepreneurial skills comes when they attempt to woo the voters during election campaigns.

It is clear that a Schumpeterian account of political innovation, as carried by leaders, undermines the equilibrium model of politics and the accompanied vision of 'reflective-transmitting' democracy. Proper leadership (that is, politically innovative) leadership and perfect (that is, open and egalitarian) competition are at odds with each other. It is true that the total lack of competition implies a monopolistic position of a single political actor, a political dictatorship. It is also true that any long lasting political monopoly is bound to have a negative impact on political innovation and progress. But too much competition is also dangerous. It destroys the power oligopolies held by major parties, fragments and divides the constituencies, destabilises the political process, and weakens the motivation of strong/large political actors (major parties and leadership candidates) to innovate. The idea of perfect political competition, in other words, is undermined by preexisting major party loyalties, and therefore by the inevitably oligopolistic nature of leadership contest (see also Santoro 1993). This is often reflected in the common-sense fear of party fragmentation and a preference for two-party politics and two-way (alternative) political competition.

What is the meaning of perfect competition in the political market? Again, in a Schumpeterian rendition it means many things: (1) a free entry and high in- and out-mobility; (2) frequent elections that maintain high mobility; (3) well-informed and competent citizens with determinate political preferences; and (4) responsiveness of government policy to the citizens' preferences. It is easy to see that such conditions of perfect competition reduce the role of leadership as autonomous political-entrepreneurial activity. Free entry of new competitors, for example, reduces the value of political investment in political innovations. It undermines motivation for political investments and destroys political progress. In addition, free entry may also increase the number of rival parties or candidates in the competition, and the proliferation of parties impedes stable government by weakening governability. In order to reduce these negative impacts, institutional and other barriers are set up against free entry: for example, entry is restricted to times of general elections, electoral rules place numerous conditions on registration and newcomers have to pay entry fees that cover the costs of organisation and political advertising, and so on.

The same applies to the second aspect or condition of perfect competition, namely frequent elections. The short term of office makes governments responsive, but it also makes them 'jittery and fickle', sensitive to the swinging moods of voters, unable to set and pursue consistent long-term strategies. Frequent elections (especially elections that may be called at any time) destabilise government and public policy. By contrast, long terms of office and considerable time lags between elections increase monopolistic advantages for the governing parties by giving them more scope for using the 'incumbency advantage'. They also encourage 'political investment' in innovations and reforms and increase the likelihood of 'long-term' planning. If election winners do not have a guaranteed time in office, they lose motivation to make any political investment in the campaign. With a degree of simplification one can say that frequent elections maximise political responsiveness at the expense of innovation, autonomy and responsibility. They encourage short-term opportunism and political conformism.

The third condition of perfect competition – a perfectly informed and competent citizenry with determinate political preferences (represented by the 'median voter') – also has some destabilising effects. As Downs (1957, 55–60) explicitly acknowledges, under such an imaginary 'perfect' condition, political candidates can win only one electoral contest. This reduces their motivation to keep their electoral promises, to respect the rules of the game and to be honest. Contrarily, in the more realistic world of Schumpeterian politics citizens are poorly informed, and they lack the technical competence that is necessary for rational evaluation of an incumbent's policy (see his famous infantilism argument 1942/1987, 262). Political leaders widen the room for political manoeuvre, but they have no incentives to inform or educate voters/citizens about their policies or broader conditions of decision making. Thus political stability and the autonomy of rulers come with a price tag of low civic competence.

Finally, perfect competition means that policy products become more homogeneous. This is equivalent to product homogenisation/standardisation in the economic market. Such homogenisation may facilitate choices (by reducing them), but has some obvious detrimental effects. It is a serious impediment to innovation, and hence to progress. Another way of putting it is that homogenisation leads to political conformism because the optimal (from the point of view of success) policy has to follow public opinion, or strictly speaking, its articulations in opinion polls and focus groups. It also means that competing leaders and parties try to differentiate their own product (i.e. policy strategies) from that of their rivals through other means like negativity, alternative framing, different rhetoric, or original advertising. Genuine innovation, however, is discouraged.

The Schumpeterian model questions the positive relation between the openness and competitiveness of the market, on the one hand, and the optimum (common good) democratic outcome on the other. Unlike in Downs' static equilibrium theory, in the Schumpeterian model higher competitiveness does not motivate the rival parties or candidates to move closer to the position of the median voter. Instead, competitiveness motivates leaders to innovate and actively reshape voters' preferences.

This reshaping may involve manipulations of agendas, inclusion and exclusion of critical issues, changing ideological orientations and interpretive frames, introducing new criteria of assessment and redefining public interest. Competing leadership candidates are also seen as actively shaping the views of their constituencies and restructuring political markets to create strategic constituencies of their own. Unlike office-seeker politicians in the Downs' model who just follow and 'reflect' public opinion, political entrepreneurs (typically oligopolistic in form) reshape public opinion in order to achieve their own policy goals and create their own visions of public good (1942/1987, 154–5; Santoro 1993). Without such active shaping and creating – or without demagogic (oratory) manipulation – qualitative change, that is authentic political progress, is impossible. According to Schumpeter, it is competition for leadership, and not a perfect political competition, that is a precondition of achieving some common good. But this achievement is never guaranteed.

The mirage of the hidden 'common good'

This point deserves an additional comment. As we have seen above, Schumpeter challenges the popular belief that democracy *necessarily* delivers the common good. There is no political equivalent of the 'invisible hand' that would provide equilibrium, no lasting balance between preferences and policies and no direct relationship between institutions, however well-designed, and political outcomes. Common good, the equilibrium between average-voter demand and policy supply, is too vulnerable to countless contingencies to be reached or even closely approximated. However, the 'good of the people' can sometimes be achieved, provided it is identified with the constructed (rather than merely identified) public interest (1942/1987, 134). This construction, or rather constant reconstruction, is done by political leaders.

In setting up a descriptive-analytical definition of democracy, Schumpeter never rejects the notion of public interest.[24] What he objects to is, first, the illegitimate derivation of common good from the statistical aggregation of individual preferences; second, its identification with the metaphysical (ergo quasi-mythical) notion of *volonté générale*, and third, the assumption that common good is stable and unambiguous. Schumpeter is a methodological individualist and a forerunner of what was subsequently labelled Public

---

24 Although Mackie (2009, 134) accuses Schumpeter of intellectual and moral incoherence, saying that he on one hand attacks the notion of common good, but on the other hand appeals covertly to the notion of common good (cf. Bellamy 1991, 502; Held 1987, 179).

Choice Theory (PCT). This makes his objections quite predictable and widely shared among the adherents to PCT. Common good or, in Schumpeter's term, the 'interest of all' is a construct that is occasionally created by successful leaders in the process of rivalry for top executive positions in the state. It may be seen as a side effect of competitive leadership, though there is nothing inevitable in its appearance or reemergence. There is no guarantee that policy innovation and its implications in a democratic regime necessarily serve the shared interests of the people, or are publicly recognised as such. If an 'interest of all' is successfully created, it is typically a result of leaders' persuasion and imposition, rather than a discovery or poll-driven approximation by responsive politicians. Moreover, success in constructing the 'interest of all' cannot be predicted. Since it depends on leadership action, its emergence – marked by mass consent and commitment – can be ascertained only *post factum*.

The core elements of Downs' and Schumpeter's theories of political market can be summarised and contrasted in a tabular form.

Table 2.1. A summary of the core elements of Downs' and Schumpeter's theories of political market

	Downs	Schumpeter
Nature of the political market	Equilibrium, possible balance	Disequilibrium, permanent imbalance
Political aim (optimum)	Perfect competition	Imperfect (oligopolistic) competition
Structural mechanism	'Invisible hand' balancing political demand and supply	Unintended consequences, perverse effects
Propellant of politics	Exogenous factors that change voters' preferences	Endogenous factors – leaders' actions and innovations
Key actors	Voters	Leaders
Political changes	Quantitative, slow, cumulative	Qualitative, sudden, revolutionary
Behavioural rules	Fixed (stable 'production function')	Fluid (constant innovation: new 'production function')
Outcomes	Predictable	Unpredictable
Common good	Determined and unambiguous: defined by median-voter views	Open and ambiguous: a construct imposed by leaders
Elected officials	Managers: aggregators and translators	Leaders: creators and proponents

The limits of the market analogy

Although Schumpeter embraces the market metaphor consistently, he does this with caution and seems to be aware of its limitations. The political market, he suggests, works differently from the economic one in at least three respects. First, the political 'market' is more volatile, more innovation-driven and more oligopolistic than the economic one. In the circular flow of the economic process you can be, but you do not *have to be*, an entrepreneur/innovator. The typical figures in industrial economies are businessmen and managers, both involved in routine and customary production and exchange. Entrepreneurs are a special and rare species, and their actions undermine the established routines. In politics, however, routine seldom brings success. There is a stronger pressure to innovate, to break the old routines and expectations, and to invent new attractive appeals. This is because the nature of political rivalry is quite specific, and the risks of innovation are low. Initial failures to attract political support do not result in political bankruptcy and forcible exclusion from the game. Moreover, the costs of political competition are 'underwritten' by parties and other support organisations. They absorb many of the initial costs of competition, especially the costs of prolonged campaigning. This transforms the leadership contest into a regulated and typically oligopolistic race in which the initial loser is motivated to introduce a new 'combination', an innovation, a newly crafted appeal in order to improve his/her chances and defeat the rivals. Politics becomes a strategic game between the (pre)selected few, but open to – and inviting – innovations.

Second, there are stronger monopolistic and oligopolistic tendencies in the political market due to the well-known and widely accepted 'advantage of incumbency' and the limited number of 'major parties' that field serious contenders. It means that in politics, unlike in the economic producer/consumer market, there is always an incumbent winner, benefiting from their position of power and exposure. It is this incumbent who typically controls the timing of the next contest and the circumstances of competition. Moreover, there is little continuous feedback from citizens (political consumers), and rare changes of leaders 'mid-stream'. The main 'feedback' from voters occurs at the discrete moments of elections, though there are also more continuous results of opinion polling.[25] Between elections (and between polls) there are long periods of uncertainty, and during these periods the monopolistic position of the incumbent leader and the ruling political party is both advantageous and secure.

---

25 Cf. 1942/1987, 263. In economic terms, political competition is similar to bidding for a long-lasting government contract (licence).

Third, citizens' political competence is much weaker than consumers' competence. This prompted Schumpeter to formulate his famous argument of 'voter infantilism' (1942/1987, 258–61). It points to different frameworks of conduct and experience among market consumers and citizens/voters. Consumers make their decisions within the familiar 'little field' of everyday life where norms and utilities are well known and confirmed by long experience. Citizens/voters, by contrast, have to make choices in the 'wider field' of political life that is separated from everyday life and seldom experienced in its complexity. However, what is the 'wider field' for ordinary voters/citizens constitutes the 'little field' for political leaders. For leaders, especially for professional politicians, politics is the familiar sphere of activity, with a strong experiential basis and clear parameters of judgement. They are familiar with the rules, conventions, choices, risks and other realities of political life. Therefore there is a wide gap between their knowledge and competence, and those of ordinary citizens. Like Weber before him, Schumpeter stresses the superior knowledge, and not the superior cognitive skills, of professional politicians. They are political experts facing dilettante voters.

It should be clear by now that Weber's vision of 'leader democracy' and Schumpeter's model of 'competitive democracy' are not only similar, but also complementary. Schumpeter 'fills in' some of the blank pages left by Weber – especially with regard to political competition and the creative-innovative role of political leaders. Taken together, the two visions provide solid theoretical foundations for an account of the modern democratic process – a very different account from the one constructed by Down and the advocates of voter-centred participatory and deliberative democracy.

Competitive Leader Democracy

Weber and Schumpeter laid theoretical foundations for what is called today 'leader democracy', 'democratic elitism' and 'competitive elitism'.[26] Both were pioneers of the leadership-agency perspective, and the key exponents of a 'disequilibrium view' that is increasingly popular in modern economics, sociology and political philosophy. Both also tried to reconcile mass democracy with the (inevitable, in their view) modern centralisation of authority in the hands of political leaders and elites.

Let us highlight the distinctive features of the 'competitive leader democracy' – as one may label the fusion of the two perspectives. It portrays politics as a domain of action full of irresolvable tensions, yet with a clear structure and predictable dynamics. Modern politics is driven primarily

---

26 See Held (2006), Higley and Burton (2006) and Best and Higley (2010).

through organised action of political leaders/entrepreneurs embedded within 'ruling minorities', within political elites concentrated at the apex of the state apparata. While the direction of political development is always uncertain – determined by 'path dependencies', complex historical contingencies, and rapidly changing circumstances – the conduct of the key actors lends itself to meaningful interpretations. In a competitive 'leader democracy', political leaders are the central actors, but not the sole actors; they always co-dominate, even if taking a central executive role. They interact with professional parliamentarians, party 'machines' and the 'officialdoms' of bureaucratic administrators, the later formally subordinate to their political masters but in possession of indispensible administrative expertise. Unlike autocratic dictators, democratic leaders always compete for their mandate-authorisation, and this competition encourages them to innovate. A victory in electoral rivalry for executive leadership in the state – and the democratic mandate-authorisation that generates mass confidence-cum-compliance – is the most important trophy in this competition. Those candidates who prove to be 'irresistible', and who appear most convincing and trustworthy, win the most votes. They do it by 'imposing themselves' on their constituencies through stirring oratory, attractive appeals and convincing images. Political action of leaders is directed mainly by their political will, determination and commitment. Most importantly, it is exercised through mass persuasion that actively shapes (rather than reflects) voters' preferences and 'public opinion'. Leaders give meaning to political processes, inject consistency to policies, integrate the highly differentiated elite, and – most vitally – establish and cultivate relations of trust with mass publics. However, in line with the democratic codes, they also take responsibility for their actions, submit to periodic tests of popularity, and 'fall on their swords' when unsuccessful in subsequent leadership contests.

This vision of the competitive and leader-centred democratic process has always provoked criticisms. In the Weber–Schumpeter theory, according to Held (2006, 135), 'leadership has to be understood as a necessary concomitant both of large-scale organisations which require firm political direction and of the essential passivity of the mass of the electorate.' This is not entirely correct. It is social complexity and wide mass enfranchisement – the core features of modern democratic politics – that necessitate large-scale organisation, representation and concentration of power in the hands of elites. Moreover, in the Weber–Schumpeter vision the enfranchised and politically organised masses are not, strictly speaking, passive. They enter modern politics in a powerful and decisive manner. But under the condition of orderly 'working' democracy, such an entry is mediated and channelled through parties, professional parliamentary institutions, and more directly through popular leaders. The direct, unorganised and spontaneous mass interventions in politics are ineffective and dangerous; they hinder deliberative rationality – thus producing bad policies – and spawn populism.

Such views cannot be seen as 'ambivalence' towards modern democracy. While Weber did not treat democracy as an autonomous goal or an end value, he accepted and approved 'mass democratisation' as an inevitable social development and therefore a 'matter of fact'. Similarly, the ageing Schumpeter devoted his intellectual energies to 'saving' democracy, redefined as competitive selection of executive leadership in the state, from what he saw as an inevitable spread of etatist socialism. He hoped to design a 'democratic method' compatible with both, liberal capitalism and the anticipated state socialism.

The Weberian–Schumpeterian vision of the modern democratic process found support in many quarters, including the theorists of representative democracy, and contemporary advocates of 'democratic elitism'.[27] But, as acknowledged even by supporters, it was more a general vision than a theoretical model. This vision needs further elaboration and updating – and this is the theme of the next chapter.

---

27 These ideas were further developed by Harold Lasswell and his collaborators (1950, 1952), and by the post–Second World War democratic theorists all of whom highlighted the role of democratic elites and the importance of political leadership in the 'vertical dimension of modern democracy': Dahl (1971), Keller (1962), Sartori (1962, 1981/1987), Welsh (1979), Etzioni-Halevi (1993), Higley and Burton (2006) and Best and Higley (2010).

Chapter 3

THE LEADER-CENTRIC TRENDS

It is not an accident that the concept of 'leader democracy' has been gaining currency only since the last decades of the twentieth century. The earlier period, especially the three decades of post–Second World War reconstruction in the industrialised West, could be well characterised as 'party democracy' – a period when the central role in political elites was played by entrenched and ideologically organised 'machines' and directorates of mass 'cleavage' parties (*Volksparteien*). There were some variations, though. Political power in America, and in other presidential systems, was always more concentrated and leader-centred than in the European parliamentary systems. It was the president who formed and led the 'core executives', coordinated the pressures within the power elite and headed election campaigns, even if presidential nomination was in the hands of party heads. The typical European parliamentary democracies, by contrast, had approximated 'party democracy' until the final decades of the twentieth century.

This postwar configuration was, no doubt, a reaction to – or strictly speaking a recoiling against – the highly concentrated, personalised, autocratic and nationalistic leadership in fascist and communist regimes that continued to cast a shadow over European politics long after their demise. The results generated a leader-phobia combined with a vigorously collectivistic and pluralistic ethos. The popular leader-phobia helped in imposing collegial constraints on political decisions and prompted the executive ruling minorities to keep a low political profile.[1] For the Western 'baby boom' generation and their East European 'post-Stalinist' equivalent, strong state and centralised leadership had highly antidemocratic connotations.

There was also a stabilisation factor in operation. As pointed out by Weber and Schumpeter, high profile leaders, especially the charismatic statesmen, reformers and innovators, tended to ascend at times of social crises and upheavals. The postwar decades of stability and growth were not

---

1 Few cared to remember that fascist regimes were defeated by regimes headed by strong liberal-democratic leaders, such as Roosevelt, Truman and Churchill.

conducive to generating such charismatic leadership – with some notable exceptions, like France, torn apart by internal ideological and postcolonial conflicts. In most Western societies, though, the postwar 'halcyon years' of stability and prosperity, steady economic growth, expanding consumption and welfare reforms reflected party-engineered political deals and 'armistices' between the major social forces. These 'neocorporatist' deals were cut and maintained by party embedded and party organised national elites (Schmitter and Lehmbruch 1979; Field and Higley 1980; Higley and Burton 2006). Politics of the 'halcyon years' resembled stable and peaceful power games, a nonviolent democratic rivalry between the major political camps – national versions of Cold War in its détente stage. Some even suggested that Western politics was undergoing a permanent shift from politics proper (that is, a vigorous power struggle) to corporatist-bureaucratic administration based on political deals, social settlements and ideological compromises – a configuration described in Germany as 'Rhenish capitalism', and elsewhere as 'neocorporatism', 'corporatist intermediation', 'consensual elite' and 'elite cartel'.[2] Naturally, there were occasional flare-ups and crises, and they spawned some towering political figures, such as de Gaulle and Churchill (or Truman in the USA). But the charisma of these leaders was anchored more in the heroic wartime past than in postwar accomplishments.

As mentioned earlier, American presidents were somewhat exceptional in this respect. They have always had much higher profiles than the European leaders – partly because of highly publicised direct elections – and prolonged, leader focused campaigns (including the primaries). But even the American presidency had its highs and lows of executive domination, with centralisation of executive power and 'imperial' tendencies increasing through the late 1960s and early 1970s (Schlessinger 1973). In Western Europe, the halcyon years of postwar reconstruction typified the rule of mass parties and governmental bureaucracies: the party officialdoms allied with the governmental 'mandarinates'. Headship, rather than leadership, characterised national politics. High profile political leaders were exceptional figures, standing out in a political world that was increasingly dominated by party-state directorates run by 'faceless men' (women have been practically absent from the top ranks of party and governmental bureaucracies). They headed the oligopolistic and largely consensual power elites that represented the organised 'neocorporatist' pillars of power, as aptly labelled and analysed by Field and Higley (1980) and by Schmitter and his colleagues (1979).

---

2 See also Dahrendorf (1967), Field and Higley (1980) and Best and Higley (2010). For a historical overview of European developments since 1945, see Judt (2005).

New developments changed the political landscape throughout the 1960s to the 1980s. First, there was a gradually declining support for major political parties, especially those relying on class cleavage, identity and loyalty. Second, almost all Western societies experienced a powerful wave of mobilisation of left-libertarian and reformist-democratic movements, followed by a backlash mobilisation of right-conservative movements. Both shook up the dominant parties and spawned strong, reformist leaders – typical articulators of mass discontent and protest. Third, the protest mobilisations, and the accompanying oil crisis of 1974–5 ended the 'halcyon years' of stable economic growth and initiated a wave of market reforms in the 1980s and 90s that were led by strong and assertive leaders. These leaders overruled or ignored the party-bureaucratic corporatist deals and refashioned party programmes, sometimes by redirecting party strategies, sometimes by creating their own parties.

Such overruling was easy in the parties that had already been weakened by the dealignment, dwindling membership and political failures of the 1970s. The 'oil shock', stagflation, economic stagnation, industrial chaos, rising unemployment and the general sense of malaise and exhaustion that had ended the postwar period of 'Keynesian consensus' and neocorporatist deals, had also triggered mass disenchantment with the established *Volksparteien* and their political strategies (Judt 2005, ch. 19). Party rule was also crumbling in 'partocratic' dictatorships of 'really existing socialism' and one-party apartheid regimes, both experiencing a wave of reformist movements. The success of these liberal-democratic reformist movements gave their leaders (such as Lech Wałęsa, Mikhail Gorbachev, Boris Yeltsin and Nelson Mandela) instantaneous celebrity status, or at least a very high media profile. They not only spearheaded the 'third wave' of democratisation (Huntington 1991), but also 'rehabilitated' leadership in the eyes of European liberal democrats. The limelight they attracted, and the democratic credentials they gained while negotiating liberal reforms and crafting new democratic regimes, had weakened leader-phobia and removed the antidemocratic stigma attached to strong leadership. This reconciliation between leadership and democracy was further reinforced by the rapid political ascendancy in Western liberal regimes of popular liberal-conservative leaders/reformers. This proliferation of such reformers, as well as their almost instantaneous political successes, could be seen as early symptoms of a shift toward 'leader democracy'.

The Drivers of Change

As argued here, this shift had been occurring both at the political surface in the form of ascendancy, and rising media profile of popular leaders, as well as underneath the surface, in the form of structural reshuffles that weakened the hold of mass party machines over their organised and henceforth loyal constituencies. One could detect the operation of four powerful 'leader-centric' trends: (1) the continuing party–voter dealignment, the social decomposition of the whole infrastructure of 'cleavage politics' and 'organised party democracy' or, as Lipset and his colleagues (2001) called it, 'the breakdown of class politics'; (2) the expansion of the mass media into the sphere of (mainly electoral) politics, and a transformation of this sphere, under the commercial imperative, into 'infotainment' – a combination of information and entertainment – and celebrity cults, and more generally, into image influenced 'media politics'; (3) further centralisation of executive power in the hands of 'core executives', 'court governments', and 'kitchen cabinets' that emerged within the expanding state power apparata; and (4) the growing focus on 'international leaders' as key actors/heroes on the global political scene. Globalisation, the growing interdependency and intensified social, economic and cultural links across national boundaries, has also increased the complexity of political issues, thus setting the stage for the emergence of high profile leaders, as well as narcissistic 'media junkies', poll-driven opportunists and populist demagogues.

The first two of these 'below the surface' trends have changed the configuration within the state-political 'quadrangles of power' (involving leaders, parliamentarians, party officials and top governmental experts/ bureaucrats). They weakened the relative power position of party officialdoms and governmental-bureaucratic 'mandarinates' vis-à-vis political leaders. These trends, one should stress, are relatively old – some dating from the 1930s. But all of them had been intensifying, accelerating and producing disruptive effects in the final decades of the last century. The decomposition of class-national constituencies has been occurring throughout the middle and second half of the twentieth century; by the 1970s it reached its peak and terminal stage.[3]

The latter two 'below-surface' trends formed a springboard for the ascendancy of assertive and media-savvy leaders/reformers and leaders/ innovators who successfully experimented with new electoral appeals and alliances. They actively used their images, stylistic idiosyncrasies, and sociocultural identities to mobilise and build up public trust and support. The result of such mobilisations was a new highly volatile voting pattern based on 'celebrity cults', personalisation and image manipulation – and the accompanied shift towards leader-centred politics and image-driven voting. Such new formatting of popular preferences became possible only with the

---

3 Its earlier stages have been analysed by Lipset (1960/1981), its final stages by Pakulski and Waters (1996) and Clark and Lipset (2001).

proliferation of popular, socially diffuse and politically intrusive mass media. The emergence of powerful mass media rostrums, and the symbiosis that developed between the publicity-hungry leaders, the news-hungry media, and the spectacle-hungry and image-sensitive mass voters, created a new form of political mobilisation, a 'new "new politics"'.

Let us examine these four leader-centric trends in more detail because they form the main theoretical underpinnings of 'leader democracy'.

Weakening parties and ascendant leaders

One can risk a generalisation that the post–Second World War generation in the West, especially in Western Europe, grew not only under conditions of ideologically organised 'democratic class struggle', but also under what Weber may have called 'party democracy'. Political leaders were dominated by the 'faceless men', the officialdom heading mass *Volksparteien*. The party executives, caucuses, party rooms and powerful heads of party factions, played the decisive role in shaping the ministerial appointments and governmental policies. They were backed by the equally influential 'mandarinate' of top governmental officials – the major 'powers behind the throne'. In turn, parties were well entrenched in the social structure or 'aligned' with loyal and ideologically organised mass voters, whose general interests were articulated and formatted by party establishments. Party-political affiliations and identifications were stable and typically transmitted from parents to children, thus creating lasting partisan loyalties and stable voting patterns.

While similar to the European one in socially anchored partisan loyalties, the American scene was slightly different in terms of party organisation. Party bureaucracies had never entrenched themselves in America and political parties there evolved into 'patronage' or 'spoils' parties. Strong regional-local loyalties and direct election of presidents, combined with intense competition during the newly instituted primaries, generated a more direct, populist and leader-centred American democracy that differed from the predominantly parliamentary Western European democratic practices and regimes. Moreover, the shadow of autocratic leaders had not reached America – or at least did not affect the American political culture. Neither intellectual circles nor the political classes in the USA recoiled against the ascendancy of strong autocratic leaders in the 1920s through to the 1940s as strongly as their European equivalents.

Yet, these differences were more a matter of degree than type. Like in Western Europe, the postwar American presidents – until the 1980s – were seen more as team leaders and 'central coordinators' than charismatic leaders/reformers. They were expected to follow the established patronage patterns and ideological-political scripts, rather than innovate. After the extraordinary success and popularity of FDR the presidential term of office was restricted to two runs, Congress gained significant veto and regulatory powers, and party bosses increased their control over local politics – including the distribution of spoils.

Thus 'party democracy' blossomed mainly in Europe. The Western European party systems (replicated also in Australia, New Zealand and Canada) were firmly embedded in the main social cleavages (class, religious, regional-cultural) described in the famous Lipset–Rokkan model. They were subsequently 'frozen', that is, organised and supplemented by ideologically consistent programmatic parties. Of course, one could always find some regional variations, but the political-ideological space in most European societies was clearly and predictably divided along these cleavages, with Right versus Left forming the political 'master' dimension (Lipset 1960/1981; Mair 1990). Political leaders were seen as loyal party heads, and who acted that way. They were bound by established ideological commitments, party programmes and electoral platforms. Moreover, the corporatist 'deals' and 'armistices' further limited the scope for political innovation and entrepreneurship. The aspiring leaders and political candidates relied on the established idioms of partisan appeal and on the support of powerful party 'machines'. It was the officialdom of these machines that dominated political decision making and shaped electoral platforms. In order to climb the political hierarchy, the aspiring politicians had to get the 'numbers' and secure support within the party factions. Even when particularly successful leaders did occasionally build a personal following and wide popularity, they were always at the mercy of the party officialdom that controlled the selection and nomination process and organised factional support in the caucuses and party rooms. Leadership, in other words, was restricted. Political autonomy of party leaders was narrow; it was largely reduced to organisational and political management with little scope for innovation and little capacity for change.

The autonomy of political leaders was also weakened by the strong position of administrative departmental heads – the top public/civil service 'mandarins'. The heads were policy experts with high-level knowledge of policies and organisation, vast experience, dense networks (transcending party circles), and the loyalty of administrative apparata. These powerful figures, according to Rhodes and Weller (2001, 1), 'worked in the shadows, advising, managing and influencing the direction of their respective countries. They were the mandarins, recognised as the real rulers, the providers of continuity.' They were seen as exercising uncontrolled hegemony over governments. In their massive study of administrative elites, Aberbach et al. (1981, 1) identified the most significant trend in power distribution in advanced Western societies as 'the steadily growing power of professional party politicians and of permanent civil servants.' The postwar extensions of state planning and interventionism have accelerated this trend. 'By 1970 civil servants throughout the West were deciding how to restructure the steel industry, how to design an actuarially sound pension scheme, where to locate airports, how to break inflation, and a thousand other such issues.' (Aberbach et al. 1981, 2). The popular British TV comedy serial, *Yes Minister*, have captured well the typical power relations between amateurish and ever-mobile politicians – typically dilettante party hacks – and the seasoned administrative virtuosi at the top of the public/civil service establishment. While the former were 'political masters' who carried major responsibilities, the latter often prevailed by controlling policy expertise and technical advice necessary for successful policy implementation. Only 'brave' (read: foolish) political masters tried to impose policies that contradicted or ignored the advice of the bureaucratic heads. The 'mandarinate', in turn, formally celebrated the ethos of nonpartisan detachment and political loyalty, while enjoying high de facto and 'behind-the-scenes' influence over policies, security of office immune from carrying political responsibility, high salaries and enormous prestige. The top public servants were recognised as key governmental figures, as core members of national elites operating the corporatist policies described as 'politics of directionless consensus'[4].

Party leaders were highly respected, and sometimes they even enjoyed genuine affection, but their autonomy vis-à-vis the party machine and governmental officialdom was restricted. Most of them, like Harold Wilson in the UK, Robert Menzies in Australia or Willy Brandt in Germany, kept a low public and media profile. They were expected to voice the established and coherent partisan position, affirm the party-ideological stance, present and clarify the party programme and follow faithfully the electoral party platform. In Schumpeter's economic analogy, they were 'political businessmen' and 'party managers', rather than leaders/ entrepreneurs. The political careers of these 'party managers' were well structured, with long apprenticeships in party-controlled bodies. Those who attempted reformist innovations without the party-factional blessing or securing the support of the bureaucratic mandarinate were typically cut short. As dozens of failed politicians were discovering again and again, without the 'party numbers', and without the support of the 'directorates', political life was brutish and short.

---

4 See Aberbach et al. (1981, 2–3) and Putnam (1976, ch. 2).

The crumbling 'party democracy'

This model started to crumble in the 1970s. The most conspicuous correlates of the crumbling were declining party membership, growing electoral volatility, collapse of cleavage voting and decline in partisan loyalties. All of them coincided with the ascendancy of new ('third', often single issue) parties, the proliferation of high-profile 'independents' – often propelled to power by protest movements – and, generally, the gradual waning of ideological idioms as effective organisers of political outlooks. It marked what Lipset and his colleagues diagnosed as the 'death of class' and the 'breakdown of class politics'. In Dalton's phrase, it was a symptom of progressive 'dealignment', the 'end of cleavage politics' and the beginning of a 'new politics' that resulted in the appearance of new actors (movements and their leaders), as well as the political demise of 'parties without partisans'.[5]

The *Volksparteien* were rapidly losing their members (Table 3.1). To make matters worse, they were also losing loyal voters. The most popular measures of party–voter dealignment, the Alford Index and the Thomsen Index of class voting, have declined since the 1960s and 1970s in all advanced societies for which longitudinal data on voting behaviour are available (Nieuwbeerta 1997). The decline varied in intensity but appeared to be universal throughout the advanced democracies. It was particularly strong in societies with an initially high level of cleavage-based identities and loyal class voting. Most importantly, the space on the political scene freed by these waning party actors and structures has been increasingly filled by new political entrepreneurs, reformers and innovators.

The leader-centred politics was budding in Europe and elsewhere. The institution of primaries, i.e. the popular selection of a party's leader and/or candidates, was spreading in Latin American democracies, but also in some major parties in Canada, Japan, Denmark, Finland, Britain, Australia, Ireland and Belgium (Carty and Blake 1999; Scarrow and Gezgor 2010). Israel, a country that traditionally has a parliamentary form of government, experimented with direct election of the prime minister. All these measures aimed at 'democratisation', but they achieved this democratisation through strengthening the hand of party leaders vis-à-vis the party machine (Pennings and Hazan 2001). Thus, Tony Blair used direct postal ballot of party members to outmanoeuvre medium-level party rank and file and trade unions in order to get through the Labour Party and Parliament innovations and reformist policies.

---

5 See Dalton and Kuechler (1990), Pakulski and Waters (1996), Clark and Lipset (2001) and Dalton and Wattenberg (2000).

Table 3.1. Declining membership of political parties, 1980–2000

Country	Period	Percentage change
France	1978–1999	−65
Italy	1980–1998	−52
United Kingdom	1980–1998	−50
Norway	1980–1997	−47
Finland	1980–1998	−34
Netherlands	1980–2000	−31
Austria	1980–1999	−30
Switzerland	1977–1997	−29
Sweden	1980–1998	−28
Denmark	1980–1998	−26
Ireland	1980–1998	−24
Belgium	1980–1999	−22
Germany	1980–1999	−9

Source: Mair and Biezen (2001, 12).
Note: Change in numbers as a percentage of original membership. New democracies, like Portugal, Greece, Spain, Hungary, the Czech Republic and Slovakia are not included. They show a very different pattern. In all of these countries, except the Czech Republic, there was a significant rise of party membership, which can be explained by the early phase of party development after the democratic transition.

Another symptom of change was gradual disappearance of party programmes and platforms from election campaigns, especially those previously containing strong ideological or class references. Instead, the campaigns have been increasingly focusing on the personalities of leaders and on current and new issues of public concerns, such as the environment, economic reform, minority rights, migration, taxation levels, and national security. Parliamentary election campaigns started to resemble presidential campaigns (hence the label 'presidentialisation') by focusing on the pronouncements of political leaders – especially on leaders' character (truthfulness, determination, reliability). Leaders' ability to win mass confidence, control the agendas of political debates and provide reassurance to anxious voters became the main focus of political commentaries. In turn, leadership contenders and candidates were abandoning ideological references and turning their attention to new issues of public anxiety and concern, especially those publicised by the mass media. It is the mass media that connected these issues/themes with public concerns on the one hand, and leadership qualities on the other. Perhaps most importantly, leaders were gradually becoming the favourite source of the news and focus of media coverage. They were increasing their advantage over political parties and programmes as dominant subjects and references, especially during election campaigns (Table 3.2).

This change has spelled the end of ideologically organised 'party democracy'. It seems party membership, party ideological programmes and party-ideological left–right polarity have been withering away together.[6] The core elements of the left–right political-ideological spectrum – the ideological 'packages' of liberalism, conservatism and socialism/welfarism – have been diminishing, thus paving the way for reformist and vague programmes of 'neoconservatism', 'neoliberalism' and amorphous 'New Labour' (Giddens 1993, 1998). They look now more like repositories of useful references than as consistent visions and blueprints for action. Successful leaders/ innovators draw from these repositories at will and seldom care for ideological consistency. An example is Ronald Reagan and Margaret Thatcher famously mixing economic liberalism and social conservatism. Kohl experimented by mixing religious conservatism with nationalism and liberal commitment to individual rights. Blair mixed communal collectivism with liberal commitment to individual success, and with conservative respect for religion. Others, like Schröder, Chirac, Berlusconi, Koizumi, Zapatero and Sarkozy, have chosen almost entirely nonideological, issue-oriented idioms of electoral appeal. Importantly, the new generation of political leaders/reformists was fiercely independent and hostile towards the administrative mandarins.

Media spectacles, celebrity leaders and the spin machines

The ascendancy of high-profile leaders/reformers has coincided with two other changes. On the 'supply side', there has been a proliferation of media-savvy politicians backed by expert PR and spin machines. They build their image by carefully cultivating their appearance, survey-testing issues of concerns, and focus group testing the main phrases and themes of electoral appeals. On the 'demand side', there has been a proliferation of image voting, impulse voting and the accompanied 'cults' of celebrities (some of whom come from the media sector). The new leaders have 'fans' as well as supporters, and they are able to generate emotional bonds that reflect

---

6 See Volkens and Klingemann (2002). In the 2000s the ideological profile of both party members and supporters became more moderate (grew closer to the centre on a left–right scale) than it was in the 1990s, as survey results show (Scarrow and Gezgor 2010, 836–9).

admiration based on image, rather than a bond of rationally calculated interest. Above all, they attract mass voters through a very short and highly mediated political contact (one even hesitates to call this contact 'political communication'). One observer described this form of campaign encounter as a momentary seduction:

> After seeing a candidate for 100 milliseconds, voters make certain sorts of judgments based on expressiveness, facial structure, carriage and attitude. Alexander Todorov of Princeton has found that he can predict 70 percent of political races just by measuring peoples' snap judgments of candidates' faces. Then, having formed an impression from these thin-slice appraisals, voters rack their memory banks...trying to fit new things into familiar patterns. Maybe John Edwards reminds one voter of the sort of person he disliked in high school. Maybe Barack Obama evokes the elevated feeling another voter felt watching John F. Kennedy... In making these associations, voters are trying to perform trait inference. They are trying to divine inner abilities from outward signs. (Brooks 2007, 1)

The diagnoses of 'presidentialisation' (Poguntke and Webb 2005) and 'personalisation of politics' (McAllister 2007) highlight some important features of the new elite–mass encounters and alliances, but they are less clear in identifying the changing nature of the leader-voter relations. More importantly, they raise more general questions of compatibility of these new trends and tendencies with the normative aspects of democratic theory. Is the mass-mediated 'linkage' between elites and the masses sufficiently rational and robust to deserve the label 'democratic'? Or should we treat it as a form of pathology that heralds the deterioration of 'democratic quality', the 'dumbing down' of democratic practices? It would be safest to leave this question open now, especially since 'leader democracy' has not exhausted its historical potential. But we take a risk of some preliminary observations and judgement about it. In the next chapter (see section on 'normative underpinnings') we provide a normative defence of 'leader democracy'.

There is little doubt that high-profile politicians and 'celebrity' leaders are to a large extent products of intensifying media coverage-cum-consumption, and the shift from print-mechanical media (the 'Gutenberg galaxy' in McLuhan's famous phrase) to the pictorial-electronic galaxy, especially the one created by TV and the internet-based digital technologies, such as blogging, Facebook and Twitter. But there are also some less obvious – and potentially confusing – corollaries of this general statement.

Saying that political leaders share the centre stage with sport and film stars carries the risk of stating the obvious. What is less banal and less discussed is the parallel change in 'political consumption' and 'political culture', that is, the norms and behaviours of mass citizens/voters who become image consumers and impulse voters. Yet, it is the interaction between the two – political actors and political audiences – that jointly produce the 'new "new politics"'. Aspiring politicians learn early about the importance of media cultivation, convincing rhetoric and self-presentation and, generally, skilful projection of electorally attractive image. In turn, the attractive visual images of leaders, especially when combined with oratory talent and staged presentation, become the major attractors of mass voters 'freed' not only from old partisan loyalties and ideological preoccupations, but also from the need to read, comprehend, interpret, inquire and analyse. When constituencies expand, and when political issues become complex, especially when these issues transcend the widely known and well understood ideological blueprints, they are reduced to simple images and 'sound bites'. This means that the most economical way of winning votes en masse is through image-based and 'sound bite' persuasion that resembles political seduction.

Seducing or 'luring' mass voters is more effective than convincing them. Seduced voters, in turn, respond rather than choose; they react rather than act. This behaviour does have a rational and deliberate component. This component, though, is restricted to image selection and choices between competing images. Under the new conditions of intensely mediated seduction politics, political decision concerns the allocation of trust in one of the competing leader-image packages. This is less a matter of change in the nature of voters (most voters have always been 'mass' voters/consumers), and more a result of a changing environment in which mass media reshapes electoral competitions into 'infotainment', the essence of commercialised and entertainment-oriented popular shows (cf. Bennett and Entman 2001; Stanyer 2008).

The spread of political 'infotainment' coincides with the proliferation of popular shows and 'mocumentaries', the fictionalised documentaries that cast political leaders as their focus and main heroes. TV series, such as *The West Wing* (US) and *The Thick of It* (UK) seem to be emulated in most countries – with similar success. TV programmes such as *The Cabinet Confidential, The Rivals, Road to War, The Downing Street Patient, Hotline to the President,* as well as the ironic *Do You Still Believe in Tony?,* and *Bush's Brain* have been enjoying the highest popularity ratings. Mass voters/viewers are fascinated with leaders, their families and their 'courtiers' as much as they are fascinated with the private lives of other media celebrities. Moreover, this fascination seems to affect voting behaviour. Voters 'invest' their interest and confidence in political leaders not only because they mistrust party programmes and ideological blueprints (both taking back seat in political campaigns), but also because the images of leaders are more accessible, available for quick identification and easily absorbed as a synthetic political vision 'with a human face'. Proliferation of these images – typically photographs with a short slogan – is an important factor in popularising politics, mobilising voters and making politics more accessible. One can even say that politics has become more 'popular-democratic' due to 'infotainment' and the cult of celebrities, though possibly at the cost of increasing simplification and declining deliberative quality. We insert this cautious qualifier 'possibly', because the diagnoses of mass media 'simplification' and 'dumbing down' are largely restricted to advocates of 'media malaise thesis',[7] recently criticised for its exaggeration and one-sidedness. Political observers like Norris (1999, 2001) and Coleman (2001), see the new media as popular channels of civic participation and complex political engagements and as potential enhancers of rational-reflexive political behaviour.

As mentioned earlier, both Weber and Schumpeter recognised some of these trends and tradeoffs, and acknowledged the inevitable shift towards representative character of democratic politics, as well as 'plebiscitary' and 'demagogic' tendencies in modern mass democracy. Mass election campaigns, they noted, made modern democratic contest increasingly and inevitably open to persuasion (that is, manipulation) through sloganeering and demagogy by skilful and popular leaders. While neither thinker anticipated the impact of the visual electronic media, they nevertheless pointed to the growing importance of leader images, leader appearances and 'oratory charisma' as a core trend in modern mass-democratic electoral politics.

However, the contemporary studies of election campaigns and electoral behaviour also show some unanticipated developments. For example, the mass media favour individual leaders in their coverage over any collective body, such as parties, governments and cabinets. Thus Wattenberg (1998a) and Dalton et al. (2000) illustrate a dramatic increase of leader-focus in press coverage of electoral campaigns (Table 3.2).[8] A recent Australian study shows a similar increase in leader-focus in the press coverage of election campaigns from 2001 to 2010 (Jones 2010), as well as increasing influence of leaders on electoral behaviour between 1984 and 2010 (Pakulski et al. 2011). Students of the press coverage note that the proportions in coverage of leaders versus their parties has been increasing rapidly in most Western democracies, particularly since the late 1970s (McAllister 2007; Dalton et al. 2000). Similarly, comparisons of presidential acceptance speeches by early presidents – such as Harry Truman in 1948 – and the more recent

---

7 For example, Patterson (1993), Franklin (1997) and McChesney (1999) stress the negative impact of commercialisation, marketisation and massification – especially in tabloid politics and commercial TV channels.

8 One should note here the cautious and sceptical voice represented by Karvonen (2009).

Table 3.2. The ratio of leader-candidate versus party mention in election coverage by the popular press, from the 1950s to the 1990s

USA 1952 – 1.7	France 1956 – 4.3	UK 1959 – 0.7	Canada 1957 – 1.2
USA 1964 – 3.0		UK 1966 – 0.8	Canada 1968 – 1.7
USA 1976 – 4.5	France 1974 – 4.4	UK 1974 – 0.9	Canada 1974 – 2.0
USA 1988 – 5.2	France 1988 – 5.4	UK 1987 – 1.1	Canada 1984 – 1.1
USA 1996 – 5.6	France 1995 – 5.6	UK 1997 – 1.3	Canada 1997 – 1.6

Source: Based on Dalton et al. (2000, 52).

ones – such as Bill Clinton in 1996 – show a rapidly shifting emphasis from partisanship to leadership, from programmes and ideological commitments, to executive performance (Dalton et al. 2000, 50).[9]

Personal focus on leaders becomes the core media idiom of dramatised and entertaining coverage. In turn, mass audiences pay attention to the drama of 'heroic struggles' and to leaders' images, the latter shaped by reported foibles, headlines and stories about their real or imaginary debacles and glorious triumphs. Moreover, the media cater to short attention spans and quickly grasped images that have to be reinforced by dramatisation and hyperbole. Consequently, mass-mediated political campaigns – especially on TV – take the form of leader-centred spectacles. Aggressive interviewers are often important actors in these spectacles, thus empowering media staff. [10]

The mass-mediated contests for leadership become a major 'stuff' of infotainment. The infotainment has to be short, simple and emotionally arousing and personality focused in order to attract wide attention. Personalisation of coverage and focus on leaders fit the template of popular dramas, and they enjoy popularity that rivals sitcoms. The focus on personalities, dramatisation and hype also suit the interests of the media, always primarily interested in maximising their audiences and improving their ratings. They are accessible, undemanding and therefore 'democratic': all people are skilled in judging character and personality; while very few would be capable of engaging in serious debate of complex issues and policy dilemmas. Judging character and developing an opinion about personality (as friendly, sympathetic, trustworthy, determined, committed, etc.) can be done by anyone in a few seconds of

---

9 Nor can the leader-focus and leader-centric trends be seen as a unique response to increased terrorism and threats to national security. The focus on leaders antedates the terrorist spectre; although there is no doubt that the concentration on leaders is reinforced by it.

10 For the analysis of a symbiosis between media and politicians and image shaping, see Meyer with Hinchman (2004), Stanyer (2007) and Denemark et al. (2007).

media exposure. Yet, such a judgement is also 'generic' or 'generalisable' in that it covers candidate's leadership abilities, and therefore can direct voting.

Leader-media relations are, of course, symbiotic. Leaders and candidates carefully mould their image as 'ordinary persons': easy to identify with, sensitive servants of the nation, and capable rulers, informed and committed. Media rely on leaders in feeding the 24-hour news cycles. Mass-mediated politics attract readymade celebrities, and growing numbers of leaders – such as Reagan, Schwarzenegger, Ventura, Estrada and Berlusconi – enter politics with an already developed media career and image. Those who have less media experience surround themselves with media-savvy advisors, PR experts and spin doctors.

The entry of the electronic media, especially live broadcasts through radio and TV, has changed the nature of electoral competitions and it necessitates a significant supplement to the original theoretical vision of 'leader democracy' offered by Weber and Schumpeter. The largely critical accounts of 'simplifications' and 'distortions' allegedly inherent in mass mediation of political coverage are themselves grossly simplified, and they call for a more balanced assessment. We offer such assessment – a supplement to a theoretical portrait of 'leader democracy' – in a short overview below.

Voting and personal trust

The new digital media of communication have facilitated the close, some even say personalised, contact between leaders and political audiences, giving the audiences a sense of 'a new kind of personal intimacy' (Thompson 1995; Schickel 2000). Leaders become close and familiar persons who deserve support because of this closeness and familiarity. Since familiarity is also the foundation of trust, the images of leaders as familiar figures – one of us – easily translates into electoral support.

The familiarity generated by mass media coverage (especially radio and TV) has been used most effectively by popular and successful leaders in creating political audiences that resemble both the celebrity 'fun clubs' and Facebook 'friends'. Tony Blair, Bill Clinton and Barack Obama used the TV and the internet to generate a sense of closeness and familiarity, and to reach the 'digital generation' of young (and often politically alienated) audiences. Clinton launched the first interactive White House website, which included his speeches, appearances, briefings and a guided tour of the presidential quarters. Downing Street followed him in early 2000. Perhaps the most expert user of these personalised digital technologies has been Barack Obama. His spectacularly successful 2008 presidential campaign utilised both Facebook and Twitter in spreading his image, generating a sense of familiarity-cum-closeness, and – last but not least – soliciting political donations.

This personalised contact often extends to leaders' families. They are drawn to the image cultivating process, often reluctantly but inevitably, always at risk of 'overexposure', as found out by the gaffe-prone Sarah Palin and her dysfunctional family. We are probably witnessing the impact of the first generation of mass voters who are more familiar with the images of leaders than with those leaders' views or political preferences, and who are more concerned with those leaders' characters than with their ideological leanings and partisan loyalties.

TV, in particular, has been changing political competition into emotionally charged rivalry of leadership images. Mass voters who can 'swing' the election results, and who vote for images rather than parties by choosing a familiar person rather that programmes and ideologies, have been targeted by the expanding PR and 'spin' apparata. Such voters are both numerous and sensitive to image presentation. They increasingly turn to leaders for political cues, explanations and – ever increasingly – for identification, hope and reassurance. The image presentation has to fit both the mass expectations and changing circumstances. Leaders have to appear genuine and sincere; at the time of crises, successful leaders have to present themselves as sensitive empathisers; at the time of campaigns they must appear as uncompromising reformers. In fact, the winning strategy seems to include a mixture of both, with balance of emphases dependent on the circumstances and the 'reading' of the audiences.

Oratory skills are also taking a different form than in the past, when leaders were less visible, when political appeals were heavily coated in ideological arguments, and when election appeals were predominantly directed to loyal followers and the educated strata – the 'political class'. Today, the winners of leadership contests have to attract mass attention without alienating the targeted 'belts'; they have to stir emotions, 'touch people's hearts' and generate and harness popular concerns – all without sounding rhetorical, detached and 'elitist'. The successful political candidates speak to everyone and address people with egalitarian simplicity tempered by respect, without trivialising the issues or sounding didactic. Above all, they have to sound *and look* convincing, combining appropriate body language, gestures and conduct scrutinised by ever-present microphones and cameras and broadcast nationwide.

The campaigns are, of course, highly competitive. During these intense competitions for votes, there is little tolerance for errors, gaffes and 'image spoiling' lapses. The latter may be related to seemingly trivial and superficial aspects of behaviour such as twitching, winking, shifting gaze or the adoption of didactic manners. In 2004, the unsuccessful American presidential candidate John Kerry, a self-made man (though benefitting from his wife's wealth) spoke and looked patrician, and was prone to occasional self-aggrandisement.

He lost to a scion of the most powerful political family, George W. Bush, who looked and sounded folksy, spoke with a drawl, walked the 'Texan way', and carefully cultivated an image of a 'simple fellow'. In the earlier presidential election, the 'folksy' George W. Bush defeated a sophisticated Al Gore, whose public persona suffered from a narcissistic and elitist image (in the eyes of media critics), in spite of Gore's Nobel Prize winning achievements. Similarly, Gordon Brown suffered a serious political blow in 2010 when his off-the-cuff response to a member of the public was overheard and broadcast.

Obviously, the investigative media quickly reveal obvious falsities in coverage and leadership 'makeovers', but this is often done too late, when the vote has already been cast. Therefore the competition of images is reminiscent of a *Blitzkrieg*: it is ruthless and instantaneous, with immediate responses – and sometimes with only moderate concern for truth and accuracy. Exposure of manipulation hurts, but it often hurts less (and at less critical moments) than hyperbole: a distorted accusation or an exaggerated claim. This is particularly important at the time when the decisive image confrontation occurs, during TV debates. Such debates leave no space for error, and are therefore carefully stage-managed.

As pointed out by Savoie (2007) and Stanyer (2008), contemporary political communication turned into a one-way leader promotion and political advocacy – more a persuasion than communication proper. While this leader-focused 'promotional rationale' originated earlier, it grew into a major preoccupation in the 1980s and 90s.

> By the time of the Reagan presidency this 'promotional rationale' can be seen as firmly established in the White House, consisting of several news management principles: plan ahead; stay on the offensive; control the flow of information; limit reporters' access to Reagan; talk about the issues the White House wants to talk about; speak in one voice; and repeat the same message many times. The Reagan administration's perspective has been widely adopted by subsequent presidents. In Britain, while some observed such promotional tendencies in the Wilson government of the 1960s, the consensus is that such a culture developed slightly later with the Thatcher government, but reached its apex with Blair government. (Stanyer 2008, 44–5)

The effects of continuous promotion, in turn, are carefully and continuously monitored by opinion polls and focus group studies. As noted by Bowman (2000), the scope of this monitoring increased dramatically at the end of the last century. While there was only one approval poll during the initial 100 days of Truman presidency, the beginning of the Clinton presidency was monitored by 37 polls, with a similar increase noted in Great Britain, especially between the Wilson and Blair governments. Margaret Thatcher, one of the key pioneers of leader-centric trends, is credited with a major increase in the use of polls and focus groups in tracking public responses to her image, statements and controversial policies (Cockerell 1988).

Cultivation of attractive public image – and therefore public trust – is not only difficult, but also increasingly expensive and time consuming. Leaders have to be able to balance their time in front of the cameras with time spent shaping policies and attending important events. If they spend too much time in the limelight, they risk being seen as 'media junkies' – the label that harms. If they do not spent enough time in front of the cameras and microphones (or blogging on web), they risk a backlash from compulsive communicators who see such time balancing as symptomatic of secretiveness or arrogant 'elitism'. Above all, the successful balancing of time and image relies on good relations between leadership candidates and the 'fourth estate', the media commentariat, and especially the star anchors and popular radio 'jocks'.

The war and postwar generations of leaders could survive low exposure, low media profile, or even occasional critical hostility of the media. They relied more on public intellectuals, the well-informed 'commentariat', and on the broad 'political class' known in Europe as the 'political intelligentsia'. The public image of those leaders was shaped more through their decisions and their outcomes than through their media images, appearances and pronouncements. Leaders could give occasional interviews and engage in in-depth conversations, but their public appearances were rare and they were capable of protecting their privacy (including keeping spooks locked safely in their cupboards). With the intensification of electoral competitions, proliferation of the media, and with the 24-hour news cycle, the discrete image shaping has given way to continuous media presence and nonstop campaigning.

The mass-mediated communication and campaigning is in many respects more superficial and one-sided than communication of a more direct nature – a point highlighted by many critics of mass democracy. Yet, such a communication also expands political audiences, widens access to politics, increases the reach of politicians and, generally, makes the elite–mass linkage wider, more inclusive and more egalitarian – one may say 'more democratic'.[11] This often escapes the attention of those critics who see mass mediation as synonymous with 'dumbing down' of political discourses. Mass democratisation also, and inevitably, simplifies political communication – as does any inclusive practice. It is simply more accessible, more personalised and more leader-centric.

---

11 The point made recently by students of 'digital democracy' and 'e-democracy' (e.g. Bellamy and Taylor 1998; Norris 2001).

The mass media, especially the electronic/digital media, are the natural partners and allies of contemporary popular leaders. The importance of media-projected images and their impact on the outcomes of mass-mediated electoral contests also increases the importance of the PR machines. Political success is increasingly a product of synergies between talented leaders, receptive audiences and skilful media/PR staffs. Because of this dependence, and because of the complexity of the leader-media-audience relations, political seductions seldom lasts long and the risks of mass publics deserting their leaders are high. Democratic leaders – even the most popular ones – are increasingly vulnerable to fluctuating media exposure and fickle public support.

Leonine leaders and their courts

One of the frequently overlooked features of the political rivalries has been the ascendancy of strong, forceful, imposing and preemptory democratic political leaders who have dominated the contemporary political scene since the 1980s, and who have displaced – in almost all advanced democracies – more moderate, conciliatory, consensus-seeking and compromise-oriented leaders. This provokes interest in the cycles of elite ascendancy and decline.[12]

The ascendancy of high-profile, tough and 'leonine' leaders such as Thatcher, Reagan, Blair, Berlusconi and Bush has been striking, partly because it started in the major and 'trend-setting' Western liberal democracies, the USA and the UK, and partly because the new tough style of leadership, constituted a striking contrast and change compared with less imposing and more conciliatory leaders, such as Jimmy Carter in the US and 'Sunny Jim' Callaghan in the UK. In fact, these 'limp' leaders set the stage for a backlash-like succession of the 'firm' and 'forceful' leaders. Jimmy Carter developed an unfortunate image of a well-meaning but weak and naïve politician. He pursued, almost to its bitter end, the politics of détente that was widely seen as encouraging the Soviet invasion of Afghanistan and the fall of the Shah of Iran (the latter followed by the fundamentalist takeover and the infamous 'Iranian hostage crisis'). Callaghan, in turn, presided over the exhausting 'Winter of Discontent', the series of strikes and protests that paralysed Britain on the eve of the 1979 elections. Both Thatcher and Reagan were seen as 'path dependent' leaders and as radical reformists, whose success came on the wave of discontentment with their predecessors, the widespread sense of malaise, and with growing mass expectations of radical change.

---

12 See Higley and Pakulski (2007, 2011) and Femia (2011).

Both lived up to these expectations. Thatcher was a seasoned, tough and combative Conservative politician recruited from the 'dry' faction of the party, with over sixteen years of parliamentary experience prior to her prime ministerial elevation. Reagan was an equally seasoned and tough activist/leader, recruited from the 'anti-détente' faction of Californian Republicans. He was also renowned for his expert communication and image-presentation skills, both honed in Hollywood. The uncompromising and eloquent 'Gipper' and the dry and determined 'Iron Lady' struck an immediate close political alliance backed by personal friendship. Above all, they jointly started radical liberal-conservative reforms combined with a forceful and combative style of implementation. Thatcher did not hesitate to authorise the use of weapons in the 1980 hostage crisis in the Iranian Embassy; did not budge under the pressure of the hunger strike of the IRA prisoners in 1981 (ten of whom died); and without hesitation responded with force to the Argentine invasion of Falklands in late 1982. She supported Reagan in his criticism of Soviet invasion of Afghanistan and took an uncompromising line on the deployment of nuclear weapons and long-range missiles in Europe. In spite of initially widespread protests, Thatcher firmly stood behind an initially unpopular poll tax reform in 1981–2, closed the deficit-ridden coal mines, and withstood a prolonged and violent confrontation with the powerful National Union of Mineworkers. In the mid-1980s she authorised a series of deregulatory reforms aiming at 'unchaining the market' and reducing welfare entitlements, thus provoking a serious backlash among voters and her Conservative colleagues. In spite of her fading popularity, she refused to back down ('the Lady is not for turning'), and earned considerable respect for her consistency and uncompromising stand, even among her political adversaries. These admiring adversaries included Labour Party 'rising star' Tony Blair, who subsequently adopted many key elements of the Thatcherite political style, especially the 'politics of conviction' combined with a high media profile.

Ronald Reagan, whose election followed mass discontent and sense of malaise in America similar to that in Britain in 1979, also adopted a similar determined, tough and combative style combined with skilful persuasion. He denounced détente, embraced policies of 'peace through strength' (which amounted to a new version of the containment strategy), and restarted the arms race, especially by funding a massive antimissile 'Star Wars' programme. This was followed by boosting American forces in Europe, thus triggering a wave of antinuclear and antiwar protests in Germany. Reagan elite changed the military scene in South Asia by supplying sophisticated weapons to anti-Soviet Mujahidin in Afghanistan and Pakistan. He also militarily aided the anti-Sandinista partisans in Nicaragua and invaded Grenada to stop a leftist takeover. The Gipper was equally aggressive in his domestic policies. He declared 'war on drugs', 'war on illegal immigration' and confronted militant air traffic controllers who threatened airport authorities with strikes. Above all, he projected a worldwide image of himself as a firm, tough and uncompromising leader.

Reagan's moment of triumph came with the peaceful decomposition of European communism. This unexpected 'victory' cemented his winning image – and the accompanied image of his strong and successful leadership. His undoing was undoubtedly the infamous Iran–Contra scandal (illegal aiding of the anti-Sandinista Contras using the proceedings from weapon sales to Iran), followed by a massive budget deficit – generated in clear contradiction to Reagan's antideficit and small-government rhetoric.

This success story, in turn, provoked emulations. Like Thatcher, Reagan became a stylistic 'role model', widely admired and copied worldwide. The tough, dry and combative political style promoted by Thatcher and Reagan became a stylistic model template embraced by countless followers and imitators. Surprisingly, these followers appeared throughout the next three decades on both ends of the political spectrum. Kohl, Schroeder, Berlusconi, Blair, González, Heider, Aznar, Koizumi, Howard, the Kaczyński twins, Sarkozy, and especially the combative George W. Bush – to mention just a few – all considered themselves the political heirs of the Thatcher–Reagan duo. They openly imitated Thatcher and Reagan, obviously with some substantive variations. Tough and uncompromising politics, as well as 'faith politics', 'politics of conviction', reformist 'neoliberalism' and combative 'neoconservatism' became the standard style of politics in all camps, from conservative Republicans to New Labourists.

The new style spread wide and fast. Jean Blondel (2005) described the ascendancy of leaders and the proliferation of leader-focused and leader-created parties in Europe from the 1960s to 2004. Such leaders and parties multiplied both in Western and Eastern Europe, especially in the 1980s and 90s. The list of leaders who gained prominence over the party machines and transformed their parties has been growing. In the West, Mitterrand, Schröder, Karamanlis, Thatcher, Soares, González, Craxi, Papandreou Jr, Aznar and Blair dominated and reformed their party machines. In the Eastern Europe, Wałęsa (Centrum), Laar, Antall, Klaus, Mečiar, Tusk, and Orbán have been described as 'strong leaders'. However, the list of leaders who have formed new parties or radically revamped existing parties into new entities is even longer: Hage, Gilstrup, Berlusconi, Haider, Le Pen, Anders, Kjaersgaard, Bossi, Fortujn, Dewinter, Olechinsky, Wałęsa (BWR), Tudor, Saavisar, Skele, Adamkus, Paksas, Simeon, Putin, Lepper and the Kaczyński brothers. The political landscape at the turn of the century was dominated by political imitators of Thatcher and Reagan and by leader-parties – the political power vehicles for ambitious leaders.

This proliferation coincides with a renaissance of interest in 'leadership'.[13] Studies of leaders and leader-parties multiply; so do political analyses of leadership and memoirs of leaders. There have been political accounts of the increasing personalisation of politics, commentaries on 'personalised' governments (the Reagan administration, Thatcher government, Blair government, Howard government, Sarkozy regime) and personalised governing styles (Thatcherism, Reaganism, Blairism, Howardism). The biographies, memoirs and autobiographies of leaders sell well and attract unprecedented advance fees from publishers.[14]

The ascendancy of strong leaders has stimulated social and political change. In a truly Weberian–Schumpeterian manner, leaders position themselves as key agents of reform. By contrast, party establishments are seen as obstacles to change, forces of conservative resistance and sources of opportunistic pandering to the status quo. Accordingly, the mass public seems to approve the new prominence of leaders/reformers as a dynamic counter balance to partisan inertia. After a slump in voter turnout, the rates of electoral participation have been increasing together with intensifying leadership competition. Satisfaction with democracy also seems to follow strong leadership, though it fluctuates with different leadership performances and economic ups and downs. Party bureaucracies tolerate the high profile leaders in the hope of winning elections. Perhaps most importantly, the popular expectations include now what is described as 'leadership capacity' – the capacity to take a firm stance, develop a clear vision, maintain consistent position, make tough decisions and to carry them through. Those who fail to live up to these expectations suffer a decline in popular trust and support.

The global connection

The increasing focus on leaders, especially the high-profile 'world leaders', is also a response to the growing global interdependency and increasing complexity of political issues. Both increase the sense of uncertainty and risk. Both also heighten anxiety among political elites and publics at large. In the complex and interconnected world, predictability declines together with national control over social processes and their outcomes. Military intervention in Afghanistan, for example, triggered not only mass insurgency, but also an unexpected increase in the use of illegal drugs, the flows of refugees and illegal migrants, and prolonged and costly interventions. In line with the famous

---

13 See Rose and Suleiman (1980), Skowronek (1997, 2008), Sykes (2000) and Helms (2005).
14 See Rhodes (1995), Blondel (1987), Norris (1999), Mughan (2000) and Farrell and McAllister (2006).

'butterfly effect', causal connections multiply and become more complex, while the number of key 'stakeholders' – whose collaboration is essential for securing control – rapidly increases. Consequently, control over processes and outcomes declines proportionately to intensifying interdependencies. The outcomes become risky and uncertain, while the likelihood of unintended consequences, side-effects and dangerous 'backfires' increase. Governing starts to resemble attempts at regulating complex weather systems – it is increasingly risky and triggers risk-related public anxieties.

The point we want to make is that governmental bureaucracies, as well as political parties and their ideological programmes, are not capable of dispelling uncertainties and allaying the anxieties of risk, such as those generated by environmental threats, terrorism and unpredictable economic turbulences. The highly differentiated and horizontal government structures were best suited to times of greater certainty and established stable 'orders', when (in the developed societies, at least) nations were relatively insulated from external influences and turbulences, national governments maintained a higher level of control over domestic social developments, policy choices were relatively clear, and policy outcomes were relatively predictable (and therefore within the sphere of effective influence, if not control, of national political executives).

But such certainties have been diminishing. At times of growing uncertainty, risk awareness, and mass anxiety about the future, political leaders – especially the assertive ones – prove much better providers of public reassurance than the bureaucratic 'mandarinates', party programmes and ideological blueprints. They are looked upon as the main problem solvers and 'order makers', and are expected to act decisively and promptly on the basis of their electoral authorisation and public trust. Moreover, the leaders offer also a clear 'locus of responsibility' – much more clear than collective bodies, party programmes and abstract ideologies. If things go well, the leaders can claim the credit; if they go wrong, the same leaders have to accept responsibility and blame – and this is seen as an essential feature of democratic accountability.

In order to further clarify this argument, a short digression is necessary. Savoie (2007, 2010) puts his finger on the central political paradox of globalisation when he points to the coincidence between two seemingly opposite trends: the concentration of executive-decisional power in the hands of leaders and their 'courts', and the accompanying dissipation of 'control power' – a diminishing capacity of national governments to secure intended (desired) effects and outcomes. This paradoxical coincidence explains why globalisation generates a sense of both (executive) power concentration and (control) power dissipation. 'It has become increasingly difficult to locate power and influence in modern society' he argues, because 'the location of power [of control] has shifted in recent years, and this shift enabled those who wield [decisional] power to sidestep responsibility' (2010, 16). The sense of weakening control in national 'power centres' to manage the increasingly complex and chaotic network of interdependent forces that propel 'globalisation' translates into a widespread anxiety about governmental control, uncertain future and the fragility of 'social order'.

The problem is that certainties and stable 'orders' (national and international) cannot be restored and risks cannot be reduced. Globalisation cannot be arrested, let alone reversed, but partial 'ordering' is possible. Such partial 'ordering' – strengthening the predictability and control over outcomes in selected policy areas – seem to depend increasingly on effective coordination of action by many diverse 'stakeholders', and therefore on effective leadership. This is why the risks and uncertainties trigger widespread demand for urgent, prompt and reassuring political leadership and action, as well as for a clear explanation of the nature of these challenges and consistent 'plans of action'. This can be delivered only if political leadership and influence extends beyond national boundaries. National leaders who effectively 'network' and lobby during 'world summits' are more successful in 'ordering', and therefore more capable of providing reassurance and generating public confidence 'at home'.

The 'summits' (regional, G7, G10, G20, etc.) are devices for demonstrating broad leadership credentials, increasing the 'ordering' capacities, and facilitating the wide coordination of action. They provide some reassurance and inject some certainty into otherwise chaotic political developments. Summits demonstrate that the 'world leaders' are prepared to tackle the world problems. The enhanced communication, coordination and cooperation among these 'world leaders' reduces anxieties – as reflected in the popularity and intense media coverage of the summits. They also raise the profiles of participating national leaders as those who deal with 'issues whose complexities lie beyond the grasp of mass publics' (Zakaria 2003, 241).

The new central circles

As stressed by Weber and Schumpeter, modern political leadership should be seen as both collective, exercised by small 'ruling minorities' and 'leadership groups', and as competitive, shared not only with close collaborators – the 'courts' – but also with some prominent oppositional rivals and contenders. For a start, there are always rival opposition leaders (and in the presidential system leadership contenders) who exercise what has often been described as 'critical leadership'. In the Westminster parliamentary system, these are leaders of the alternative governmental teams, whose profile parallels the high profile of government leaders. In the presidential systems, there has been a similar profile enhancement of leadership contenders, including those who actually contest the leadership (during the primaries), and those who are just jockeying for position. Thus, Al Gore and Sarah Palin have maintained a very high political profile both during and between presidential campaigns. Such contenders stay in the limelight, make important (and widely reported) pronouncements, and participate in what has been described as 'permanent campaigns'. In this respect, the parliamentary and presidential systems do not differ in a significant way. In both systems, the leaders/contenders critically assess governmental strategies and do not miss any opportunities to pick holes in the performance of government leaders and their teams. They continuously keep the incumbent leaders in their political crosshairs. All (real or imaginary) weaknesses and failures of government leaders are under constant scrutiny – and under challenge. Characteristically, even problems caused by persons quite distant from the core leadership are now attributed to 'leadership failure'. It is this critical 'leadership failure' that is seen as most politically damaging for governments.[15]

This upgrading of oppositional 'rivals' accompanies the shift towards 'leader democracy'. While the political influence of parliaments declines, the weight of 'checking and balancing' leaders gradually shifts to their rivals – the leadership contenders. It is these contenders, typically 'leaders of the opposition', who provide a critical scrutiny of leadership performance, and who keep the governing leaders and their teams 'on their toes'. They take over (mainly from parliaments) the role of critically 'overseeing' governments, and complement the investigative media in muckraking.

The second corrective concerns the role of leaders' 'governing teams' and 'core executives' – the groups of closest political advisers and confidants that surround national leaders. The weakening of the party apparata and the ascendancy of strong leaders accompany the concentration of political power also in the collective hands of leader-centred 'central circles' (Higley et al. 1979), 'core executives' (Rhodes 2005), 'court governments' (Hennessy 2000; Savoie 2007), 'inner circles' (Useem 1986) and 'kitchen cabinets'.[16]

---

15 These features should not be confused with 'dispersion' or 'dilution' (Kane et al. 2009). While there are hierarchical 'chains' and 'lattices' of leadership – as well as a degree of functional specialisation – national leadership is progressively concentrated and centralised, even in countries with strong federal traditions, like the USA, Australia and Canada. This is particularly transparent during emergencies (terrorist attacks, national disasters, etc.), when the 'central' leadership becomes prominent – and is critically tested.

16 The term 'kitchen cabinet' is the oldest of all. It was first used in the 1830s by political opponents of President Jackson to describe and condemn the unofficial advisers Jackson appointed after purging his official ('parlour') cabinet.

In America, such a concentration and centralisation of influence in presidential trusted 'inner circles' was diagnosed relatively early (Schlessinger 1973; Useem 1986), but it has intensified since the 1980s. In Europe, the strengthening of governmental executive teams is a more recent and less uniform development. On both sides of the Atlantic (as well as in Australia) the general centripetal and centralistic trends in power distribution have accompanied the ascendancy of strong leaders and their 'courts'.[17]

There is little doubt that 'core executives' and 'inner circles' form easier under assertive leaders, especially those who have come to power since the 1980s. This is because executive appointments at the apex of political hierarchies include faithful political supporters ('people like us' in Thatcher's famous phrase), trusted formal and informal advisers, and the reliable PR spin and image experts – and are easier to make when leaders have strong power position and wide 'executive prerogative'. Similarly, the 'shallowing' of the neutral civil/public service, that is, the executive appointment of top governmental advisors, facilitates such leadership-executive appointments and makes governmental bureaucracies more responsive to leaders – but also more politicised and less neutral.

Savoie (2007, 16) describes the leader-centred state executives emerging in the Westminster systems of Britain and Canada as analogous to monarch-courtier relations, whereby

> effective political power now rests with the prime minister and a small group of carefully selected courtiers. I also mean a shift from formal decision-making process in cabinet and, as a consequence, in the civil service, to informal process involving only a handful of key actors… Courtiers are drawn from the cabinet, from partisan political staffers, from the bureaucracy, and from outside, including selected lobbyists and think tanks.

Under the pressure for urgent reform, and under pressure of leaders' preferences, the executive branches of government increasingly usurp and concentrate executive prerogative. The executive groups created by Margaret Thatcher, Reagan's informal advisory teams (famously including

---

17 While students of power elites have always pointed to the influence of semi- and informal 'ruling minorities', the mainstream political analyses tended to ignore them and focus on the formal institutional governmental structures. The renewed interest in informal leader-centred 'courts' has been diagnosed more recently mainly in the context of 'presidentialisation' (Poguntke and Webb 2005), the declining role of the public service (Savoie 2007), and the formation of executive PR apparata (Helms 2005; Stanyer 2008).

his wife, Nancy), 'kitchen cabinets' formed by Tony Blair and the exclusive and radical 'Vulcans' surrounding George W. Bush are the most publicised recent examples. Their (re)emergence, as persuasively argued by Hennessy (2000) and Savoie (2007), has coincided with the waning influence of parliamentary committees, party caucuses, top public servants and even 'large' cabinets. The governmental 'manadarinates', in particular, have been gradually circumvented by – and subordinated to – executive appointees. The latter become the main sources of influence and policy advice for leaders.

The progressive concentration of executive power gives some political advantages to governments. Decisions are made faster, strategies are more coherent and execution is more prompt – no doubt in response to public pressure for urgent and effective action. If leaders are successful in exercising their leadership, governmental strategies are more consistent because they emanate from a single decisional centre and reflect a coherent vision of the leader. There is also a clear authorship, and therefore a strong and personalised sense of responsibility for success and failure. As famously noted by Weber, both the credit and the blame can be apportioned more clearly when the decisional centres are small, when the decisions are transparent and when key policy announcements are monopolised by elected leaders rather than usurped by party coteries of unelected 'faceless men' (and increasingly also women). Consequently, it is 'leaderlessness' or weak leadership that are seen as most serious political liabilities today.

The final corrective concerns the scope of contemporary 'leadership groups'. Contemporary political leadership is subject to intense competitive pressures. While we often use the singular to describe national leaders, we also stress that modern leadership is plural (leadership groups) and permanently contested. This ongoing contestation, extending far beyond electoral campaigns, has been institutionalised. Thus, national political leadership is not only 'shared' between incumbent and opposition rival(s) but also subjected to continuous critical scrutiny. The 'principal critics' of governing leaders are supposed to keep the rulers 'on their toes' through constant critical scrutiny. They also play an important role of 'leaders-in-waiting' (Uhr 2009). Thus the increasing centrality of national leaders accompanies a rising centrality and profile of oppositional rivals/contestants. In spite of obvious differences between the parliamentary (especially the Westminster) and presidential models, high profile opposition, relentless opposition and political polarisation of the contest become common features of both systems. This permanent – and increasingly sharp – competitive contestation of leadership is another feature of contemporary 'leader democracy' and, as argued in the next chapter, one of the sources of its vulnerability.

Leaders Rule OK

The arguments presented by Weber and Schumpeter, and the evidence of leadership enhancement discussed above, suggest that the ascendancy of strong and high profile leadership groups coincides with the declining centrality within political elites of the main leaders' 'competitors' – party officials and top bureaucrats. Public confidence in parties and parliaments has declined (although this decline has recently been arrested). Under the increasing burden of legislation, which becomes an ongoing business and preoccupation of parliamentarians, parliamentary 'supervision' of governments becomes a fiction – thus expanding the autonomy of leaders and their 'central circles'. Similarly, the top echelons of the public/civil service have also experienced a decline in influence and public confidence, reduced to an advisory role. The relative power position of the bureaucratic mandarinate, seemingly unassailable in the postwar era, has been diminishing particularly fast since the 1980s, mainly as a result of 'rival' executive-advisory appointments made by political leaders. This coincided with a change in voting behaviour. Voting became not only 'personalised', leader-sensitive and increasingly image driven, but also gradually turned into the political equivalent of 'impulse buying' of goods under the momentary impact of attractive presentation. In relational terms, the new 'personalised' and fleeting alliances between leaders and the mass constituencies started to resemble short affairs and one-night stands. The resulting fleeting alliances have been described as electoral 'belts' ('oil belt', 'sun belt', 'Bible belt'), which are less structured and more fickle, and usually the result of rhetorical formatting by media-savvy leaders rather than the reflection of 'frozen' structural cleavages. The key factors of the success in such alliances are image projection and rhetorical affinity.

The new political alliances have been arranged, shaped, consummated and refashioned fast and in an unceremonious fashion. Leadership candidates, who are good persuaders and skilful political communicators, are capable of quick seduction of mass publics stripped from old party loyalties. Those with an attractive image and high media profile are therefore in high demand and are increasingly perceived as the 'winning horses' that guarantee electoral success. They are also backed by professional experts in political communication – or strictly speaking – persuasion. The leader-appointed advisory teams may include an odd senior bureaucrat – but they certainly include trusted campaign strategists, media advisors, polling/public opinion experts and other members of the PR ('spin') machine.

The leader-centricity also reflects the symbiosis between political leaders, the media and the mass publics. Skilful leaders are able to use the media as a means for imposing their images, agendas, interpretive frames and even formulas and phrases on mass audiences. While Facebook and Twitter open the way for public feedback, for a more 'horizontal' and dialogue-like communication with political audiences, the rapidly expanding 'spin machine' (PR experts, campaign strategists, pollsters, etc.) reinforce the 'vertical' and 'persuasive' nature of this communication. In turn, the media need leaders as accessible and authoritative sources of news and commentary. This also means that leader-voter relations change. Leaders are able to shape public perceptions in a more efficient and systematic manner. Mass constituencies, in turn, expect successful candidates to display both 'leadership' and 'celebrity' qualities – above all confidence, consistency, determination and firm convictions combined with readiness to face cameras and microphones. The widespread public approval of narcissistic, decisive and innovative-transformative leadership, as well as a critical disapproval of those political heads who fail to act decisively, are clear symptoms of the changing form of contemporary democracy, a shift towards a more representative and indirect, more mass-mediated and elite-driven – yet welcomed by mass publics – 'leader democracy'.

The shift towards a leader-centred democracy naturally triggers concerns, especially among those who consider the leader-centric politics as undemocratic. It is hard to see, though, why the leader-centric trends should undermine democratic principles (popular sovereignty and ruling with public authorisation and consent), or why it should be considered as less democratic than the 'party-centric' politics that preceded it. In 'leader democracy', popular sovereignty is exercised in a representative way, predominantly through electoral mass-mediated competition but also through more active management of mass confidence and concerns. Importantly, leaders succeed in building elite–mass linkages based on trust and confidence. As argued in the next chapter – and as originally suggested by Weber and Schumpeter – these linkages, even when mass mediated, place contemporary 'leader democracy' firmly within the 'democratic family'.

CHAPTER 4

'LEADER DEMOCRACY' AND ITS RIVALS

In the previous chapter we highlighted some trends that reinforce the central role of political leaders: the centralisation of executive power; the decline of mass parties and electoral dealignment; the expansion of the mass media and the accompanied revolution in political communication; and the globalisation-driven complexity of political decisions, increasing risk, and the high profile of 'world leaders'. Together, we have argued, they result in a shift in contemporary democracies towards leader-centred, trust-based and highly mediated politics. It is time now to look more closely at the theoretical model of 'leader democracy' and compare it with its main rivals/competitors: the *aggregative-pluralist* and the *deliberative-participatory* models. This comparison is undertaken not so much to question the ideological attractiveness of these rival models as to assess their descriptive accuracy, consistency and adequacy in accounting for actual political developments. Moreover, we also highlight the normative underpinnings of 'leader democracy' – mainly in response to those critics who see the model as 'insufficiently democratic'.

It is worth stressing again that this is more a juxtaposition than a comparison because the rival models of democracy we overview below are only partly commensurate. The model of 'leader democracy' is predominantly descriptive-explanatory, while the compared models are predominantly normative. The *deliberative-participatory* model, in particular, aims primarily at setting up criteria for the normative justification of democracy, and it addresses – above all – the question of desirability of democracy. The proposed model of 'leader democracy', by contrast, aims mainly at portraying the contemporary democratic practices and capturing the recent trends. It aims primarily at explaining how democratic politics actually works, rather than why it is desirable. Nevertheless, there are some comparative plains. 'Leader democracy', we argue, has some solid normative underpinnings; it is based on a minimalist definition of democracy. The aggregative-pluralist model of democracy is located somewhere in between the other two; it is partly normative and partly descriptive-explanatory. What makes the proposed juxtaposition and comparison both interesting and relevant is that each model, regardless of its main aim, makes some claims for validity on both normative as well as descriptive grounds – though in different degree in each case. Thus even the deliberative-participatory model, although predominantly normative, does not withdraw into an ivory tower of normative political philosophy. Its advocates claim that it has some descriptive relevance and empirical validity. On the other hand, we claim, the model of 'leader democracy' also claims 'minimal' normative validity and credentials – something worth stressing, especially in response to those critics who confuse it with guardianship or even modern Bonapartism.

The Competing Models

John Plamenatz's (1973, 56) observation from a generation ago that 'the idea that there is something inherently undemocratic about the mere fact of leadership...has attracted both democrats and sceptics about democracy' seems still relevant in contemporary debates. This was confirmed 15 years later by Giovanni Sartori (1987, 171) who pointed to the fact that 'the vital role of leadership is frequently acknowledged', and yet nonetheless 'obtains only a negligible status within the theory of democracy'. Remarkably, three decades later leadership is still regarded by democratic theorists as either an anomaly, or as a necessary evil. Moreover, more than a century after Weber's convincing arguments about incompatibility of direct forms of democracy with the requirements of large-scale, organised and complex societies, many contemporary democratic theorists still embrace a problematic view of democracy on the national level as 'participatory' and 'direct'. These views accompany normative standards according to which the quality of democracy and the strength of democratic credentials depend primarily on persistent mass involvement, wide public participation in ruling, and popular control of government. The assumption underlying these views and standards seems to be: the wider the public involvement, the stronger the citizens' control of office holders, the narrower the decisional autonomy of leaders and elites, the better – that is, more democratic – the governance. By contrast, strong and autonomous leadership heralds creeping autocracy, arbitrariness and personal bias, all incompatible with the principles of popular sovereignty and 'rule by public consent'. Let us look at the two most popular versions of these direct-democratic views: deliberative and 'neoclassical'.

Deliberative democracy

Contemporary democratic theory seems to be dominated by the popular and fashionable discourse on deliberative democracy.[1] As John Dryzek (2000, 1) notes, this discourse spread in the final decade of the twentieth century. Deliberative democracy is mainly a normative concept, a radical-utopian project, but it also contains a descriptive-explanatory model of democratic arrangements and practices. The essential features of democracy, according to deliberative democrats, are (a) wide and equal participation of citizens and (b) open and rational discussion of political issues. These two features allow for continuous and consensual transformation of citizens' preferences. The novelty of this vision is that it is consensus-oriented and centred on discussion. In those respects it differs radically from the traditional interest-oriented aggregative theory of democracy that focuses on voting.

The participants in the deliberative debate are in the 'ideal speech situation' to use Jürgen Habermas's (1990) famous phrase. They are not supposed to represent territorial, social or religious interest groups, or segmental interests, but rather present their own personal opinions. In John Rawls' *A Theory of Justice* (1971) the role of the original view or position taken, and the veil of ignorance under which the public operate, ensure or at least closely approximate these conditions. The participants are construed as impartial and rational individuals, whose purpose is to find the right opinion – an unequivocal answer (truth) for any public issue on the agenda – in order to achieve consensus and thus to identify the authentic 'public good'. Wide publicity and the rational quality of debate are the key guarantees of finding the best judgement whereupon political consensus rests. The discussion transcends the prior views of the participants and leads to the recognition of truth, or at least to a consensus of opinions.

It is claimed that deliberative democracy avoids the pitfalls of representative democracy, such as the tyranny of the majority and the problems of a dominant 'principal agent' (Dryzek and Dunleavy 2009). Since decision making is not passed to or through representatives or elected leaders, the classical ideal of self-rule of the people is more likely to be achieved. All citizens are entitled – and expected – to take part in deliberations about policy decisions. Equality and civic involvement are also maximised because decision making is not the privilege of a narrow specialised elite or elected representatives (politician, plutocrats, etc.) but a right and an obligation, a civic duty of all citizens. The close identification of decision makers and citizens bridges a gap that

---

1 See Bohman and Rehg (1997), Elster (1998), Fishkin (1991), Dryzek (2001, 2006) and Fishkin and Lasett (2003).

traditionally existed between representatives and the represented, between the ruling minority and the people. Political leadership, which typically accompanies unequal distribution of power, is seen as a threat to equality and to liberty; hence it is not welcome in this highly idealistic view of politics.

Deliberative democracy also promises to avoid two further 'deficits' of representative government. First, it provides an answer to Joseph Schumpeter's (1987, 258–61) argument about 'mass infantilism' that points to the limited knowledge and technical incompetence of ordinary citizens. Drawing on John Stuart Mill's reasoning, deliberative democrats claim that participation in a free deliberation not only engages and informs citizens, but also improves their political knowledge and competence. Second, it resolves the problems related to aggregation (e.g. the paradoxes of voting) through shaping citizens' preferences 'horizontally' (rather than hierarchically), and through generating a consensus without manipulation. As Jon Elster (1997, 11–12) stated, 'there would not be any need for an aggregating mechanism, since a rational discussion would tend to produce unanimous preferences... Not optimal compromise, but unanimous agreement is the goal of politics on this view.' In other words, participants in the deliberation 'stand for' the whole community, society and nation.

This model of democracy, as many critics (including Max Weber) point out, is not only unrealistic in large-scale societies but also contradictory. Thus placing a citizens' assembly at the centre of the decision-making process does not necessarily produce rational 'deliberation' and egalitarian consensus. Unanimity rarely emerges in public discussions, even if these discussions take the form of prolonged deliberations. In fact, instead of creating a consensus, such discussions often deepen divisions and entrench conflicts (Elster 1997, 14). Deliberations are expensive; they take time, energy and resources that few organisations can afford. Moreover, group discussions of this sort are far from egalitarian. Plato and other classical authors in the era of Athenian democracy dismissed public discussion as the birthplace of sophistry or demagoguery. Equal participation is an attractive idea in line with modern egalitarian ideology, but like this ideology, it is unrealistic – especially in large-scale, complex societies. It is persuasion and manipulation that prevails in public debates, even if carried out in a tolerant and egalitarian manner.

This is not, one should stress, just a problem of scale and complexity. Effective rational deliberation, that is, a discussion that brings rational and consistent decisions, is not possible beyond a small number of informed and equal participants. It can be applied in homogeneous professional groups and organisations, in small-scale communities, in local politics or in collegial bodies (such as academic senates) and in groups capable of meeting face-to-face. It presupposes social homogeneity, cultural similarity and minimal information and decisional competence. Beyond a certain size and certain level of cultural diversity, deliberation becomes illusory and it inevitably breaks down 'with speech-making replacing conversation and rhetorical appeals replacing reasoned argument' (Goodin 2000, 83). In cases of national referenda, this breakdown has been clearly diagnosed. Instead of rational deliberation, we observe mass persuasion, media impact and partisan campaigning sponsored by large pressure groups. Dominant interests and vocal minorities capture the stage, emotions run high, and 'moral panics' overwhelm rational debates. Therefore, national referenda conducted without elite consensus (and persuasion) typically polarise already divided electorates or produce decisions that are subsequently regretted and criticised. They also inevitably produce disgruntled minorities whose views are bound to be 'overwhelmed' or altogether ignored. The decisions made by canton and commune referenda in Switzerland illustrate these problems well.

Could we get closer to genuine deliberation in a small group or forum, as a few deliberative democrats suggest? The results of experiments (like those conducted in Australia in 1999 and 2003) are not encouraging. First, deliberative decisions are bound to be illegitimate for those left outside the discussion forum. And by bringing more than a few people into the forum, one inevitably turns deliberations into oratory contests or demagoguery (Parkinson 2003, 181). Second, equality seems to be an idea that cannot be achieved even in small groups. A contemporary political theorist, Adam Przeworski (1998, 145), points out that deliberation in itself presupposes inequality of influence:

> If everyone had information of the same quality, and the same capacity to interpret this information, then deliberation as normally understood would be pointless. If beliefs are to be modified as the result of deliberation, it must be because individuals have unequal access to information, and/ or they see themselves as having unequal reasoning capacity.

The mere existence of deliberation entails recognition of certain differences *and* inequality, either of information or of the ability to process it, as Przeworski argues. Third, although it is true that public deliberations typically transform individual preferences, they do not necessarily transform them through force of reason or in a consensual direction. As Joseph Femia (2009, 74) reminds us, results of social psychology research suggest that social interaction in a small group or community usually produces not unanimity, but conformity, 'group thinking' or 'mutually reinforcing bias' (cf. Elster 1997). People are ready to conform to the majority in the group and to abandon their own personal beliefs and opinions, even when discussions are conducted in an atmosphere of freedom and respect. Encouraging direct political interaction may intensify this conformist tendency.

The deliberative model also assumes that individuals have the capacity and willingness to argue with reason, thus disregarding our knowledge about human motivation and behaviour. We know, however – both from social psychology and observation – that human preferences are grounded in custom, habit, emotion and instinct. Some streams of political theory ground their models of mass behaviour in Paretian and Freudian assumptions about principally nonrational foundations of human conduct. Deliberative democrats either ignore these streams, or regard 'nonautonomous attitudes' as an illegitimate source of citizens' opinion making, that should be excluded from the deliberative process (presumably, by those who conduct the debates). This, paradoxically, gives deliberative democracy a paternalist flavour (cf. Femia 2009, 76).

Most deliberative democrats also overlook the problem of representation. They prefer the so called 'deliberative forums', such as citizens' councils and assemblies, citizens' juries, mini-publics, and so forth to large-scale representative institutions, such as parliaments or legislative assemblies. Such established representative institutions are often dismissed by deliberative theorists as improper, as arenas of bargaining between political parties and competing interests, rather than forums for deliberation. They distort deliberative democracy. It is not accidental that for John Rawls the ideal site for deliberation is not a political assembly, like national parliament, but rather the Supreme Court (1993, 231–9). For other deliberative theorists, the ideal sites for authentic deliberation are informal groupings, such as associations, focus groups, citizens' juries, deliberative opinion polls or 'consensus seeking conferences' (Saward 2000, 71). To put it succinctly, for the advocates of deliberative democracy, representation is a 'nonissue' – representativeness is subsumed in authentic and free deliberation.

Leadership is also treated by advocates of deliberative democracy as a 'nonissue'. Deliberation is located in an abstract 'leaderless space', or a leaderless egalitarian assembly. This is because leaders may distort egalitarian deliberations by introducing the element of authority. This part of an argument is particularly utopian because in real life situations leaders emerge spontaneously, even in small groups like juries, focus groups or debating societies, and even when the discussions approximate 'free speech conditions'. Eloquent or highly motivated speakers emerge as 'natural' group leaders and they inevitably dominate the discussion. Studies conducted on jury deliberations reveal that 'some kinds of people routinely speak more than others in free deliberative settings', hence participation is not equal, even if freedom and respect are enforced by rules (Sanders 1997, 365). Therefore most jury deliberations begin with the selection of a group leader, a 'chair' (usually a white male with a college degree, in the American setting). Speaking confidently and eloquently and sitting at the head of the table enhances the chance of being chosen as such 'chair'.

Another problem lies with the fact that any decision-making body, even if it is free, egalitarian and respectful of minority views, is seldom autonomous or self-executing. The classics of liberal political thought – like that of Locke and Montesquieu, not to mention the authors of the Federalist Papers – showed awareness of this fact, and envisaged an executive branch of the government as a means of effective enactment. Since then, the 'practical' consideration of prompt and efficient decision making was placed at the very centre of political theory. This theory concentrated on both consensus and consent, and on conditions of effective exercise of executive power. This is because even the most deliberative processes grind to a halt without some form of executive conclusion or solution to frequent gridlocks. The participants/discussants cannot escape the question of 'who leads' and 'who acts' when it comes to the enforcement of deliberative decisions. Enactment generally requires an actor/leader and relies on a decisive, prompt, informed and clearly directed action – the qualities that deliberative decision-making bodies cannot deliver simultaneously (Kuyper and Laing 2010, 6–8).

To continue the list, the model of deliberative democracy also faces the 'problem of collective action'. If deliberative groups are to provide public goods and benefits to their members, their creation and sustenance has to come from some form of energising entrepreneurship. Even ongoing deliberation, let alone conclusion, requires leadership. Leadership works to stimulate action and overcome collective action problems because leaders have different incentive structures and motivations that are independent of those held by the followers (Cho 2004, 218–22).

Deliberative democrats, like Jürgen Habermas (1989) and John Dryzek (2000), often refer to civil society as an arena of free, unconstrained and contested discussion – a 'free speech situation' writ large. They regard nonhierarchical structure and the activity of civil society movements or organisations as the embodiment of the ideal deliberative process. Yet, this is misleading. As Kuyper and Laing (2010, 13) point out, civil society always contains power asymmetries and therefore has leaders. Most civil society organisations build up some form of organisational hierarchy that gives direction, provides appropriate means for operation, and makes it possible to achieve their aims more effectively. The deliberative democratic faith in natural egalitarianism and 'leaderless' nature of civil society fails to recognize the fundamental role that leadership has played in overcoming collective action problems in civil society (Crozier et al. 1980; Tarrow 1994). Great leaders, like Winston Churchill, Franklin D. Roosevelt, Mahatma Gandhi, Martin Luther King and Nelson Mandela, were able to mobilise people for collective actions by persuading, convincing, exhorting, directing and prompting. Without these leaders and their persuasion, exhortation or prompting, collective action would not eventuate – or succeed. This problem is widely recognised by Weberian sociologists and collective action theorists, but seldom addressed by the advocates of the deliberative model of democracy.

Finally, there is a neglected issue of cost and capacity. The deliberative forums organised in Australia confirmed their expensive and exclusive (in the sense of tasks and issues) nature. It took thousands of dollars to bring the participants together and free them, for the period of deliberations, from their daily preoccupations, tasks and chores. Yet, without such periodic (at least) liberation from daily tasks, the civic focus and deliberation would be impossible. As critics noted wryly, the 'Athenian' civic deliberation relies also on Athenian slavery.

What enables systematic civic deliberation, and what motivates 'ordinary' people to participate in collective discussions? Deliberative democrats seldom give clear answers to these questions. They rarely address the conditions and 'practicalities' of broad civic debates. They seldom acknowledge that even if citizens do have equal political rights, they are still different in their character, personal interest and outlook. Even if wide debates are organised (e.g. through the new infocommunication technologies), there is no guarantee of rationality and equal levels of motivation to participate in the process. 'The fact that only some of the population will be motivated to overcome their rational lack of participation leads to some degree of self-selection and de facto leadership and hierarchy in undirected deliberative processes', as Kuyper and Laing (2010, 10) argue (cf. Femia 2009). It looks like there is no escape from hierarchy and leadership, no refuge from differences in skill, talent, power and authority. Theoretical models of democracy that seek such a refuge typically end in ideological nirvana, where reality does not count.

The neoclassical model(s)

The neoclassical or *aggregative-pluralist* model and the underlying 'adaptation theory' of democracy could be seen as contemporary updates of the 'classical' Athenian model. According to the adaptation theory 'the institutions of political representation *indirectly* fulfil the same functions that were previously exercised by direct democracy in the context of the *polis*' (Zolo 1992, 76). The adaptation theory of representation adjusts these practices to the circumstances and conditions of large-scale societies.[2] In the neoclassical

---

2 Representation is considered as a necessary means to the end in this view of democracy (Dahl 1989, 13–33).

model it is the people, the electorate, who decide the political issues and who then choose their representatives to ensure that their preferences are enacted and their decisions carried out. The people choose their representatives to carry indirectly their will. In that sense, the adaptation theory takes the approach labelled five decades earlier by Joseph Schumpeter as 'classical' and 'popular' (Körösényi 2009b). Schumpeter (1987, 250) also defined the core of this democratic model as 'that institutional arrangement for arriving at political decisions which realizes the common good by making the people itself decide issues through the election of individuals who are to assemble in order to carry out its will'. Because of some modifications introduced by various thinkers (including Sartori and Dahl), it is more accurate to refer to this model as 'neoclassical'.

Critics of Schumpeter were right in saying that there is no *single* classical theory or model of democracy. The 'neoclassical model' is, in fact, a family label for diverse empirical, analytical and normative theories. We limit attention to only three prominent members of this family, namely the economic-aggregative, the pluralist and the mandate views of democratic politics. Our aim is highlighting the similarities within the family, as well as differences that set the family apart from 'leader democracy'.

Unlike deliberative democracy, all versions of the neoclassical democratic theory have strong roots in an empirical-descriptive view of social democratic politics, and they reflect the era of 'party democracy' that lasted from the beginning of the twentieth century to the late 1970s (see Chapter 3). They were elaborated within mainstream political science of the post–Second World War era and endorsed by social democratic practitioners. Today they still lay claim to being the 'mainstream' analysis of democratic politics.

The image that lies at the heart of all these models combines (1) pluralism of interests inherent in society, and (2) the key role of parties in articulating-cum-aggregating those plural interests, and in simplifying-cum-clarifying political choices.[3] Robert Dahl and other pluralist authors regard social groups as the starting point of all political actions. In this regime, political players are no longer unbiased individuals but interest organisations and parties, both representing the particular interests of social classes, communities and groups. The party composition of parliament reflects the multiple cleavages of class and interests in society. In developed party systems, all major social interest groups are represented, but none of them become dominant. The purpose of

---

3 This was the mainstream view on democratic representation for decades in the second half of the twentieth century. The classic proponents of this approach are Harold Laski, Robert Dahl (1956, 1989) and Anthony Downs (1957); for critical interpretations see Carl Schmitt (1991) and Jürgen Habermas (1962).

parties in parliament is to articulate and represent the interests of the social groups as clearly and efficiently as possible. Politics is an instrumental activity; the fundamental logic of democracy is utilitarian. Unlike in the deliberative view, parliament is not the forum of rational debate in search of truth and consensus, but rather a forum for interest articulation, rational bargaining, and reconciliation or harmonisation. Consequently, politics based on interests does not result in a consensus but a compromise. This compromise is possible to establish because the confrontation/competition of interests eventually creates equilibrium. Due to this, proportional representation is an appropriate electoral system to reflect the political composition of the society, the whole nation, and to achieve a dynamic political equilibrium/outcome. The proper composition of the legislature is the guarantee of the representativeness and stability of the system.

On a more abstract theoretical level, there is a more sophisticated version of the pluralist approach: the aggregative model of democracy. It also represents the 'bottom-up' view of the democratic political process. But while the pluralist model regards social groups as the starting point of political action, the aggregative view regards individual citizens with exogenous preferences as the basic actors of politics. Anthony Downs (1957), the founding father of this aggregative model of democracy, popularised the useful concept of the median voter, the average voter. He assumed that politics is instrumental in nature, and that citizens vote to maximize their individual welfare. In order to win their vote, office-seeking politicians adjust their electoral-programme appeal to the median voter's views, outlooks and issue concerns. To put it another way, politicians formulate their political programmes opportunistically, so to speak – in order to win elections – rather than fight elections to carry out their programmes.

We have seen that the normative concept of deliberative-participatory democracy aims at eliminating leadership from politics, since it regards leadership as an imposition, an impediment to equal participation and rational discussion. The neoclassical theory of democracy does not do that – and therefore it is more realistic. The advocates of this theory admit that leaders play a role in democratic politics, but they also restrict this leadership role in a significant way, and this poses a number of problems. Here, we highlight four such problems, selected because of their centrality and because they allow us to highlight the differences between 'leader democracy' and its neoclassical rivals.

The first one is the neoclassical portrayal of the political process as principally occurring in a 'bottom-up' direction. In the neoclassical doctrine, the starting point of the political process is the autonomous 'will of the people', which is usually interpreted as popular will or 'original views' of the people on major issues of public policy and the accompanying preferences. This will is expressed through the issue-votes of citizens in elections, and democratic governments must be responsive to the will and corresponding votes/preferences. The 'responsive rule', as John May (1978) calls it, must prevail even if citizens formally give their votes to representative candidates and, unlike in referendums, do not vote on individual issues or specific policy preferences. Democratic procedures must ensure a way – either through the mechanism grasped by the mandate theory, through delegation or through proportional representation – of recognising and implementing public policy decisions according to the expressed preferences of the people.

In the neoclassical view, the office holders (the elected representatives of the people) are principally delegates or deputies – the key articulators and executors of the popular will – and not representatives in the traditional sense. Politics resembles a demand-driven market where demand is identical with actual choices of citizens. The aggregative model of democracy thus portrays the political process as continuing responses of the government to the preferences of the citizens. Representation is achieved through the mirroring of social groupings and aggregating individual preferences – it is representation in a descriptive sense. Underlying this view is the assumption that if an assembly is descriptively representative, then it will act (and the government will act as well) in the interests of the represented. Political representation in the legislature aims at the accurate depiction of the composition of society in terms of preferences and outlooks.[4]

The second problem – and the main reason for the neglect of political leadership by advocates of aggregative view – is the special role given to elections. The aggregative theory shares with other members of the neoclassical family the assumption that the crucial criterion of democratic government is the responsiveness of public policy to the preferences of citizens as revealed through elections.[5] The central role is reflected in the concept of 'mandate'. A government is deemed representative, and therefore democratic, only if it is responsive to the citizens' will expressed in elections; this responsiveness gives politicians and governments a democratic mandate. The mandate amounts not so much to generalised authorisation to rule, as to a specific approval to carry out the policies promised in the electoral platform or manifesto. The function of elections in this view is not only the democratic selection and 'mandating' of politicians, but also the selection of policies to be implemented by the future

---

4 See, in particular, Pitkin (1967, 146), Dahl (1971, 1–2; 1989, 109–13), Manin et al. (1999, 31–32) and Judge (1999, 23).
5 This wider assumption is broadly shared in empirical political science, see Page and Shapiro (1983), Jacobs and Shapiro (1994) and Hobolt and Klemmemsen (2005).

government. If public policy is in accordance with the electoral mandate of the government, then the will of the people is realised. Such view fits well into the wider frame of the neoclassical doctrine, since elections are seen as a linkage between the people's will and public policy. The main function of elections is determining policy choice or policy direction, not just the selection of leaders – and this is seen by critics as unduly constraining and unrealistic, especially under the conditions that call for fast and flexible reactions.

The third problem comes from the closely related assumption about citizens' competence. Democracy, as self-rule of the people, assumes equality of citizens in various respects. The neoclassical doctrine in general and the mandate theory in particular assume that citizens are equally well-informed and competent in public policy matters. Only competent and autonomous citizens are able to set up a preference order for major policy issues. This is highly problematic – for obvious reasons. Similarly problematic is the assumption of a *symmetric-egalitarian* relationship among citizens. It excludes the notion of leadership because every form of leadership implies asymmetry between leaders and followers, as well as inequality. Moreover, this exclusion of leadership also eliminates the major source of dynamic.[6]

The fourth problem appears in neoclassical accounts of political responsibility. Liberal political philosophy regards individuals as autonomous and hence responsible agents. Individually, everybody is responsible for his or her own choices and actions. The meaning of this is clear in ethics, in private life and especially in the world of private goods. A collective choice derived from the citizens' preferences through an aggregative procedure, however, does not establish public or political responsibility in any way or respect. If democracy means complete responsiveness to citizens, then the responsibility of political leaders for public policy vanishes. Leaders turn into delegates/deputies, the pure transmitters of preferences, rather than autonomous representatives. Therefore the neoclassical theory of democracy does not regard politics as an autonomous sphere and so is reluctant to see political leaders as autonomous agents. It abolishes both leadership *and* political 'public' responsibility. This is apparent, for example, in Dahl's (1989) version of democratic theory that is oblivious to leadership and political agency.

These criticisms are not new. In his *Considerations on Representative Government*, John Stuart Mill emphasised that even the members of an assembly do not feel personal responsibility to the same degree as the members of the executive, like ministers, who held individual and personal 'public responsibility' in their jurisdiction (2007, 74). The problem is multiplied in the case of large-scale societies. The nature of collective, democratic decision making always faces

---

6 See Blondel (1987, 13), Burns (1978, 18) and Tucker (1995, 7).

a pitfall of collective irresponsibility, exemplified in the widely publicised tendency to increase public expenditure and deficit. Norberto Bobbio (1987, 39) sees this as a problem of *ungovernability*.[7] It is only responsible leadership that can challenge the policy of uncontrolled profligacy, public expenditure and debt accumulation.

The models compared

As argued in Chapter 2, a very different view of modern democratic leadership and politics was suggested by Max Weber and Joseph Schumpeter. Both theorists put leadership at the centre of the political process and also at the centre of their accounts of mass democratisation. Both also challenged the view that nation-level democracy could take a direct form, that public policy might be based on the issue-preferences of autonomous citizens, and that leaders could be held accountable for their *specific* policies. Instead, they suggested that modern democracy, especially the 'working' mass democracy that was emerging in Great Britain and the United States, is inevitably mass-representative, indirect and leader- and elite-centred. All these characteristics do not weaken its democratic character – mass 'leader democracy' could assure a rational and deliberative decision making as well as broad (one could say general and strategic) public responsibility of political leaders and elites towards their voting constituencies. Deliberative rationalism, they argued, is secured by elite-centred, rather than mass- or public-centred, policy deliberation and decision making. Similarly, public responsibility is exercised through regular (nowadays even continuous and permanent) and open electoral competition for executive leadership in the state. This does not diminish the role of voters/citizens, nor does it reduce them to passive objects of authority, encourage autocratic rule, reduce public trust, or free ruling minorities from public responsibility. Weber and Schumpeter saw the key role of citizens as participants in the electoral contests – as dignified umpires in (then periodic and now ongoing) leadership competition, who provide broad and general 'authorisation' to rule and periodically evaluate political outcomes. These citizens/voters are regularly informed, influenced, directed and persuaded – one may even say manipulated – by leadership contenders. But these contenders have to compete in their persuading appeal, and they rely on securing mass trust and confidence of the voters. In modern mass democracy 'public opinion' does influence the process of ruling, but it is largely an artefact – a product of leadership competition and elite persuasion – rather than an autonomous force. It is leaders and their

---

7 See also Brittan (1975) and Crozier et al. (1975).

'staffs' who actively, but also competitively, shape the amorphous and fickle 'public opinion', propose themselves to (and impose themselves on) mass voters. Those who are most successful – that is, most forceful, convincing, confident and spectacular – win public trust and confidence, obtain a broad authorisation to rule and to take responsibility of the outcomes. If they fail to secure the trust and confidence of a sufficient number of voters, they are stripped of authorisation and removed from position of political power (and responsibility). Let us elaborate this model further by contrasting it with deliberative and neoclassical 'rivals'.

In the model of 'leader democracy' the struggle for national power and leadership concentrates in the political domain of the state (as suggested by Weber). Political leaders, embedded in broader political elites, emerge in competitive elections (as stressed by Schumpeter). The political process is not energised by the political preferences of the electorate or the interests of social groups, but rather by the aspirations and ambitions of political leaders who compete for public trust and votes. The objective of leaders is not to reach consensus or compromise, but to obtain mandate-authorisation and sustain broad (mass and elite) political support. Rival politicians and their elite factions attempt to win public support not by accommodating the political preferences of the electorate, but by trying to shape voters' perceptions and preferences in line with their (leaders') will. In that sense, leaders produce and shape the electoral preferences of the people themselves – but they do it competitively in open rivalry. The active players of politics are not the constituents but the politicians/leaders. The former are reactive; the latter are active. This is because in the model of 'leader democracy' political action is based neither on truth nor on interests, but on the will, resolve and persuasive power of leaders who are seen as central political actors and as political entrepreneurs/ innovators. Therefore, the means to acquire political support is always strong conviction, oratory skill and persuasive talent – the key ingredients of charismatic appeal.

Also, the meaning of political representation is quite different in 'leader democracy' than in the other models. Representation is not achieved by public deliberation, aggregation, or mirroring of mass opinions, but rather through active leadership. Leaders lead – that is gain followers/supporters – by proposing attractive new visions, goals and policy directions. This point, central for our theoretical argument, needs more clarification. 'Leader democracy', to use Przeworski's term (1999, 23), rests on a 'minimalist concept of democracy' that is sceptical about the feasibility of democracy in the sense of self-rule by the people. It also abstains from assuming the predominant rationality and autonomy of citizens and – unlike deliberative and aggregative rivals – does not assume a high level of cognitive competence among voters/citizens.[8] Such views contrast sharply with the assumptions of the 'rival' models and, while acknowledged as more realistic, trigger frequent criticisms from advocates of direct and deliberative democracy. Even today Weber's views are characterised as 'ambivalent' towards democracy, and Schumpeter is criticised for 'underestimating' the mental capacity of voters/citizens.[9] Joseph Femia (2001, 83) rightly asks whether in this situation, when 'democratic will' is, in fact, manufactured, or at least shaped by the leaders, can we 'really say that those who prey upon their weaknesses are being held to account?' The advocates of 'leader democracy' respond in affirmative, but they add some important qualifications: political responsibility and accountability are always restricted, not just by rules and conventions, but also by the very fact that proper public evaluation of ruling (political strategies embraced by the leaders) – and the act of 'holding the leaders accountable' – occur retrospectively, after the outcomes (including the unintended consequences) become apparent and publicised through electoral campaign.

Giovanni Sartori's distinction between opinion and knowledge opens the room for a balanced account of the political capacity of the people and for a more respectful interpretation of voting. According to Sartori (1987, 117), ordinary people do not necessarily have sufficient or proper *knowledge* for governing. But they may have *opinions* that enable them to make competent retrospective judgements of the outcomes of government policy. In 'leader democracy' it is assumed that although citizens are less competent than politicians in deciding on specific policy issues, they are capable of articulating overall *retrospective assessments* of political outcomes, that is, the overall judgements of achievements or failures of leaders and governments. Thus the mass public is not excluded or marginalised in the leader-democratic model. But its role is circumscribed as an ultimate and retrospective political arbiter/authoriser and as a source of the ultimate political 'judgement' in competition for leadership and power authorisation.

Five elements of the leader-democratic model deserve special attention: the nature of the political process, the role of elections, the leader–citizen relation, the nature of political responsibility and the notion of the common good. They are not only central, but also most frequently misunderstood by critics.

We have seen in a previous section that deliberative democrats portray the political process as a continuous discussion among equal participants in an idealised free speech situation. Equality – that is, a horizontal symmetric

---

8 See Chapter 2, as well as Sartori (1987, 119–20), Santoro (1993, 131–2), Przeworski (1999, 20–5) and Femia (2001, 80–3).
9 See Best (2008), Bellamy (1991), Held (1987, 134–8, 172–9) and Plamenatz (1973, 95–129).

power relationship – prevails among the participants of deliberation. Deliberative democrats also envisage a bottom-up perspective of decision making, even if they note the executive role, initiative and prerogative of leaders. They concentrate on the ideal condition of the deliberation and assume that the executive branch of government does not have autonomy, but rather carries out the decisions of the deliberative public bodies. Officials and elected representatives are delegates or deputies, 'executors' of the popular will, and not representatives in the sense given to the concept of representation by Edmund Burke, John Stuart Mill or more recently Hanna Pitkin (1967, 146).

'Leader democracy' portrays the political process as animated mainly by politicians, especially political leaders. Power and influence flow predominantly in a 'top-down' direction. Policies and strategic programmes are created and formulated by leaders; citizens merely accept or reject them and retrospectively judge their effects (Cunningham 2002, 64–5, 186–96). This view approximates the realities of contemporary politics more closely than the rivals, and it facilitates a more adequate and realistic account of the political process (elections, representation, etc.) In this view, the political process itself is generated mainly by the rivalry of political leaders. The principal players in the political process are not political parties representing social groups, the PR professionals, or the corporate CEOs (as another, rival image suggests) – though they are obviously involved in policy making – but national political leaders, including the oppositional leaders-in-waiting. These leaders are the key actors, the main – though never sole – shapers the political process. In this view, agenda setting, interpretive frame alignment, active persuasion and manipulation are amongst the normal and expected tasks of leaders. To put it bluntly, leaders lead, citizens follow and judge. The neoclassical theory of democracy, by contrast, portrays elections as rational policy choice made by the people. Elections form the crucial moments of the political process in specifying public policy and achieving the will of the people. In deliberative democracy, elections have, at most, a secondary role. Democracy is not about elections and majority rule, but about participation in a free and deliberative discussion from which a consensual view (the truth) is bound to emerge.

In 'leader democracy', elections are portrayed as highly personalised candidate-driven voting; the electors vote for persons rather than for issues. Leaders, who emerge from the ranks of ordinary citizens, compete for power by presenting their visions, parading their egos and will, and convincing voters about their trustworthiness, superior leadership capacities and decisional skills. They mobilise followers with all means at their disposal: rhetoric, image, personal charisma, ideological appeal, competence or issue position.[10] Those who succeed in winning sufficient votes gain a broad mandate-authorisation to rule – and a broad autonomy to govern and 'prove themselves' worthy of further support. Leaders rule while citizens participate in the periodic (but increasingly frequent in the era of opinion polling) evaluations of the outcomes. Although leaders may be responsive to certain wishes of voters/citizens, 'leader democracy' does not aim at or encourage a responsive government per se. It typically produces responsible governments in the sense of leaders accepting broad public responsibility for the outcomes of their rule. This responsibility is primarily discharged as public accountability in and through the subsequent electoral cycles.[11]

The theory of 'leader democracy' contains an account of the relation between political leaders and citizens that differs sharply from the one offered by its rivals. Deliberative democrats assume that free and equal participation of citizens in deliberative decision making produces consensus – and makes leaders superfluous. Representation does not pose a problem either – it is achieved automatically through identification of representatives and the represented. It is further assumed that if deliberative bodies bridge the gap between the people and the decision makers, leadership is unnecessary and representation ceases to be relevant – consensus rules OK. No place is left for leadership, except in the administrative-technical domain where it may be necessary for the effective implementation of consensual collective decisions by expert 'heads'. The neoclassical view assumes the existence of an autonomous and specific people's will. It can be identified and articulated through aggregation from the preferences of rational and autonomous individuals or from group interests. It is taken for granted that each citizen has stable preferences on policy issues and that groups have a clear sense of their interests. Anthony Downs (1957) and Robert Dahl (1989) assume that citizens collectively affirm their political will, groups voice their interests, and that they jointly articulate a 'political will' that, in turn, evokes the reaction of politicians. Democratic elections motivate office-seeking politicians to be responsive to this 'political will' as articulated in voters' preferences.

The theory of 'leader democracy' is sceptical of this view in three respects. First, it challenges the assumption of Downs and Dahl that each citizen

---

10 The theory of 'leader democracy' is based on an image of democracy which claims that politics is less about content and policy issues and more focused on image-creation. Efficient communication of planned media messages to the electorate becomes the principal means of obtaining political support. This does not necessarily mean, however, that the packaging should become more important than the product.

11 See Plamenatz (1973, 109–14, 184–5), Bobbio (1987, 24–5) and Przeworski (1999, 23–55)

has stable, *ex ante* or 'given' preferences, and that individuals and groups spontaneously articulate any specific 'political will' other than amorphous (and often enigmatic) collective approval or disapproval of the 'state of affairs'. Second, it also rejects the view that diverse public preferences can be meaningfully aggregated, synthesised into a coherent entity. Kenneth Arrow (1951) and other authors of the social choice literature (e.g. Riker 1982) are particularly adamant about this point. Finally, leader democrats assert that the active volition of political leaders, rather than 'popular will', prevails in the political process. Leaders are autonomous actors in politics. The political will of leaders moves political actions and energises the entire political process.[12] Moreover, the mass public expects and approves such active role by directing their voters to the most confident, committed and appealing contenders.

The problem of responsibility is closely connected to the nature of the relation between citizens and their representatives. Collective deliberation and consensus building blur the responsibility for decisions, and therefore fail to generate responsible political actors. In the neoclassical approach, the bottom-up nature of decision making ensures continuing responsiveness but not responsibility of the government to the will of the people, the latter identified with parties and pressure groups. Democracy is seen as a kind of self-government achieved through multifaceted (mainly territorial and functional) 'representation'. Representation is considered as a means to identify balanced preferences.[13] Using a Schumpeterian market metaphor, democracy resembles an interest- and demand-driven political market where politicians are producers and managers responsive to preexisting 'consumer demand'. In 'leader democracy', by contrast, the problem of responsibility is closely connected to the concept of representation through leadership. As in the liberal view of representative government, the relative autonomy and responsibility of leaders is emphasised as a necessary condition of such representation.[14] Weber and Schumpeter regard political leaders, and not citizens, as the main subjects of responsible political action. Unlike citizens, leaders have to develop a sense of public responsibility because they care about the outcomes, and therefore about the potential impact of policy propositions. Their institutional accountability is realised through what Carl Friedrich (1963, 199–215) called

---

12 The faculties for various arts are not evenly distributed and neither is the ambition to carry out these faculties. The model of 'leader democracy' therefore assumes that political leaders are different from ordinary citizens in this respect.

13 See, in particular, Dahl (1971, 1–2; 1989, 13–33, 109–113).

14 This liberal view is best represented by Mill (2007), Birch (1964) and Plamenatz (1973). The difference lies in the question of the extent to which leaders can be held accountable. While the liberals are more optimistic, Weber and Schumpeter are more sceptical in this respect.

'the rule of anticipated reactions'. Ordinary citizens, by contrast, have only a limited sense of (civic or political) responsibility; they do not rule but assess political outcomes and judge the rulers.

Finally, we can compare the interpretation of 'public interest' and 'common good' in the discussed models. The leader-democratic model cannot give a clear and unambiguous answer to the question of what constitutes the common good. In deliberative democracy, 'public interest' and 'common good' are clearly defined: they are identical with the consensual outcomes of free deliberations. Since rational argumentation must prevail in the discussion of disinterested individuals, deliberation also generates a rational consensus. In the neoclassical theory, public good is also defined in a clear way. It is achieved through bargaining or through aggregation of competing interests: a majority coalition of interests prevails. This is not the case with the model of 'leader democracy'. As we have seen above, Arrow's voting paradoxes, Downs' thesis of rational ignorance, Schumpeter's argument on mass infantilism, and Olson's free-rider arguments all demonstrate that social choice and collective action cannot be based solely on citizens' preferences. This means the claims of aggregative and deliberative theories of democracy, and their constructs of 'common good' are not only idealistic, but also epistemologically suspect. Political decisions are typically made with incomplete information, and they have a contingent nature. The outcomes of political processes are therefore highly uncertain. Moreover, the ever-growing complexity of the world increases the unpredictable nature of political actions.[15] Thus one does not (and, indeed, cannot) know the 'objective' or 'true' common good or public interest. Due to these limitations, volition inevitably shapes every political action seeking to achieve the common good, and political leaders play a crucial role in creating alternative visions of 'public/national interest' and 'common good'.

All these comparative points, especially the contrasts, can be summarised in a tabular form (Figure 4.1).

Normative underpinnings

It is true that the model of 'leader democracy' is not free from normative underpinnings and normative ambiguities. It also has its typical vulnerabilities – highlighted mainly in the last chapter. However, it is equally important to stress that it is incompatible with – and it does not endorse – demagogic mass manipulation, tutelary autocracy or arbitrary rule. It is compatible with minimal norms of democracy understood as public responsibility and constraint, and it reflects a sober but realistic view of 'working' democratic

---

15 As noted by, among others, Femia (2001, 102–109) and Zolo (1992, 4–14, 54–64).

Table 4.1. Three models of democracy compared

	Deliberative	Neoclassical	Leader democracy
Direction of political processes	Horizontal, bottom-up	Vertical, bottom-up	Vertical, top-down
Role of elections and nature of vote	Election secondary; voting independent of issue deliberation	Election important; issue/party voting according to interests	Election crucial; personal and trust-driven vote for leaders
Nature (essential features) of democracy	Participation in free deliberative decision making	Aggregating citizens preferences/interests into collective decisions	Approving, selecting and authorising trusted leaders to rule
Leader-citizen (voter) relation	No leadership (headship in technical administration and/or execution)	Functional, bound leadership and restricted mandate (leaders = deputies, delegates, executors)	Autonomous leadership and broad mandate (leaders = autonomous actors with wide authorisation)
Nature of representation (P–A relations)	Participation rather than representation; deliberative consultation	Representation of groups and organised interests (adaptation theory)	Leaders held responsible and accountable to voters through electoral cycles (= political representation)
Meaning of 'public good'	Consensual decision	Aggregative optimum	Contingent, ex-post state

politics. In this view, all politics – democratic and nondemocratic alike – are inevitably dominated by the central power actors: leaders and elites. These central power actors are the main creators of meaning, the key shapers of notions such as 'common good' and 'public interest', and the principal users of these notions in political contests for leadership. Democratic leaders and political elites, however, are not free from public responsibility, accountability or control. They rely on regularly renewed public mandate-authorisation, they subject themselves to open, free and fair electoral competitions, and they are publicly responsible – and therefore removable – in regular electoral cycles, though these evaluations and their political consequences (further authorisation or removal) are retrospective and made under the conditions of massive persuasive influences coming from power contenders.

There is nothing embarrassing or frightening in this conclusion for democrats, including liberal democrats. Indeed, the leader- and elite-phobia prevalent in the democratic ideological camp is itself a form of historical residue-bias, the result of peculiar circumstances rather than a deep theoretical reflection. As argued earlier, it is largely due to the fact that the post–Second World War debates about democracy were conducted in the shadow of fascism and Stalinism. The current debates are largely free from this distorting shadow. Moreover, we have been witnessing a 'practical reconciliation' between leadership and democracy in at least two critical instances: the emergence of prominent democratic leaders in advanced liberal democracies, and a leader-inspired and elite-crafted wave of successful democratisation that has been taking place since the late 1970s. These two experiences should help in negotiating the reconciliation, both in popular perceptions and theoretical discourses.

More specifically, the concept of 'leader democracy' should be defended against rather unfair normative critiques that are often levelled against Weber, Schumpeter and other authors who share the 'top-down' perspective on power, as well as the procedural view of democracy. One may start with the issue of equality. The theory of 'leader democracy' restricts the notion of political equality to equal citizenship rights (as opposed to equal power or influence), and to a specific 'collegiality' of political rulers, who co-dominate jointly, though always led by political *primus inter pares*. 'Leader democracy' challenges the desirability of political equality understood as equal power on theoretical and practical grounds. Due to incomplete information and the differences in citizens' competence, the common good cannot be revealed or realised in an egalitarian-aggregative way. Because of its importance, political leadership should reflect political talent, merit and superior performance. More importantly, the representative form of democracy – the only viable form in large and complex social settings – is necessarily and inevitably hierarchical. The selection of political leaders reflects and constitutes an unavoidable asymmetric distribution of political talent, skill and performance, and therefore the asymmetry of authority and responsibility. Equity, rather than equality, prevails in democratic political competition and selection.

Second, 'leader democracy' acknowledges inevitable power differentials and elite rule, but does not reject democracy as a key political value. Principles and norms of democracy, though, are general – they involve the formal sovereignty of the people and governance with the approval of the ruled – and therefore can be reconciled with leader-centrism and the rule by competitive-elective, and therefore publicly responsible, elites. To repeat: democratic political leaders accept the sovereignty of the people, carry public mandate-authorisations and rule by consent of the voters. They rely on public trust and confidence acquired through regular, free, open and fair competitive elections of top office holders, and they are removable through electoral defeats. Such regular electoral contests, together with continuous contestation provided by leadership contenders, also safeguard the public accountability of political leaders.

In this respect, leader-democratic theory opposes the 'downgrading' of elections in the theory of deliberative democracy.

Third, the model of 'leader democracy' stresses the public role of leaders as energisers of collective action. Successful political leaders mobilise and direct collective action. They also play a key role in reducing the complexities of politics (through agenda setting, framing and other means of persuasive influence), which makes politics more accessible and comprehensible to ordinary citizens. Perhaps most critical is the role of leaders as creators or formulators of competing visions of 'public/national interest' and 'common good'. These visions are not revealed through aggregation. While built on the foundations of realistic assessments of public views and perceptions, the successful visions of public interests are formulated and successfully advocated by innovative leaders. Some of these visions gain popularity and approval; others are rejected and wane into obscurity. Regardless of their fate, however, they constitute leadership products and leadership accomplishments.

Fourth, successful leadership always involves clear allocation and acceptance of public responsibility. Responsibilities are safeguarded, and accountability is maintained through two parallel processes: first, through regular electoral contests, whereby leaders present their visions and open their records to public assessment; second through ongoing political rivalry, systematic political contest built into the institution of critical opposition. Both are reinforced by sensitivity to 'public opinion' that is increasingly tested through polls, focus groups and other forms of 'interim assessments'. Even if this 'public opinion' is recognised as an artefact – the result of competing persuasion – it provides a form of constraint of rule. Too strict constraint, though, is counterproductive.

In order to carry responsibility (take credit and accept blame) leaders and elites have to enjoy sufficient autonomy, sufficient freedom from immediate pressures and sufficient freedom of manoeuvre. Otherwise, they cannot be held responsible for the 'enforced' – rather than their – action.

Finally, 'leader democracy' admits and encourages democratic representation, but this representation is anchored in leaders' actions. Leaders actively represent by securing trust and confidence of their electorates, by winning electoral support, electoral authorisation and mass consent. Such representation through active leadership cannot be dismissed as less real than, or inferior to, the representation claimed by the neoclassical theorists, be it in the mandate or pluralist version. Representation in the theory of 'leader democracy', unlike in other doctrines of democracy, is also interpreted as an accomplishment of political actors, rather than passive 'reflection' of social characteristics or (often arbitrarily) imputed interests (Körösényi 2005). Citizens voters play a most dignified role as ultimate judges and 'king makers'. Although they do not shape – and are not supposed to shape – specific policies, they are the key participants in the political processes. 'Leader democracy', in other words, is compatible with a representative and responsible government (Plamenatz 1973), and is in line with a minimalist conception of democracy (Przeworski 1999).

Confusions and Clarifications

Weber and Schumpeter were not only the critics of 'democratic illusions' – that is, the unrealistic views of democratic governance – but they also explored political pathologies accompanying political modernisation and mass democratisation. They identified these pathologies mainly with impaired rationality, reduced responsibility, arbitrariness and illegitimacy. Such pathologies are detectable in various political configurations, some of them close cousins of 'leader democracy': political guardianship/tutelage in the form of dominant 'technocracy' and 'bureaucracy', autocratic Caesarism or Bonapartism, and the most familiar 'cult of personality', which is commonly associated today with the 'totalitarian' despotism of Stalin, Hitler, Mao and Pol Pot. The superficial similarity of such nondemocratic forms to modern 'leader democracy' is a major source of confusions.[16]

The oldest form of authoritarian government in political thinking, based on meritocratic values, is guardianship or technocratic tutelage. In guardianship, legitimate rule is based on superior knowledge, as it was laid out first in Plato's

---

16 Due at least partly to Weber's own frequently oblique, confusing and fragmented presentation often mixing references to pre-modern and modern forms (e.g. 1978, 268–9), as well as inevitably selective uses of the rich Weberian legacies.

Republic. A classical argument for guardianship and against democracy is the notion of the superior knowledge of a minority. Technocratic guardians are 'qualified to govern by reason of their superior knowledge and virtue' (Dahl 1989, 52). As the advocates of this form of rule argue, it is in the public interest, if individuals with superior, 'parental' or 'tutelary' knowledge rule.

Three important features of 'leader democracy' set it apart from guardianship (Körösényi 2009b). The first feature is procedural. Leader-democratic selection does not favour any substantive criterion other than leadership skills and credentials. The institutional method for leadership selection prescribed by the model of 'leader democracy', namely an open (we add 'free and fair' as well) competitive election, is incompatible with the selection norms of guardianship. In turn, the idealist model of guardianship does not tolerate open competitive election. Since we are not able to say how to select the guardians, guardianship cannot be distinguished from arbitrary rule. The second difference lies in epistemological assumptions. Each democratic theory has a different concept of substantive political knowledge, because each theory regards and favours certain types of knowledge as a foundation for political action. In the theory of guardianship the basis of political action is *epistemé*, that is, absolute or theoretical knowledge. The principal players in the political process carrying this type of knowledge are the philosophers in Plato's Republic, and scientists or experts in modern technocratic visions of society. In contrast to this, the theory of 'leader democracy' insists that the basis of political action is *praxis*, that is, practical knowledge and accomplishment. The motivation for political action in 'leader democracy' is provided not by absolute knowledge (truth), but by opinion and will or volition 'proven in action'. In other words, there is no superior political knowledge in the sense Plato understood it, or as the philosophers of the Enlightenment assumed. Politics is the realm of consideration and decision about action, and therefore inevitable risk. It is about the future, and future is contingent. Political action is therefore subject to conditions of contingency, and political leaders have to choose and take the risk of decisions 'without certainty'. They also bear the responsibility for the consequences of their actions, even the unintended consequences and outcomes. The subject of this sort of practical knowledge, or *praxis*, is the politician/leader or the statesman, and not an expert. The third differentiating feature, as noted by Weber, is the functional-political embedding of leaders. Weber portrays 'leader democracy' as an elite configuration in which leaders are prominent in the sense of executive prerogative held, and as key generators of public confidence. But this prominence should not be confused with exclusive or unchecked or monopolistic power. Leaders always rely on their staffs – on the 'ruling minorities' in which they are embedded. They *co-dominate* with other members of the state-political 'quadriarchy' (the most senior professional parliamentarians, party 'directorates', and the top government-bureaucratic 'mandarins'). As Weber often stresses, modern democracy cannot function without those collective leadership 'supplements': without a 'working' parliament, organised parties and effective government bureaucracies. It parallels the vision of bureaucratic rule to the extent that modern technocratic tutelage attempts to diminish the role of parliaments and parties, the governance by policy experts – criticised by Weber as a threat to democracy and as an ever present 'perversion' of democratic rule.

In a similar way, modern 'leader democracy' should not be confused with autocratic Bonapartism or Caesarism. Caesarism is often associated in a wider sense with an absolute or autocratic system of government or political authoritarianism in general. In a stricter sense it refers to military or imperial dictatorship, unconstrained and unchecked power exercised by a single person who declares himself a repository of popular will.[17] In Caesarism or Bonapartism there is no competition for leadership – just usurpations of power through *coup d'état*. There are no elections but plebiscitary acclamations – the historical ancestors of democratic elections. There is no rivalry, no public responsibility, no obligation to renew trust-based mandate-authorisation. Plebiscitary acclamation constitutes a proto-election, a mass acknowledgement that a particular person is acceptable. Therefore Bonapartist leadership merely resembles modern 'leader democracy' and, in one of Weber's renditions (1978, 268–9), constitutes one of its historical predecessors relying heavily on the 'raw' charisma of the ruler. In all other respects, though, it departs from the ideal type of modern democratic politics and mass democracy, including 'leader democracy' (Weber 1919/1978, 1126–29).

Using a Weberian idiom, one can say that charismatic leadership is open-ended – and this constitutes one of the vulnerabilities of all forms of leader-centric politics. It may evolve and 'routinise' either into autocratic rule, which violates the key principles of democracy, or it may develop into a modern democratic electoral competition, whereby plebiscitary acclamation becomes

---

17 Bonapartism is a modern version of Caesarism. It is modelled on the imperial regime established by Napoleon I and III in France; it is associated with centralised government by a military dictator, who enjoys popular support that is articulated through plebiscites (rather than competitive elections). Perhaps the best sociological diagnosis of Bonapartism was given by its vocal critic, Alexis de Tocqueville (1862/1980). Like Weber, Tocqueville noticed the proto-democratic features in what he described as 'despotic democracy', and the democratic impulse that generated Bonapartism. Despotic rule, he argued, arises more often than not from a democratic impulse. It evolves out of democratic (in spirit) public acclamation that produces leaders with such a powerful public mandate that is difficult to check, constrain and curtail their power through laws and conventions.

open competitive election. As long as open electoral competition for leadership prevails and democratic institutions function, democracy survives – even if elected leaders acquire charismatic support, and even if the electoral contest is bordering on a 'plebiscitary' 'pledge of allegiance'.[18]

'Leader democracy' should not be confused with a 'cult of personality' or a Nietzschean worship of individual heroism. Such cults appeared in the last century in the form of Stalinism, Hitlerism, Maoism and the more recent cults of North Korean communist leaders. All these cases involved not only autocratic and exclusive, but also totalitarian rule. The rulers are treated as 'personal geniuses' and 'universal experts' (Weber's labels), and they aspire to shaping individuals and society in all aspects of life, including the domains regarded as private. Most such leaders combine the elements of autocratic Caesarism, and therefore military rule, with technocratic tutelage. Weber referred sarcastically to such leaders as 'personal geniuses' who usurp power by rejecting the principle of 'popular sovereignty' and replacing it with a mixture of 'class' (Mao), 'racial-national' (Mugabe), 'ethnonational' (Mussolini) or religious-national (Gaddafi) sovereignty – which they claim to realise personally and exclusively. Like the Caesarist leaders, they not only exceed the modern political confines of power, but also refuse to compete and prove 'irremovable'.

Obviously, such 'cults' have little to do with modern democracy, including 'leader democracy'. They are also incompatible with the conditions of modernity, especially with the growing social complexity and progressive rationality. Some elements of 'hero worship' and 'personality cult' may appear under conditions of political crisis, but they evolve into illiberal dictatorships, some superficially resembling democracies. Illiberal popular dictatorships may look democratic and resemble 'leader democracy'. But they rely on military discipline, rather than persuasion, eliminate authentic leadership competition and fail to 'circulate' their leaders.

How does our updated model of 'leader democracy' fare, not only in comparison with the rival theoretical visions (the 'deliberative-participatory' and 'neoclassical'), but also when confronted with popular long-term scenarios of social and political change? This is the main question addressed in the next chapter.

---

18 According to Weber (1994, 220–1; 1978, 1129), active democratisation of the masses has shifted the selection of the leader in the direction of Caesarism in a sense of approximating a plebiscite. Every democracy displays this tendency. But if there is a real choice between candidates, and if there is a competition among them for votes, it is not a plebiscite but an election in a normal sense.

Chapter 5

THE FUTURE OF (LEADER) DEMOCRACY

What is the future of 'leader democracy' – and the democratic system of government in general? In a short run, we expect a continuation of leader-centric and leader-democratic trends, as charted in Chapter 3. In the longer run, we should consider two popular but alternative scenarios: a 'demo-optimistic' one predicting a further spread and evolution of democratic values and practices, and a 'demo-pessimistic' vision forecasting a decline of democracy.

Considering the central role mass parties have played in the process of democratisation, the coincidence of current party decline with 'demo-optimistic' visions may be considered as a paradox. It is less paradoxical if we remember that the demo-optimistic visions are strongly coloured by direct-participatory ideals (allegedly ignored, if not corrupted, by parties), and that their spread has coincided with a powerful 'third wave' of democratisation. Fukuyama's (1992) announcement of the 'end of history' – the ultimate victory of liberal-democratic ideology – followed a worldwide political restructuring that put, for the first time in our history, the majority of countries and world population in the 'free' or 'democratic' category. Few readers noted a sceptical note in Huntington's (1991) famous diagnoses of the historical democratic waves (he predicted that each historical tide eventually ebbs) and the optimists dominate the field predicting a continuation of the 'wave' in the Middle East and China. They forecast not only the continuous spread of democracy, but also – and more controversially – a shift towards direct democracy and participatory engagement. Demo-optimists point to four developments supporting their scenario: (1) the worldwide expansion of democratic values carried by pro-democratic movements; (2) the spreading dissatisfaction with – as they interpret it – bureaucratic, indirect and representative forms of democratic practice in the West, especially among the young and educated urbanites; (3) the popularity of direct forms of political activism and growing participatory expectations among the educated 'new middle classes', especially those with self-expressive 'postmaterial values'; and (4) rapid proliferation of digital technologies that facilitate direct-participatory action (digital democracy, e-democracy, EDD, etc.).[1]

This optimism needs to be tempered by a more balanced analysis. The successes in Central and Eastern Europe in installing democratic regimes resulted mainly from the strength of pro-democratic orientations among the emergent leaders and elites. The determination of these leaders to combine national liberation with democratisation and liberalisation, and to emulate the representative-democratic Western institutions, led to a prompt 'consolidation of democracy'. This has not necessarily been the case elsewhere – and it should not be assumed that it will be the case in the Middle East and North Africa. The revolutionary turmoil there may give rise to democratic order only if pro-democratic leaders, in the mould of Wałęsa, Havel, Mandela and Yeltsin, emerge there and direct the process of reform. Otherwise the movements may pave the way for an Ayatollah, or a nationalistic dictator or populist strongman – as it happened in Iran, Belarus, Russia and Venezuela. There is no guarantee that Western interventions and spread of information necessarily help in installing pro-democratic regimes. Western interventions, especially military 'assistance', often provoke a nationalistic backlash. Similarly, the spread of digital communication does not necessarily help in democratisation. Digital technology serves both pro-democratic activists and antidemocratic forces well. Twitter has been used by pro-democratic dissenters, as well as religious militias, extremist vigilantes and the military. Mobile phones are used by Taliban and Hezbollah in coordinating their rallies, planning terror attacks and exploding bombs. That should make us more sceptical about the Western capacity to graft democracy, and more cautious about the prospect of infocommunication technology bringing 'digital democracy'.

The main grounds for scepticism, however, lie elsewhere and concern the *type* of democracy predicted by 'demo-optimists'. While participatory forms naturally dominate in the mobilisation stage of all movements, most of these movements settle for representative forms of democracy – typically following the Western templates. When this does not happen, when there is a prolonged instability – protests, demonstrations, marches and rallies – there is a danger of military/autocratic backlash. This is because autocrats impose order in a ruthless and effective way and any order – democratic or not – is more acceptable than prolonged chaos. The point is that direct-participatory forms of democracy do not serve well in restoring social order and reconstructing effective governments – for

---

1 See, for example, the triumphal popular accounts like Mitchell (1997), and the more balanced analyses like Dryzek (2000, 2006), Bellamy (1998), Norris (2001) and the *Economist* (2008) – as well as http://digital-democracy.org/ and http://en.wikipedia.org/wiki/E-democracy (last accessed 26 September 2011).

reasons that are well known and understood. They may form temporary governments, local administrations and 'transient' authorities, but prove ineffective as permanent political-administrative frameworks.

Demo-sceptics promote an alternative popular scenario, a reverse image of 'demo-optimism' predicting a spread of 'democracy incorporated' (Wolin 2008)[2], a 'winter of democracy' (Hermet 2007), or even the 'death of democracy' (Keane 2009) and 'post-democracy' (Crouch 2004). This sceptical vision is either deduced from dystopic accounts of globalisation, seen as market deregulation and corporate ascendancy, or it is projected from observations of public disaffection and civic atrophy: declining trust in governments, parliaments and politicians, falling civil engagement, declining social capital, eroding party loyalties, declining voting turnout, widening radical activism, and so forth. According to these scenarios, best exemplified by Colin Crouch's *Post-Democracy*, democratic governance is withering away under the combined impact of market globalisation, deregulation and declining civic engagement. Consequently, the rule of democratically elected leaders and elites is gradually replaced by the domination of unelected corporate executives anchored in transnational corporations. Power, in other words, gradually slips out of the hands of democratically elected state politicians and into the hands of transnational business elites, global corporate elites, or a global plutocratic 'superclass'. Citizens become compliant consumers, voters are manipulated or ignored, and democratic procedures are reduced to ritual electoral acts. Democracy survives only as a ritual façade for global corporatist or 'superclass' domination.[3]

Most of these scenarios are as unlikely as their sanguine rivals. They emerge from exaggerated and one-sided interpretations of globalisation, understood as progressive trade liberalisation, corporate expansion and other processes that increase the resources and power, perhaps even autonomy, of corporate elites. Such portrayal of globalisation – as a triumph of market over the state and as a domination of transnational corporate elites over

---

2 Wolin argues that the emergence of the corporate state in the USA does not just undermine democratic institutions but establishes an unprecedented repressive power machine fused with manipulative media. The fusion produces an 'inverted totalitarianism' that threatens citizens' liberties but operates within the democratic institutional frameworks (less and less liberal). There is also a growing literature on general discontent with contemporary democracy, reviewed by Pippa Norris (2011). Perhaps the best known examples are Nye et al. (1997), Norris (1999), Putnam (2000), Phar and Putnam (2000), Dalton (2004), Torcel and Montero (2006), and Hay (2007).

3 For a portrayal of the ascendancy of global 'superclass', see Rothkopf (2008). The rise of corporate 'global elite' and 'global bourgeoisie' is discussed by neo-Marxist scholars, such as Sklair (2001), Robinson (2004) and Sassen (2007).

elective governments – is partial and biased. It ignores the fact that even under the neoliberal regimes state powers expand and state budgets continue their growth, both in absolute terms and as a proportion of GDP (*Economist* 2011a). Moreover, national identities, pride, commitments and political focus do not wither away in the process of global expansion of trade and investment; in fact, they seem to gain strength (Norris 2011). Political leaders and elites do become more interdependent, but their democratically founded mandates and influence persist, rather than decline. When threatened by economic crisis, even a mild recession, private corporations hide under the protective wings of 'their' democratic states – and most are bailed out, though grudgingly, by national leaders with the support of politicians and the approval of national constituencies. If power relations are best revealed in crisis, then the wave of bailouts and business stimuli that accompanied the recovery from the global financial crisis demonstrates that democratic political elites still hold the upper hand.

As one may guess from this short overview, we are critical and sceptical of both rival scenarios. Both the gloomy and the sanguine visions look inconsistent and implausible. But before such a verdict is presented, let us examine the arguments of 'demo-pessimists' and 'demo-optimists' in more detail.

Demo-pessimism Writ Large: Post-democracy

Colin Crouch (2004) sees democracy as withering away, gradually to be replaced by the domination of business-corporatist elites. He is not impressed by the growing number of formally democratic regimes in the world, since he regards free competitive elections – the standard indicator of democracy – as a rather unsatisfactory and superficial criterion of actual or genuine democracy. The latter relies on effective public participation, on the capacity of the masses to register their voice and preferences in a more direct and regular way than that permitted by formal electoral mechanisms. Electoral democracy, as left-leaning critics often conclude, can easily turn into de facto rule by and for plutocracies and corporate elites.

According to Crouch (2004), the term 'post-democracy' describes a new and gradually developing power configuration, and a new era when formal electoral democracy gradually turns out to be a veil for domination of business-corporate interests. In post-democracy, he argues that

> while elections certainly exist and change governments, public electoral debate is a tightly controlled spectacle, managed by rival teams of professionals expert in the techniques of persuasion, and considering a small range of issues selected by those teams. The mass of citizens plays

a passive, quiescent, even apathetic part, responding only to the signals given them. Behind this spectacle of the electoral game, politics is really shaped in private by interaction between elected governments and elites that overwhelmingly represent business interests. (2004, 4)

Post-democracy is a withering away of real or authentic – what turns out to be ideal – democracy, a form of liberal democracy as seen from a social democratic and egalitarian-participatory perspective. The procedural-institutional forms of representation and electoral contest are portrayed as a façade. The central argument is that 'while the forms of democracy remain in full place... politics and government are increasingly slipping back into the control of privileged elites in the manner characteristic of pre-democratic times' (2004, 6).

The term of 'post-democracy' also reflects a specific view of history, widely embraced by the thinkers of the social democratic left, contrasting a 'democratic moment' of democracy with the new age of democratic decay. The 'democratic moment' is located in the post–Second World War decades; the period of decay is broadly coincidental and overlapping with globalisation. In the more robust and authentic democracy that allegedly prevailed in social democratic regimes during the post–Second World War era of Keynesian economics, strong trade unions, welfare consensus and entrenched old Labour, power was broadly dispersed. This helped in achieving a certain balance between the interests and orientations of the major classes: organised labour and big business. It was also a time of mass industrial production and mass consumption embodied in 'Fordism', neocorporatist political deals and expanding welfare rights. And it was the only period, according to Crouch, when important groups and organisations of ordinary people were capable of influencing political agendas in a systematic way. This golden era ended in the 'postindustrial' age, and its demise was heralded by the rise of 'neoliberalism', corporate expansion, deregulation, and the resulting dominance of business-corporate interests.

Post-democracy has four major features (Crouch 2004, 19–26). The first is a decline of active and positive citizenship combined with the dwindling of effective (constructive) mass political participation. The political activity of citizens is gradually replaced by apathy and alienation, punctuated by sterile protests that allow for venting mass frustration and disillusionment, but not for genuine reforms. The second feature is the dominance of exclusive elite circles, especially those representing business interests. With the spread of neoliberalism, powerful minority interests become far more politically active, sophisticated and effective than in the past. They dominate politics through a combination of manipulation, exclusion and imposition. Therefore, post-democracy can be characterised by the domination of new corporate elites in a climate of deregulation, weakening trade unions, waning Keynesianism and rolling back of welfare rights. The neoliberal deregulation facilitates the emergence of a 'stakeholder economy' – which is, in fact, an economy driven by, and in the interest of, corporate elites and plutocracies. The third feature of post-democracy is increasing persuasion and manipulation. The neoliberal reforms coincided with a boom of the advertising industry and increasing sophistication of political propaganda. The means of mass persuasion, the mass media, have been expanding their influence and they now reach every area of social life. The new elites have learned how to use this means of persuasion, and how to manipulate both public opinion and consumption demand. With the ascendancy of new digital technologies, new means of information and communication, new forms of advertising and new polling techniques, all the highly sophisticated means of mass persuasion and manipulation are available to pressure groups, political parties and media corporations. The corporate sector can easily outspend its rivals in media campaigns and engineer public support for neoliberal reforms. Moreover, the manipulation is facilitated by the increasing receptivity and vulnerability of mass publics. The growing technical complexity of the policy issues have confused and alienated many citizens by reducing their capacity to work out what their interests are. People are increasingly persuaded to act in line with media-generated recipes, promotion and publicity campaigns. The fourth trait of post-democracy is the decline of the social democratic regimes and welfare safety nets. The 'social rights', including a broad range of welfare entitlements, have been curtailed – and these curtailments have been justified in terms of financial prudence, cutting waste and restoring incentives for 'responsible' conduct. The state withdraws from taking responsibility for the lives of people, especially for providing security and welfare support. Unsuccessful attempts to arrest this erosion of social security nets contribute to the widening disaffection and apathy, thus enhancing the domination of corporate interests.

Crouch identifies three major causes of the drift towards post-democracy: economic, social and political. The economic driver of postdemocratic trends is closely linked with globalisation, especially with corporate growth, mergers and expansion. Global business expansion and deregulation strengthened transnational corporations vis-à-vis national governments and weakened trade unions that defended the interests of working people. 'Global firms' become the dominant institution of the postdemocratic world. The owners and managers of global firms form global corporate elites, and these elites (that may merge into a single global corporate-capitalist elite) owe their loyalty to no specific community, nation or country. In the intensified global competition for investment, profits and markets, the corporate rulers gain an upper hand not only vis-à-vis their workforces, often shifted to low-wage regions, but also in relation to nation-states, the latter always hungry for business investment, the accompanying tax revenues, as well as employment opportunities. While global firms gain increasing political weight as key investors, employers and taxpayers, they also increase their influence on national and regional governments. They successfully lobby for privileges such as reduced taxation, hidden monopolies (or oligopolies), exemptions from standards, subsidised energy supply, shared costs of infrastructure, and freedom from union pressures. As governments oblige, the hidden costs and fiscal burdens shift from firms to individual taxpayers – the latter incapable of resisting corporate takeovers.

There are also some social causes of the drift towards post-democracy. Crouch points to the decline and social decomposition of the manual working class(es), and the 'confusion' of the whole occupational or class structure. The manual working class is shrinking, while the complacent and consumption-oriented middle strata have expanded. The whole working population in advanced societies has been individualised and fragmented. The new movements and radical groups are more interested in defending and protecting cultural identities than interests of the lower strata and 'working people'. In addition, the 'working people' are betrayed by contemporary reformist parties: the New Labour, Neue Mitte and Socialisti Riformisti. The latter represent the outlooks and interests of consumers and upwardly mobile categories, and not the interests of workers and the disadvantaged.

Finally, 'post-democracy' has some specific political roots. The first and foremost is the changing relationship between political parties and the electorates or, if you prefer, class–party dealignment. The political muscle of ordinary working people – trade unions and social democratic parties – has weakened. This atrophy deprives the ordinary working people of their political voice and influence, without representation of their interests. The Labour and SD parties have become *Volksparteien*: mass parties for all, without a particular and loyal social base, and therefore without a clear political direction. The 'newly confident corporate interests have rushed to fill' this vacuum, especially in the case of New Labour in Britain. But Crouch sees this 'takeover' as a broader phenomenon affecting all reformist social democratic parties (2004, 64–5). Moreover, the fragmented political parties that emerge from the dealignment process are dominated by their own power factions and bureaucratic apparata.

If we extrapolate from recent trends, the classic party of the twenty-first century would be one which comprises a self-reproducing inner elite, remote from its mass movement base, but nested squarely within a number of corporations, which will in turn fund the sub-contracting of opinion-polling, policy-advice and vote-gathering services, in exchange for firms that seek political influence being well regarded by the party when in government. (2004, 74)

Thus a new political alliance of the influence-seeking corporate elites, party bureaucracies and organised lobbies has been established. This alliance forms the social and political base of post-democracy.

The problems with postdemocratic vision

As we can see, the concept of post-democracy is anchored in some widely recognised aspects of social change we have witnessed in the last three decades, including the decline of the manual working class, class–party dealignment and the end of class-based partisan loyalties, the expansion of global firms, and the shift of the political behaviour of the voter/citizen from the ideological to the more pragmatic. The problem is not with the accuracy of these observations – most are quite uncontroversial – but with their exaggeration, selective juxtaposition and interpretation.

First of all, Crouch overestimates the political role of the global firms and business-corporate elites. Their importance is, doubtless, growing, but not to the extent – and not in the form – suggested in *Post-Democracy*. Perhaps the most controversial is the claim about business-corporate lobbies overriding the authority of politicians and state executives. Corporate interests do count in political decisions, corporate executives do dominate boards (often at the expense of shareholders and investors) and sometimes vote themselves astronomical salaries and bonuses, but they do not dominate contemporary 'power elites'. Most students of the contemporary power structure point to the persisting centrality of elected political executives, that is, leaders and elites who are subject to regular mass electoral competitions. It is those popularly elected political leaders and elites who determine the investment permits (or refusals), who regulate investment patterns, who determine the types and levels of taxation – and, perhaps most importantly, who either bail out or let sink the companies that find themselves in financial trouble. And this continued dominance of 'political masters' is widely acknowledged. Even the most staunch advocates of 'global elites', for example, include top politicians in their lists of 'superclasses', 'global elites' and top power holders (Rothkopf 2006). There is no list of power holders that would not place at its apex presidents, prime ministers and influential state executives: people like Obama, Merkel, Sarkozy, Cameron and their executive teams.[4]

---

4 There are also more conspiratorial versions of the ruling elite, which argue that the 'real' power-holders are hidden behind the formal institutional 'facades', especially in the corporate boardrooms (as well as international organisations). But these versions rely on the familiar – and largely discredited – 'logic of conspiracy' backed by gossip and fear. Respectable analysis should stay clear of this 'logic of conspiracy'.

It is also true that political power is concentrated in the hands of 'power elites', especially the 'core executives' of modern states. If anything, this is a banal statement. But Crouch has difficulties in demonstrating that (1) this is a *new* phenomenon, that such power elites had not existed during the postwar 'golden age' of social democracy; and (2) that business-corporate elites gain an upper hand in the new power elites, that they rule and dominate contemporary politics, at least to a higher extent than in the past. Critical readers may not be convinced by his arguments that this allegedly new power concentration implies systematic playing down, if not exclusion, of certain nonbusiness interests, and therefore that it is incompatible with modern democracy. He rather presumes and assumes both.

Yet such assumptions, while popular among the left-leaning critics, are hard to defend on empirical grounds. After all, the best known diagnoses of 'power elites' (e.g. Mills 1956; Guttsman 1958; Higley et al. 1979) appeared during the alleged social democratic 'golden age'. Moreover, it is widely accepted that contemporary power elites are 'open', 'strategic' and 'widely integrated' (to use sociological jargon), that is, that they are accessible to a wide variety of lobbies and interests (Keller 1962; Putnam 1976; Higley and Burton 2006). Among the top power holders there are corporate business elites, party/parliamentary elites, professional elites, media elites, leaders of influential social movements, as well as various actors of national and global governance. It is true and obvious that unorganised segments of electorates have less impact on governmental decisions. But this does not exclude the 'interests of working people', or those who rely on welfare. Except for the USA, which experienced a stagnation of average incomes and salaries (and significant widening of income gaps), wages and salaries have been increasing more or less proportionately to the GDP in most advanced economies. State budgets, including welfare budgets, have also been increasing, both in absolute terms and as proportions of the GDP – in spite of some attempts of neoliberal regimes to arrest this growth (*Economist* 2011a, 2011b). To repeat: power inequalities, power concentration in the hands of elites, and disproportionate influence by leaders of large corporations are all beyond doubt – they are the standard features of all regimes, including democratic ones, regularly diagnosed and analysed over the last century or so. It is not clear how and why this power configuration should drift towards post-democracy, especially towards some form of exclusive corporate domination.

Second, Crouch strongly underestimates the role and autonomy of political leaders and the influence of the organised nonbusiness groups within elites (2004, 64–7). He contends that the decline of class-based mass politics and the rise of global capitalism have produced a new manipulative and self-referential corporate class/elite more concerned with building links with global corporate interests than with pursuing national policies which meet the concerns of national voters. He also claims that 'for a party to have no particular base is to exist in a vacuum' (2004, 64). All three claims are, to say the least, incompatible with the conclusions of mainstream political studies and with the views of mainstream political observers and analysts. These analysts accept the view of politics as state centred, if not increasingly leader centred. And they turn to political leaders as the key political actors. As argued throughout this book, it is political leaders and state-based core executives that emerge as the central figures in decisional and power networks – and they always have been there, as shown by the classic students of power and influence from Weber, Pareto, Michels and Mosca to Dahl, Scott, Higley and Savoie.[5] These central power actors are subject to competitive electoral 'tests of public confidence', as well as institutionalised checks and safeguards of public responsibility which are widely seen as warrants of democracy. If we really drifted towards post-democracy, if power were really slipping out of the hands of elected politicians and state executives, this – presumably – would have been widely registered by students of elites and democracy. Yet elite studies point to the continuous centrality of state executives, and studies of public attitudes demonstrate mass commitment to democracy, and mass satisfaction with 'how democracy works'. This apparent disparity between empirical diagnoses and the conclusions of advocates of post-democracy – as well as the confinement of such conclusions to the ranks of radical critics – undermine the plausibility of Crouch's claims.

There are also some problems with the argument about political parties and voter manipulation. Crouch suggests that political parties are defective if they do not represent specific 'class interests', especially the interests attributed to 'the working people'. Similarly, he regards political leaders as principally representatives of specific (if ignored) class constituencies, rather than autonomous political actors, with independent roles, interests, values and political outlooks. This is an old fashion view, already criticised as unrealistic and implausible over a century ago. Voter's views may be manipulated, but they are not easily duped, especially in retrospective assessments of political outcomes. 'False consciousness' is more frequently than not suffered by ideologically biased analysts, by observers/attributors, rather than the audiences/attributed. Moreover, political parties have never been anchored in classes alone. They have always been anchored in a wide variety of 'social forces' – property and occupational classes, sectional interests, social strata, ethnoreligious and ethnocultural 'status groups', cultural-territorial minorities, regional groupings and their alliances, religious movements, and

---

5 The latter exemplified by Scott (2000), Higley and Burton (2006) and Savoie (2007).

so forth – and their constituencies have frequently changed. Modern mass parties, as argued in Chapter 2, rely on 'captured' or 'seduced' voters, rather than loyal supporters, and they are highly dependent on attractive leaders who 'seduce' and build confidence, rather than on interest representation of property or occupational classes. Furthermore, political leaders, whether backed by parties or allied 'independents', have gained significant power-political autonomy – the core fact-observation legitimising the concept of (power) elite. To paraphrase Robert Michels, if one says 'elite' (corporate or otherwise), one acknowledges the power of organisation and the autonomy of power-political actors.

The accompanying claim about the withering away of social democratic parties is true, but so is the claim about the weakening of non–social democratic *Volksparteien*. Most mass parties have been weakening and losing grounds. Moreover, most of party officialdoms have always been quite independent of their mass constituencies (even loyal constituencies) and all parties have been undergoing constant adaptive change in the way they cultivate their mass support. They have gradually modernised their structure and electoral appeal, shed the class idiom of mobilisation – or failed electorally – and morphed successfully into mass centrist 'catch-all' parties: more universalistic, better organised, more complex (with diverse factions), and above all more active in organising political support and soliciting votes. Crouch correctly identifies an increasing dependence of these parties on electoral funds and spoils of office (government), but he provides no evidence of takeovers of such modernised parties by 'global corporate elites'.

Moreover, there is no convincing evidence that such a supranational 'global corporate elite' exists as a real (versus nominal) social-political entity – that is, that transnational corporate executives form more than a mere social category. Those who deploy the concept of 'global corporate elite' do not demonstrate that corporate executives are also sufficiently integrated, organised and self-conscious to form a coherent and potent political force (the elite).[6] Nor do they convince the reader that the top corporate executives, the core of the alleged 'global corporate elite', are losing their national power moorings, ethnostate identities and loyalties. To continue this long list of doubts, Crouch and his colleagues[7] do not demonstrate that there has been a change power structures

---

6 To remind, such integration, organisation, self-consciousness and, generally, minimal social cohesion-cum-'groupness' has been seen by all elite theorists as a necessary condition of elite power, indeed, the condition of elite existence (Bottomore 1964/1993; Parry 1969/2005; Putnam 1976).

7 The arguments about the domination of 'global corporate elite[s]' are also presented by other neo-Marxist scholars, such as Sklair (2001), Robinson (2004) and Sassen (2008).

and power relations that justify their claims of corporate domination. The claim that some political leaders favour certain business interests (e.g. energy, automotive, armament), and that there is a growing financial dependency on large corporate donors (or plutocracies), may be accurate in the US where the G. W. Bush administration was accused of selective bias, and where Republican-controlled Congress waived control over political donations. But they would not be valid for other advanced democracies, especially the European regimes, most of which maintain impartiality combined with strict controls over political funding. One should not uncritically assume that these democracies will follow the American practice (which attracts heavy criticism).

The third criticism of Crouch's analyses flows from his radical approach to democracy. He embraces a radical-egalitarian view of democracy anchored in neoclassical and Marxist political theories. Similarly, his vision of post-democracy is a product and a contemporary rendition of radical democratic theory (democracy as government of, for and by 'the people') fused with classical Marxism (politics reflect class interests, especially the interests of the capitalist versus working class). It represents a familiar, one may even say perennial, Marxist perspective that always predicts the inevitable degeneration of modern capitalism, together with its political democratic 'superstructure'. Hence the implied (and predictable) dynamics of capitalist degeneration: after a period of neocorporatist deals and compromises between major class interests, the class struggle has been lost by the working classes. These classes, the large majorities of 'the working people', have disintegrated and/or declined numerically, and their political agencies – the labour and the social democratic parties – have been captured by the newly emerged arch-capitalist global corporate elites. Electoral politics, in fact, the entire infrastructure of modern democracy, becomes a façade of new corporate domination. Competition is superficial in the face of overwhelming corporate domination mobilised and exercised 'from behind the throne' with the help of the persuasive media. 'Electoral competition then takes the form of a search for individuals of character and integrity. The search is futile because a mass election does not provide data on which to base such assessments', he notes (2004, 28).

These arguments are open to many critical questions. Why would the electoral competition be superficial; superficial in what sense and compared to what? It is true that democratic elections produce a 'mixed bag' of leaders: sometimes 'individuals of character and integrity', sometimes lesser figures. In the past, electoral competitions generated some great and successful leaders, as well as mediocrities – as does any form of leadership selection (though typically these choices are of better overall quality than those generated via nondemocratic forms of selection, including those employed by radical movements). Moreover, heavily mass-mediated competitive (s)election has no match as far as the leadership qualities of candidates are concerned. Even if mediocrities slip in, they are promptly 'recalled'. In that sense, competitive democracy is more than just a façade, and – as noted by Weber – it has proven itself as a successful method of (s)electing and 'circulating' 'individuals of character and integrity' (1978, 1414–15).

Finally, one notes a curious nostalgic twist in the postdemocratic scenario. The alleged 'golden age' of democracy was the post–Second World War period, the time of strong labour parties, social democratic regimes, Keynesian consensus, and the redistributive welfare reforms. Some aspects of this statement are obviously correct – the postwar period decades were very successful in terms of economic growth, increasing prosperity, economic security, employment, political stability and a widespread elite consensus about growth strategies. Yet, on sober reflection, this was not the time of democratic-participatory fervour or the time of wide and egalitarian political involvement. The golden social democratic era was welfarist, but not necessarily highly democratic in the sense of civic engagement and public trust. It was a period of stable, organised and representative democracy. As famously noted by Almond and Verba (1963/1989), the democratic civic culture balanced participatory aspirations with the fair amount of passive approval and complacency based on trust and persuasion. Some critics saw this form of democracy as highly exclusive and 'neocorporatist'. In that sense, in the sense of a historical contrast between the allegedly democratic-participatory past, and the allegedly nondemocratic manipulative and passive present (and future), the label 'post-democracy' seems to be rather confusing.

One must stress again that our criticism is not directed towards the claims about the influence of corporate interests on political decisions; it is quite clear that this influence is, and has always been, very high. Nor is it directed towards claims about the increased influence of large corporations on democratic governments and elites – there are good grounds to believe that such an increase has accompanied the growth in the size and resources of these corporations, especially in the USA, Great Britain, Japan and some of the 'Asian Tigers'. Nor is it a criticism of the diagnoses of disproportionate benefits enjoyed by the corporate elites – it is quite obvious that corporate CEOs, especially in the largest corporations and 'strategic' sectors (energy, finance, weapons, etc.), were the winners in the recent global expansion. The criticism is directed against the claim that these developments constitute a weakening, a crisis or failure of democracy, that this failure-cum-crisis is widespread and progressing, and that the atrophy of democracy is leading to a 'postdemocratic' (that is nondemocratic) future. It is also directed against the assumptions – highly questionable – that democracy was somehow more egalitarian and robust in the past; that it is incompatible with wide inequalities in power distribution, power concentration in the hands of elites (including elective state executives); and that it is at odds with policies that benefit (though not exclusively) the powerful and the wealthy. The leader-democratic forecast we propose offers an alternative scenario of constantly evolving and altering democracy, democracy under a continuous stress of contradictory pressures and constant change. In our view, it is more realistic as a diagnosis, and more plausible as a prognosis, than the 'postdemocratic' scenario.

Instead of analysing 'postdemocratic' arguments as an accurate reflection of political change, one can interpret it symptomatically, as a reflection of a specific ideologically coloured outlook, and as a symptom of a widespread anxiety, and disappointment with the social outcomes of globalisation. Seen that way, Crouch's arguments accurately reflect the discontent of the Old Left with New Labour, its disappointment with the gradual decomposition of social democracy (as a political force and ideological outlook), and the dissatisfaction of the left-leaning intellectuals with the neoliberal strategies, as represented by a generation of political leaders and elites ascendant since the 1980s. To many observers on the Left, these developments look either as a reversal of history, a regression and degeneration of liberal democracy – one of the few progressive aspects of modern capitalism – or as the signs of a (perhaps even ultimate) crisis of capitalism, as predicted by Marx. While popular among critical left-leaning audiences, such anticipations are more ideological than based on empirical diagnoses and realistic assessments. Their predecessors – the perennial diagnoses of terminal illness and inevitable collapse of modern capitalism produced by the Old Left – have proven wrong many times in the past, thus seeding a widespread scepticism as to their accuracy. But they should be taken seriously as symptomatic of widespread disaffection, uncertainty, and public anxiety about globalisation and its outcomes. Increasing trust placed in democratic leaders, as we argue below, is also a reflection of these uncertainties and anxieties.

Global Elite(s) versus Democracy

The predictions of post-democracy form a proverbial tip of the iceberg of proliferating gloomy visions of democratic deterioration. They are a part of a broad family of critical forecasts that link the diagnosed decline of democracy with the ascendancy and domination of a 'global corporate elite(s)'. Those who diagnose such ascendancy – either as a warning or a lament – suggest that globalisation leads to corporate domination combined with withering away of democratic forms of state-political governance and public control. This is because the global expansion and mergers of business corporations takes them outside the regulatory framework of nation-states and their democratically elected governments. When combined with the deregulatory liberal policies adopted by a growing number of state governments, this is leading to the emergence – and gradual domination – of an informal corporate ruling group, a 'denationalised' global corporate 'superclass', a new power actor that increasingly shapes the direction of world affairs: political, economic, military, etc. Its power is anchored in global transnational corporations, rather than national governments, and it is increasingly freed from democratic controls that operate only within national state jurisdictions.

This family of visions and scenarios is quite broad. At the very outset, we must distinguish here between conspiracy theories of undemocratic 'world government' (which we ignore), some perennial neo-Marxist predictions of the atrophy of democracy in the hands of ascendant 'global corporate elites', and more sober, but often exaggerated, visions of national-corporate ascendancy through superpower (typically American) domination-cum-hegemony – the latest being quite uncontroversial, if not banal, and therefore ignored here.

Perhaps the best known are the arguments about the emergent global 'superclass'. This 'superclass', argues David Rothkopf (2008), gradually overshadows national governments and influences the direction of social change. It includes the top politicians of the largest nation-states, globalisation-spawned 'super rich' and other influential supranational figures: CEOs of the largest transnational corporations, heads of the most powerful military establishments, heads of the largest religious movements, and so forth. Controversially, Rothkopf (2008) adds to this list also heads of the most notorious transnational terrorist and criminal groups. He argues that their social coalescence (contacts, meetings, consultations) indicates progressive social integration and organisation into a single 'global elite' or 'superclass without a country' – an international version of the Millsian 'power elite – that gradually dominates world affairs. The 'superclass' is a product of the rapid concentration of wealth in transnational funds, mergers and the expansion of transnational corporations, widening of information and communication networks, and mobilisation of global movements.[8] Moreover, like the American 'power elite' analysed by C. W. Mills (1957) half a century ago, it is an 'abomination of democracy'.

Rothkopf's (2008, 10–11) arguments sound plausible because two out of the four premises on which the argument rests are relatively uncontroversial. First, Rothkopf (2008, xiv) correctly identifies some centripetal trends in wealth and power distribution, and he argues that these trends coincide with globalisation. Wealth concentrates in the hands of new billionaires and

---

8 Note a link with some popular 'global power rankings', like the one presented in *Newsweek* (5 January 2009).

'superfund' directors; business-corporate power concentrates in the boards of largest transnational corporations, especially following the 'merger-mania' at the end of the twentieth century. Similarly, political-executive power concentrates in the hands of leaders and their 'court governments', and influence in the large religious churches and movements concentrates in their charismatic heads. Consequently, Rothkopf can argue convincingly that fewer people have now 'the ability to regularly influence the lives of millions people in multiple countries worldwide.'

The second premise is equally uncontroversial. Rothkopf argues that the global elite/superclass consists of predominantly new and self-made plutocracies and power wielders, whose power – derived from recently accumulated wealth, financial and business innovations, newly acquired political influence, centralised executive control, widening communication and broadening networks of control and influence – has been either created in or enhanced by the recent processes of globalisation.

Much more problematic is the third premise, namely that the members of the superclass are deracinated and 'denationalised', that they lose national identities, interests, commitments and loyalties – and therefore fall outside the democratic control of national governments. This claim has a shaky theoretical base and its empirical backing is weak. The international scope of interelite communication, consultation and coordination – something that is widely known and publicised by the media – does not necessarily indicate 'denationalisation'. In fact, the key figures on Rothkopf's list of superclass members – Obama, Gates, Hu, and Merkel – represent the power and interests of the largest nation-states. They identify with their nations, push their specific national interests, and legitimize their power in national terms – as elective heads of nation-states and governments. It is true that they meet, coordinate their strategies and collaborate with each other, but this international consultation is pursued primarily in national interests and in response to 'transnational problems': environmental damage, climate change, terrorism, uncontrolled migrations, drugs trade, and the like. To argue otherwise would risk ignoring overwhelming evidence of strong national commitments (frequently criticised as 'egoistic', 'parochial' or 'protectionist'), especially among the leaders of 'superpowers': the USA, Russia, China and India. It would also ignore overwhelming support given by national governments at times of crisis to 'their' nationally embedded businesses and nationally anchored corporate interests. National banks, financial institutions, top employers and 'strategic' military or energy or food producers, especially those with high economic profiles (in employment, technology, innovation, import-export, etc.), have been protected and supported (usually at the taxpayer's risk and expense), even if they are privately owned and their ownership and operations are international in scope. If they find themselves in trouble, like Northern Rock in 2007, AIG in 2008, or the Royal Bank of Scotland in 2009, national political leaders bail them out or at least help them to get 'off the hook'.

Some qualifications are necessary here: the process of globalisation has undoubtedly weakened some aspects of national loyalties and identities by giving more influence to both regional (subnational) organisations and supranational ones, including transnational religious and secular movements. However, the power and influence of such organisations and movements is typically proportionate to the support they receive from national elites in powerful nation-states. One needs only to mention here the critical importance of the US backing for the IMF, the World Bank, WTO and NATO. Similarly, it is widely recognised that the anti-Western Islamist movements, such as the Hezbollah and the Taliban, depend on support of national elites in Iran and Pakistan respectively. Their strength seems proportionate to the enhanced influence and power leverage they offer to the Iranian and Pakistani political elites.

This leads to the most problematic claim made by Rothkopf, namely, that the members of the superclass form a group or a cohesive collective, rather than a mere statistical category. The author does argue persuasively that they share similar lifestyles and rub shoulders at social gatherings.[9] But that is not enough to transform a loose social category of powerful and privileged individuals into a cohesive grouping, the global equivalent of a national 'power elite'. Genuine elites, we are reminded by elite theorists, are real groupings, rather than mere nominal categories. In order to acquire and sustain power and influence, they have to develop a minimal level of social integration – that is 'groupness', cohesion, identity and solidarity. After all, it is internal integration, cohesion and identity (and not mere lifestyle commonalities and occasional social interaction) that create and enhance collective power and influence of an elite. Yet, Rothkopf fails to demonstrate this minimal integration, he fails to show the existence of common purpose, identity and group solidarity, the capacity of these individuals to act as an elite. In spite of this lack of evidence, or even a strong argument backing his assertions, Rothkopf (2008, xiv) describes his superclass as a 'group'. Moreover, he compares the superclass to the American 'power elite' as famously depicted by C. W. Mills (1956), overlooking the fact that, according to Mills, the members of the American 'power elite' were

---

9 'The influence of this transnational superclass is often amplified as the members act in clusters knit together by business deals, corporate boards, investment flows, old school ties, club memberships and countless other strands that transform them if not into the conspiring committees of legend then at least into groups that are proven masters at advancing their aligned self-interests.' (Rothkopf 2008, xvii)

anchored in coherent national institutions and, above all, that they were well integrated by overarching national interests and unified by shared 'American values'. None of this integration, unity and solidarity could be attributed to the superclass – and this makes this construct akin to a sociological chimera.

The theme of 'global elite versus democracy' also appears in neo-Marxist analyses of the 'transnational capitalist class' (or, in some versions, classes), some of them similar to Crouch's scenario of 'post-democracy'. The professional and executive 'apex' of the new global corporatist class (or classes) forms a 'transnational (corporate) elite' of corporate leaders, professional experts and their political sponsors – all supporting a common interest of the global bourgeoisie in deregulation and expansion of global markets. The class-embedded transnational and global elite also includes the top political executives and bureaucrats in international associations and alliances (e.g. EU, NAFTA, ASEAN), as well as heads of regulative and coordinating bodies promoting 'global economic governance' (e.g. WTO, World Bank, IMF). The members of this elite are supposed to operate as a 'management committee' of transnational bourgeoisie by promoting its common and vital interest in business expansion, profit maximisation and minimisation of interference-cum-regulation by elective state governments. The ascendancy of the class-based elite is symptomatic of the withering away of democratic governance (Chase-Dunn 1998; Sklair 1995, 2001; Robinson and Harris 2000; Robinson 2004; Boswell and Chase-Dunn 2006; Sassen 2007).

The neo-Marxist scholars offer a more detailed analysis of 'global elites' and a more plausible scenario of change. They depict 'global elites'[10] as quite sizable and diverse, and also dependent on economic globalisation. Globalisation promotes the worldwide or global social formation of both, global classes, especially the 'denationalised' transnational bourgeoisie or the corporate-capitalist class, and the class-embedded 'global elites'. This follows the logic of capitalist development, as originally charted by Marx and updated by the 'world-system' theorists, such as Wallerstein, Frank, Chirot and Chase-Dunn. The global expansion of capital, according to them, has resulted in a gradual detachment of class interests and identities from their national 'moorings' and the accompanied detachment of elites from nation-states. The neo-Marxist theorists tend to analyse the alleged worldwide 'globalisation' and 'denationalisation' of ruling classes and elites as a standard aspect of contemporary (global) capitalist development and expansion – increasingly undermining state-located democratic controls (Robinson 2004, 49–57).

---

10 While the authors often use plural (elite*s*), they typically qualify it by the adjectives 'transnational' and 'global', thus clearly distancing themselves from the classic concept of (multiple) national elites.

As noted above, the neo-Marxist accounts of erosion of democracy and ascendancy of 'global elites' differ in details. Thus, Robinson (2004) sees transnational class integration as asymmetric, whereby in the last half-a-century 'capitalist globalisation has increased the relative power of global capital over global labour by acting as a centripetal force for the capitalist class and a centrifugal force for the working class'. By contrast, Sassen (2007, 168–9) sees transnational integration as occurring on both ends of the class spectrum, and therefore generating new class conflicts and confrontations. She distinguishes three emergent global and at least partly 'denationalised' classes: transnational corporate professionals and executives, top state executives embedded in 'transnational networks of government officials' (experts, judges, law enforcement, etc.), and 'an emergent class of disadvantaged or resource-poor workers and activists'. The process of 'denationalisation' and integration occurs, according to Sassen, mainly at both extremes of the class spectrum (2007, 173–5). The 'middle' classes remain less globalised and more 'nationalised'. The top globalising classes spawn 'powerful transnational elites' anchored directly in their organisational hubs, and indirectly in wider transnational classes. The organisational hubs form 'a kind of operational infrastructure for corporate economic globalization', and are run by groups of 'professionals, managers, executives, and technical staff members' – a 'new transnational profcssional class' of controllers of the main class organisations.[11] The key assets of controllers include expertise, information and networks (social capital). They intertwine with the second constitutive component of 'global elites', namely, a transnational network of top government officials 'in charge of critical work in the development of a global corporate economy'. Their main function is facilitative and deregulatory (2007, 179). Finally, there are also informal networks of economic and financial experts and advisors operating outside transnational corporations and intergovernmental regulatory bodies, and political directorates. They aim at promoting and implementing the international 'deregulatory project' by generating mass consent and administrative backing.

The critical point for us is the portrayal of the relation between these developments and modern democracy. All neo-Marxists see globalisation, especially the market liberalisation and corporate expansion, as primarily serving the interests of the corporate classes. These classes undermine democracy in multiple ways: by exerting class domination (more effective because exercised transnationally), by thwarting regulatory attempts of

---

11 This is in clear parallel to the original arguments of Berle and Means (1932) and the Frankfurt School thinkers who suggested that owners and corporate managers/executives formed two separate class categories.

nation-states and their elective governments, and by engineering mass consent. The 'global elites' are portrayed as partly autonomous, detached from national interests and political institutions, and therefore freed from national (in scope) democratic controls. The fact that they form within the dominant classes – that is, within international corporations, financial organisations, government networks, regulative and facilitative bodies – shapes their orientations and directs their actions in the way that is independent of democratically established national interests. This is reflected in the shared elite commitment to the globalist market liberalisation and the accompanying 'deregulatory projects'– both undermining national interests and democratic controls.

Almost all criticisms directed towards Crouch's vision of post-democracy apply also to the neo-Marxist visions of 'global' classes and elites. There is no point in repeating these criticisms here. Instead, we highlight some more specific problems faced by these visions. First and foremost is the problem of 'commonality of interests' and 'transnationality'. All neo-Marxist accounts seem to ignore the sharp competition between different national corporate interests – American, Chinese, and so on – for example, in securing international contracts, exclusive rights on certain territories and various financial (tax, infrastructure use, etc.) privileges. Studies of business elites show the strength of national links and the paucity of international connections (Carroll and Fennema 2002, 2004). They also suggest that there are differences between corporate interests that rely on free global expansion and those who depend on national protection. The latter oppose deregulation, reject liberalisation of trade and criticise unconstrained capital circulation. These cases cannot be dismissed as marginal or exceptional. They concern quite powerful interests and industries, including farming and automotive industries. Yet, they do not seem to 'fit' the neo-Marxist theoretical framework and accounts. Moreover, these accounts seem to overlook the 'alliances' between corporate interests and some segments of organised labour that jointly support or oppose globalisation (often described as 'exporting jobs'). This variation in attitudes towards the 'neoliberal project' – largely overlooked in neo-Marxist accounts of globalisation – explains why there is little correlation found between corporate 'upper status' and pro-globalisation attitudes (Davidson et al. 2009).

The neo-Marxist students of globalisation seem to accept quite uncritically 'denationalisation' of global companies. But how real is this 'denationalisation'? As the Western 'rescue through bailout programmes' demonstrate, national protectionism is alive and kicking among the highest echelons of political and corporate power. Nation-states continue to promote and protect 'their' business-corporate interests, in spite of declared commitment to free trade and laissez-faire. But in order to promote and protect successfully, national leaders and elites widen and broaden their interactions; and the international, interstate arenas provide privileged forums for such broader elite interaction, consultation and coordination of their action. This is why international (rather than transnational) links and networks prevail among elites, in spite of persisting commitments to national interests.

This should not be read as a dismissal of the importance of globalisation and a denial of change in international power relations. While power remains politically anchored and democratically legitimated in nation-states, it also flows globally, becomes more complex – and therefore more difficult to wield effectively. This is why globalisation – the increasing interconnectedness between nations, regions and localities – coincides with increasing interelite international communication, interaction and coordination. Such coordination is necessary to sustain the effectiveness of governance in the globalising world. It increases the effectiveness of elite actions, enhances security and reduces risks, especially the risks of undesirable and unintended consequences. International interelite power alliances, political coalitions and protective cartels became routine risk-managing strategies adopted by contemporary rulers. Thus there is evidence of wider and more frequent contacts between national leaders and elite groups, not only those sharing sectional or regional interests, but also those competing for influence and advantageous positioning worldwide.

This is why elite summits, consultations and G8–20 deliberations are more frequent. But it is far-fetched to argue that they undermine democracy or diminish the public accountability of political leaders and elites. Moreover, these international contacts seldom reduce competition among national leaders and elites, especially the competitive struggle for power that sustains modern democracy. To repeat: the intensified interelite interactions should not be confused with 'global elite' 'denationalisation' and integration, and should not be seen as symptomatic of 'global elite' domination. The proliferation of international (rather than transnational) interactions and consultations does not radically alter the state-centred power structures. It does not undermine the power and centrality of national leaders and it hardly weakens representative democratic systems.

Let us turn to 'demo-optimistic' scenarios, especially to those arguments that are more relevant for our discussion of the future of democracy, while noting that the very popularity of such scenarios is in itself indicative of an arbitrary character and problematic credibility of the 'demo-pessimistic' visions.

Demo-optimists: Transnational and Cosmopolitan Democracy

The advance of economic globalisation, the emergence of networks of multilateral regulatory organisations, as well as the proliferations of transnational

NGOs and other institutions of the 'global civil society', seem to impose serious constraints on the autonomy of nation-states. National governments, some critics argue, lose influence vis-à-vis regulatory regimes of emerging global governance. Sovereignty of democratic nation-states is weakened and citizens of national polities often bear the brunt of decisions made by governments of other states, transnational bodies (such as WTO), multinational firms, multilateral regulatory agencies or other global actors. Globalisation undermines the principle of self-determination, that is, the founding principle of democratic nation-states and the 'Westphalian' international order established in the seventeenth century. But it also spawns new visions of 'transnational' and 'cosmopolitan' democracy that attract the attention – and commitment – of 'demo-optimists'.[12] David Held's (1995) works and arguments represent and illustrate well the demo-optimistic projections of democracy spreading into the international domain reinvigorated by wider, increasingly global and cosmopolitan democratic awareness and civic engagement. These arguments, however, are also typical of 'demo-optimistic' family in another respect: they are strongly, if not predominantly, normative. They propose and promote a new 'ideal of democracy', and they champion this ideal through thought experiments combined with normative clarifications – both containing a fair degree of advocacy (Archibugi and Held 1995). Such orientation towards advocacy also transpires in the reform proposals 'in search of solutions' to the problem of the alleged 'democratic malaise' and 'democratic deficit' in Europe (Schmitter 2002a; Schmitter and Trechsel 2004). We outline these arguments and proposals in turn.

Held and other theorists-cum-advocates of cosmopolitan democracy assume that under the impact of globalisation, the maintenance of the world order transcends the capacities of sovereign nation-states. The search for general principles and structures that can sustain a more harmonious and humane world, in which stability and satisfaction of people's needs take precedence over the implementation of interests of state apparata, take them to a new philosophical and theoretical territories. Held suggests that the Westphalian order of sovereign and 'egoistic' nation-states has to give way – and actually but gradually gives way – to a new one, a more interconnected world in which complementarities and interdependencies are recognised, respected and collectively cultivated. Nation-states cease to be the only source of moral and political foundations of world order, and this order is increasingly formed and sustained through coordinated, publicly consulted and legitimated – in a word, 'democratic' – principles and practices.

---

12 See also Archibugi and Held (1995), Beck (1999), Habermas (2001) and http://en.wikipedia.org/wiki/Cosmopolitan_democracy (last accessed 26 September 2011).

Held's (1995, 159–67) vision of such a cosmopolitan order and cosmopolitan democracy rests on the philosophical arguments formulated by Jürgen Habermas and John Rawls, although it also includes some elaborations and concrete institutional proposals. The aim is predominantly normative – the advocacy of the proposed model as effective and desirable – but he includes also some fairly specific descriptive claims. His major theoretical aim, though, is to elaborate moral-political justifications for a cosmopolitan model of democracy and his practical aim is to refresh democracy by facilitating the extension of its operation into the international public realm, into the relations between and across nation-states.

Cosmopolitan democracy seeks a 'political order of democratic associations, cities and nations as well as of regions and global networks' (1995, 234). It is based on respect for the autonomy of individuals and political communities and this respect is to be upheld through a cosmopolitan democratic law. The purpose is not to establish a centralised world government but rather a complex global authority system, 'a system of diverse and overlapping power centres shaped and delimited by democratic law' (1995, 234). Cosmopolitan democracy would rest on the foundation of a confederation of sovereign local, regional and national authorities sustained by an overarching legal framework. Within this framework, civic associations may also be self-governing at all levels.

This is a compelling vision, but it is also widely criticised for its internal inconsistencies and lack of realism (Dahl 1999). Rather than repeating those criticisms – many of them quite obvious – we may just highlight the key critical points. First and foremost, the cosmopolitan vision fails to bridge the gap separating his normative vision and his ideal of democracy from the contemporary state of the world. It is based on an abstract theoretical reasoning rather than on extrapolation from any empirical trends. Therefore it resembles the utopian visions of 'Christian order' as championed in medieval Europe or their modernised versions of 'industrial order' as proposed by Saint-Simon and Comte two centuries ago. Moreover, the model of cosmopolitan democracy is built on neoclassical foundations (a bottom-up perspective on power), and this foundation reinforces its utopian nature. In Held's vision, democracy not only operates in a 'bottom-up' direction, but is also cleansed of power inequalities, hierarchies and political leadership.

This poses many theoretical problems. Held's vision is unable to identify the major social or political actors who would be interested in, and capable of, reforming the world order in line with the cosmopolitan-egalitarian vision. Such a reform would include the consensual adoption of a global legal framework (presumably, a new civil law), formation of a global parliament with limited revenue-raising capacity, and above all, creation and coordination of assemblies and the establishment of effective chains of accountability. These global institutions would have to be quite different from the current international and transnational agencies and NGOs, and they would have to secure income for all adults, irrespective of whether they are engaged in market or household activities (Held 1995, 279–80). A vision of that order transcends the reality in a very radical way. It is this gap between what exists and what is proposed – not just a mere transcendence – that makes the vision utopian. Held does not seem to be concerned by this utopianism, probably because he focuses on the desirability of the proposed cosmopolitan-democratic order. But this lack of concern causes further problems, such as overlooking some basic economic and political conditions of implementation. Who would undertake such massive restructuring of the world order? In what way could this be done? Who would lead and direct such a massive undertaking? Who would fund it? More specifically: how are jurisdictional conflicts between different layers of political authority to be managed and reconciled? How should we build supranational 'cosmopolitan' identities and commitments? And so on.

Held seems to assume that the vision of 'cosmopolitan democracy' has some realistic foundations, mainly in the processes of globalisation and extension of democracy worldwide. Cosmopolitan democracy appears to supplement those accounts of globalisation that stress the liberal aspects and outcomes of the widening interdependency: the spread of human and civil rights, liberalisation of social order, and expansion of liberal-democratic institutions. But how realistic are such assessments, and how consistent are they with the democratic visions? In order to answer these questions, we must leave the abstractions and normative constructs and look more carefully at the actual democratic practices and the related public attitudes. Our overview is based on empirical (mostly survey) studies of democratic values, attitudes, commitments and declared practices. Its aim is not so much the critical assessment of the cosmopolitan-democratic vision, as an evaluation of its realism and plausibility and its distance from the current configurations and trends.

Contemporary Democracy and Its Discontents

This is a short overview because the basic 'facts and figures' about public attitudes, aspirations, democratic practices, and so on – are well known. Our intention is not to summarise them, but rather to highlight some of them as a springboard for concluding arguments about the relative plausibility of 'cosmopolitan democracy' and 'leader democracy'.

Judging by the tone of contemporary diagnoses of the 'state of democracy', the 'demo-sceptics' seem to prevail, especially in Europe. There is no shortage of alarming diagnoses of 'democracy in crisis' – and proposals for reforms.

This most recent alarm has been triggered by a 'second wave' of critical diagnoses pointing to a decline of trust and dwindling civic engagement. This second wave of concerns follows the first wave voiced in the 1970s and coinciding with mass protests, urban dissent and the widespread counterculture movements. This time, at the turn of the century, concerns about democracy – its quality, viability and sustainability – have been based on diagnoses of declining electoral participation, shrinking support for major parties, the rise of the 'third forces' (including independent candidates), low levels of confidence in parties, parliaments and politicians and a general decline in 'social capital' – all reinforced by widespread mobilisation of radical populist movements: antimigration, nationalistic and antigovernment.[13] More recently, these concerns have been fuelled by the alleged ebbing of the worldwide wave of democratisation as indicated by a widespread fundamental-traditional 'backlash' against modern pro-democratic orientations and aspirations.[14]

As mentioned before, all these concerns are real, perhaps even justified, but the diagnoses on which they are based are often distorted. A more accurate and balanced picture of the state of democracy today emerges from most recent worldwide surveys of democratic freedoms, public values and attitudes. They do not support the diagnoses of democratic malaise or atrophy, though they indicate that the spread of democracy may have slowed down (Norris 2011). While the democratic tide may have ebbed, there is precious little evidence of the mass citizenry or its educated strata losing their trust in democracy, let alone turning their backs on liberal-democratic values and practices. Similarly, there is no evidence of elites, especially in the established democracies, deserting democratic creeds and games; in fact the opposite seems to be the case. While the democratic wave has slowed down, largely as predicted by Huntington (1991), there is no evidence of significant reversal. In fact, the recent antiautocratic effervescence in the Middle East and North Africa may herald a renewal of democratic reforms. There is discontent (of highly varied and uncertain nature), and even a sizable 'democratic deficit' in advanced democracies, but both discontent and deficit do not look like undermining pro-democratic orientations among the citizens of established and new democracies. There is an antidemocratic, antimodern and anti-Western backlash from traditional and religious movements and regimes, but it is worth remembering that this backlash has been triggered by the rapid,

---

13 See Nye at al. (1997), Norris et al. (1999), Putnam (2000, 2001), Dalton (2004), Dogan (2005) and Hay (2007).
14 See Haerpfer at al. (2009), Kapstein and Converse (2008) and Freedom House's *Freedom in the World* report, available online at: http://www.freedomhouse.org/images/File/fiw/FIW_2011_Booklet.pdf (accessed 27 September 2011).

wide and successful expansion of democracy. If anything, it indicates the strength of the democratic tsunami that swept the world in the final decades of the twentieth century.

Let us look in more detail at the picture that emerges from the surveys of democratic awareness, knowledge and attitudes towards democracy and democratic commitments, as summarised by Norris (2011). Knowledge and understanding of democracy is not very high, even among the citizens in democratic regimes, and it varies widely. The widest knowledge and the greatest understanding of democratic institutions and processes are found, unsurprisingly, among the best educated citizens of the most established and oldest Western democracies. Also as expected, the most knowledgeable and sophisticated among those citizens are those who are interested in politics and are most ardent consumers of independent media. This is important to note, because the strength of democratic cultures also correlates with the same pair of factors: knowledge/education and media consumption/interest. Both increase quite rapidly, thus boding well for democratic competence and sophistication.

Satisfaction with the 'really existing'[15] (i.e. largely representative-electoral) democracy and democratic practices ('how democracy works') is high across the board, along with commitment to democratic values and the endorsement of democratic attitudes, both combined with a firm rejection of autocracy. Predictably, both attitudes are also strongest in the established democracies and among the educated segments of these democratic societies. Thus, if anything, democratic values, orientations and practices – especially those related to representative forms of democracy – seem to strengthen and self-reinforce. They increase with the duration (consolidation) of democratic regimes. Particularly telling and striking in that respect are the results of surveys of democratic values and practices in the 'new' democracies: those societies which stepped onto the path of democratic reforms in the late 1970s to 1990s. They show a firm endorsement of democracy, but also growing concerns and anxieties about political-economic outcomes. Thus contemporary democracies – in their predominantly liberal and representative-electoral form – seem not only safe and entrenched in societies with established democratic regimes, but also taking roots in new democracies, where such regimes and institutions are still in the process of consolidation and development.

Paradoxically, one may say, the commitment to democratic values is also strong outside the democratic family of nation-states. Publics living under

---

15 The term 'really existing democracy' alludes to a term 'really existing socialism', and refers to the attitudes towards actual institutions and practices, rather than normative constructs or ideals.

autocratic regimes are also strongly committed to democratic values, though they also tend to be more etatist and nationalist in their attitudes, and less clear in what they mean by 'democracy'. This is not surprising. Globalisation works well in facilitating the spread of liberal-democratic values, aspirations and attitudes, thus making them universal. Yet, such universalisation inevitably leads to a dilution of meaning and semantic confusion. Thus many people identify (confuse?) democracy with economic prosperity, gender equality and civil rights. That would explain not only the rapid and 'wave-like' spread of 'pro-democratic' orientations and movements in China and most recently in the Middle East, but also the appearance of curious 'autocratic interpretations of democracy' (Norris 2011, 176). It may also explain why even autocratic regimes desperately try to disguise themselves as democracies (claim public mandate, pretend that they have competitive and open elections, etc.) in order to secure mass approval and to increase public legitimacy.

Even a brief perusal of survey results leads to a conclusion that democracy 'as it exists', as a set of actual value commitments and electoral practices, is in a good shape and it is strongly identified with representative forms – the misconceptions notwithstanding. It is well entrenched in established and liberal Western democracies, widely accepted in young democracies, and embraced as a popular aspiration (often misunderstood) even under autocratic regimes. Moreover, the somewhat sombre predictions of democratic regress, the ebbing of the democratic tide, may be premature: if the current pro-democratic movements in the Middle East succeed especially in Egypt (considered as a regional linchpin and trend setter) and Tunisia, the resulting spread of democracy will alter significantly the Freedom House record and the direction of recent trend, which at present point towards 'stalling and partial reversal' as seen in Table 5.1.

The results of longitudinal studies and time series analyses of public attitudes and values do not indicate a decline of democracy, either. Satisfaction with democratic performance in European countries remains high (Figure 5.1). While confidence in parliaments (and to a lesser extent, parties) was declining in the last decades of the twentieth century, this decline seems to have been

Table 5.1. Freedom House 2011 classification of countries and their regimes (%)

Year	Free	Partly free	Not free	Total	N
1980	31	31	38	100	162
1990	40	30	30	100	165
2000	45	30	25	100	192
2010	45	31	24	100	194

Source: Based on Freedom House (2011, 21).

arrested in the last decade, at least in Europe. Above all, there are no signs of decline in overall satisfaction with 'the way democracy works', no signs of democratic atrophy in the sense of declining support for democratic practices, no symptoms of endorsement or approval of autocracy. There is what Norris (2011) describes as 'trendless fluctuation' in the strength of public satisfaction, as well as significant variation between times and regimes. The overall satisfaction with democracy, though fluctuating, has remained on the same level over the last 30 to 40 years (which is the span of comparable survey data). Younger democracies show more diversity and wider fluctuations, as well as wider disparities between public expectations and perceived performance of democratic regimes – but this is rather expected and predictable. So is the correlation between public satisfaction and the key 'outcomes': economic performance and political stability. Thus the relatively high satisfaction with 'democracy' in partocratic China and Vietnam clearly reflects the spectacular growth in the economy and prosperity in both countries – claimed as credit by partocratic regimes and their leaders. It also reflects the highly guarded social and political stability, as well as the overwhelming government-controlled propaganda (including suppression of vocal critical opposition).

What is particularly worth noting, especially as a background for the discussion in the second part of this chapter, is that public trust and confidence in the democratic system remain relatively high and stable, even when trust in parliaments is declining. This is true especially in the largest and most established Western democracies (such as the USA and Great Britain). Democratic aspirations also remain very high. The last World Values Survey shows that the mean score in the scale of importance (ranging from 1 = 'not at all important' to 10 = 'absolutely important') was about 8.5. In the established liberal democracies, including the United States, Great Britain, Japan and most Western European countries, the mean score was 8.9; in younger liberal and 'electoral' democracies, such as Argentina, Mexico and Brazil, it was 8.5. Surprisingly, even people living in partocracies and autocracies, such as China, Iran and Russia showed very high democratic aspirations averaging at 8.4 (Norris 2011, 15).

Perhaps most interesting, and to some extent counterintuitive, are the findings about the correlates of democratic aspirations, satisfaction and discontent. Thus, democratic aspirations do not grow in line with the general human development index (HDI) that is widely seen as an index of societal modernisation. Nor do they correlate (inversely) with age, as suggested by an image of eager young democrats confronting conservative oldies. In fact, the older generations and societies with moderate to lower levels of HDI scores show the highest democratic aspirations. Similarly counterintuitive (though in line with the leader-democratic model) is the finding that media exposure –

Figure 5.1. Satisfaction with democratic performance, Europe 1973–2008

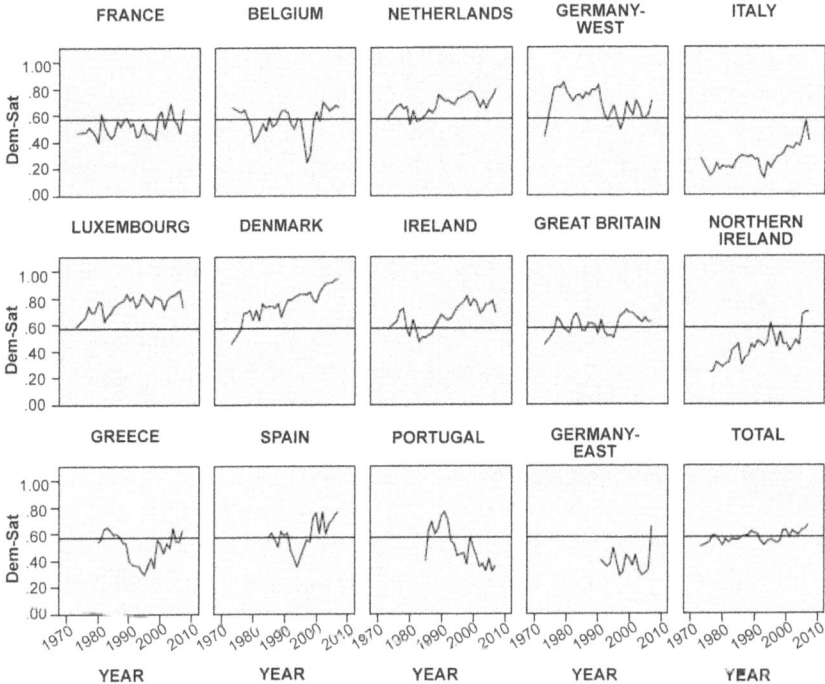

Note: "On the whole, are you very satisfied, fairly satisfied, not very satisfied or not at all satisfied with the way democracy woks in your country?" Proportion who are 'fairly' or 'very' satisfied.
Source: Norris (2011, 21).

which is often seen as excessively critical of democratic governments and focusing on scandals – in fact, strengthens democratic aspirations. The intense users/consumers of radio, TV and newspaper news are more satisfied with democracy than lesser users – in clear contrast with the popular image of mass media feeding into demo-scepticism by publicising corruption. More predictably, high education, high levels of trust and high levels of political activism are also positively correlated with democratic aspirations. This is an important finding throwing some new light on the popular view that already frustrated political activists may grow disenchanted with 'really existing democracy'. But the main and perhaps the most significant finding is the positive correlation (most likely also a causal link) between democratic aspirations and high education. It explains a somewhat surprising negative correlation between education and lower satisfaction with the working of democracy – and increasing 'democratic deficit' among the most educated (and aspiring) strata.

Thus the 'democratic deficit', a gap between democratic aspirations and democratic satisfaction, turns out to be a result of growing democratic-participatory aspirations among the best educated citizens. To repeat: it is not the growing dissatisfaction with the democratic performance, but the result of increasing education and aspirations. The aspirations are strongly affected by the level of education: those with high education grow higher aspirations. As a result, the gap is widest in the most educated societies. Perhaps most significantly, high political knowledge and media use (regular consumption of news) seem to reduce the strength of 'democratic deficit' by narrowing the gap between expectations and perceived performance – a finding which is particularly relevant in forecasting the 'future of democracy'.

But what does democracy mean? What are the popular understandings of democracy? What are the connotations and denotations of this popular term and concept? It is fair to say that 'democracy' continues to be a 'hurray' concept – as positive and widely approved as it is vague. Yet there seems to be a 'modal' meaning, especially among citizens in advanced societies – those nations that have the oldest and most established democratic regimes. Democracy there is commonly associated with electoral procedures and practices, and with popular elections of leaders, equal gender rights and civil liberties. Thus the popular understandings, expectations and aspirations concerning democracy are less 'participatory' and more 'representative'. They are also predominantly procedural and liberal – that is, involve respect for citizenship rights, including equal gender rights. If we focus on two of the most popular aspects associated with this dominant procedural understanding of democracy – 'equal gender rights' and 'free popular election of leaders' – their worldwide strength and distribution is quite telling. The procedural and representative understandings are most predominant – most widespread and strongest – in Scandinavia, newly democratised Central and Eastern Europe, and Western Europe. It is less prevalent in Africa and the Asia-Pacific. Africa and the Asia-Pacific are also the two regions where democracy is most often (mis)understood as 'military responsibility for government' and 'religious interpretation of laws'.

These findings are compatible, in our eyes at least, with both the picture of persisting democratic commitments, increasing democratic aspiration (generating 'deficit'), and with a shift toward a representative 'leader democracy'. It is worth remembering that the shift toward 'leader democracy' constitutes simultaneously a shift away from 'party' democracy, that is, away from the form of democracy in which parties (with their ideological programmes) provide the key 'democratic linkage' between elites and the masses, and away from the configuration in which parties and professional politicians are the key generators of trust and confidence of voters/citizens. The role of the main generators of public confidence, as we suggest, is increasingly taken by democratically elected leaders, the key 'representatives' who are high profile winners of democratic leadership contests. In 'leader democracy' these leaders serve as 'representatives supreme', the principal builders of trust-based linkages between the elite and the masses. Their prominence also lifts the role of competitive elections by giving them the status of being the most important form of democratic mandate-authorisation. The widespread public recognition of this fact – the fact that electoral contests constitute the foundation of democratic 'coupling' between elites and the masses – seems to transpire in the results of the surveys.

The results also suggest that leaders and governments have largely sustained public trust and confidence, while parliaments, parliamentary and party politicians have not. A declining (in the last decades of the twentieth century) public trust in parliaments and parties, in other words, did not affect confidence in democracy and satisfaction with the 'way democracy works'. Similarly, the fact that the high consumption of the media news and reports – in which leaders dominate – accompanies high satisfaction with the working of democracy, seem to be consistent with the suggested shift toward 'leader democracy', and inconsistent with the rival scenarios.

It must be noted, though, that the leader-democratic scenario is less compatible with some conclusions reached by Dalton (2004) and to a lesser extent Norris (2011). This incompatibility is most conspicuous in the interpretations of democratic aspirations and 'democratic deficit'. Dalton and Norris suggest that public aspirations have a largely participatory character and that democratic deficit' concerns mainly increasing participatory aspirations of educated and politically competent voters. The leader-democratic interpretation suggests that mass aspirations are less participatory and more representative, more leadership focused. In other words, voters/citizens do not aspire to, expect or desire more direct participation in politics, especially in deliberative processes of policy forming. Rather, they expect, desire or aspire to 'having their voice heard', their preferences registered, respected and represented by trusted leaders. This is particularly important at times of crisis and uncertainty, when public confidence in the 'old' institutional repositories of trust (ideologies, parties and parliaments) declines. Under such conditions, elected political leaders become the key repositories of public trust. If such leaders prove weak or incompetent, the trust and confidence are withdrawn and the failed leaders are 'recalled', that is, they lose the subsequent electoral contests. But such 'recalls', our model suggests, do not undermine a faith in the working of democracy. Strong commitment to democracy and high satisfaction with democracy survive high leadership and elite 'circulation'.

It is hard to decide which or whose interpretation is more plausible. The survey data collected by major research agencies cannot provide more than a very general 'plausibility' test – after all, they had not been designed to test the claim about 'leader-democratic' shift.[16] But a simple observation of electoral cycles gives us some important clues. The cycles seem to indicate that democratic 'recalls' lead either to a renewal of trust in new leaders or occasionally to a leadership vacuum, feared by Weber and Schumpeter, but not necessarily to dissatisfaction with how democracy works. As demonstrated by Norris (2011), the 'democratic deficit' diagnosed in most advanced democracies seems to reflect, above all, the increasing expectations – and possibly unrealistic expectations – directed towards democracies. The substance of these expectations is not entirely clear, though it may involve: increasing expectations of better outcomes (prosperity, economic and political security, stability), increasing expectations of honesty and competence, or increasing expectations of firm leadership. In our eyes, this democratic disaffection is now primarily dissatisfaction with the strength and quality of leadership. In other words, it is caused by high leadership expectations and conspicuous leadership failures. Such failures may not undermine faith in democracy in general, but they have other dire social, economic and political consequences registered by disaffected voters.

Toward Participatory Democracy?

Partly in response to the alarming diagnoses of democratic atrophy, citizens' dissatisfaction and the deepening 'democratic deficit', a group of international scholars and political practitioners, headed by Philippe Schmitter and Alexander Trechsel (2004), produced a discussion green paper with recommendations for some radical participatory reforms. The paper was commissioned by the Council of Europe, and it contains 28 recommendations for institutional reforms to increase citizen participation and improve the quality of democracy in Europe. It is worth considering (briefly) here, because it is sophisticated and contains a vision of future European democracy that is highly participatory in nature and close to 'cosmopolitan democracy'. Alas, it is also highly problematic. The key assumption behind the proposed plan of 'revival of democracy' is that the current malaise is caused by insufficient civic activism and restricted opportunities for direct participation – not

---

16 In fact, the way the questions in the EU surveys have been formulated, may lead to serious confusion. For example, the respondent is asked to assess 'democracy versus strong leadership'. Needless to say, this formulation assumes – incorrectly in our view – the incompatibility of 'strong leadership' with democratic commitment, trust, and satisfaction.

necessarily in line with the results of empirical analyses. The widely diagnosed 'democratic deficit', in other words, is seen as reflecting 'performance failures' (rather than growing aspirations) and allegedly frustrated desires for civic engagement and participatory activism. As argued here, this assumption may well be incorrect – and therefore the reform may prove misdirected.

Let us looks at some details of the proposed reforms as contained in the green paper (Schmitter 2002a, 2002b). The major concern of the green paper is declining citizens' trust in politicians and political institutions and declining citizens' participation in parties and party-managed political processes. In order to increase voter turnout, stimulate membership in parties and civil associations, improve confidence in their representatives (elected politicians or appointed experts), and generally strengthen the legitimacy of the democratic process (weakened over recent decades), the report proposes participatory overhaul. It is clearly a *participatory* reform; its aim is not to improve existing *representative* institutions, but to introduce new, mostly direct participative procedures and institutions that would change the nature of current democratic systems. Most of the recommendations aim not only at increasing civic involvement and participation, but also at establishing direct deliberative institutions, including citizens' assemblies. They are aiming not just at improving representation and strengthening trust through more comfortable and accessible postal and electronic voting, but also at widening the use of referenda and 'citizens' initiatives', deliberative assemblies, voting lotteries, participatory budgeting, specialised elected councils, and an extensive use of vouchers for funding organisations in civil society and for financing political parties.[17] Special measures are scheduled to open participation for immigrants and foreigners (citizenship mentor, council of denizens, voting rights for denizens). Citizen/civic education (education for political participation) is boosted and extended. Citizen/civic information is widened and intensified through installing 'democracy kiosks' and promoting involvement through media campaigns.

A separate group of recommendations is intended to make democracy more vibrant, qualitatively different from the 'really existing' democratic practices. Civic duties are to be articulated more clearly. Compulsory civic service modelled on military conscription is proposed to increase young people's commitments to the political community. Universal citizenship would grant full political rights to all persons born in a polity. Even children are registered as nominal voters, though until they reach adulthood, the child's vote is cast by their parents.[18] Discretionary voting gives citizens the chance to express their

---

17 Citizens, selected by lottery, are entitled to make public policy decisions after hearings of public and semi-public agencies.

18 A similar proposal to introduce universal citizenship has been discussed during the recent constitution-making process in Hungary.

preferences in a more sophisticated way through transferable and/or NOTA (none of the above) options. In addition, there are reform measures to set up and impose constraints on professional politicians: the incompatibility of mandates, the variable threshold for elections (higher electoral threshold for incumbents than for new candidates) and selective rewarding of most popular parties with public funding.

Some recommended measures seem controversial. Universal citizenship, for example, is bound to undermine equality of citizens; 'civic service' is bound to violate individual liberty. Direct democratic institutions, like 'lottery', lack legitimate means of distributing public duties, powers and responsibilities. The discretionary vote makes voting more interesting but more complicated at the same time, thus increasing the likelihood of electoral errors, manipulations and fraud. Moreover, it blurs political responsibility and may fail to increase voter turnout, which currently serves as a sensitive measure of citizen (dis) satisfaction. Citizens' assemblies and specialised deliberative councils are bound to be used by politicians in stalling decisions, 'subcontracting' difficult choices, and shedding responsibility for controversial policies – the pathologies well recognised and widely condemned by mass publics. Most importantly, the use of referenda, seen as exemplars of participatory democracy, may easily backfire. Unless supported by elites, reforms proposed by referenda are typically rejected. Media publicity ('moral panics') affect referenda decisions making them 'populist', and referenda campaigns are widely criticised as 'manipulated' by sectional interests.

The most problematic aspect of all these recommendations, to repeat, is the underlying (and not explicitly justified) assumption that citizens are dissatisfied with inadequate or insufficient opportunities for participation and engagement. This may not be the case. As we suggested before, and as Figure 5.2 indicates, the mainstream understanding of democracy is procedural, the key civic virtues are 'representative' rather than 'participatory', and popular aspirations seem to be directed to the outcomes (good governance, consistent leadership, economic security) rather than processes. To simplify, citizens want better leadership and outcomes, and not participatory opportunities and practices. And, assuming our interpretation is correct, if the aspirations of the European publics are more representative than participatory, the participatory reforms are not likely to work.

This leads to the last critical comment. The advocates of the 'dawn of participatory democracy' seem to make two assumptions: that popular mobilisations and protest movements, such as those in the 'Arab Spring', are pro-democratic, and that the democratic aspirations reflected in these movements are predominantly civic and participatory, rather than traditional and representative. These assumptions are shaky. Not only are the popular

Figure 5.2. Importance attached to six civic virtues underlying modern democracy in the United States, Western Europe and Eastern Europe (%)

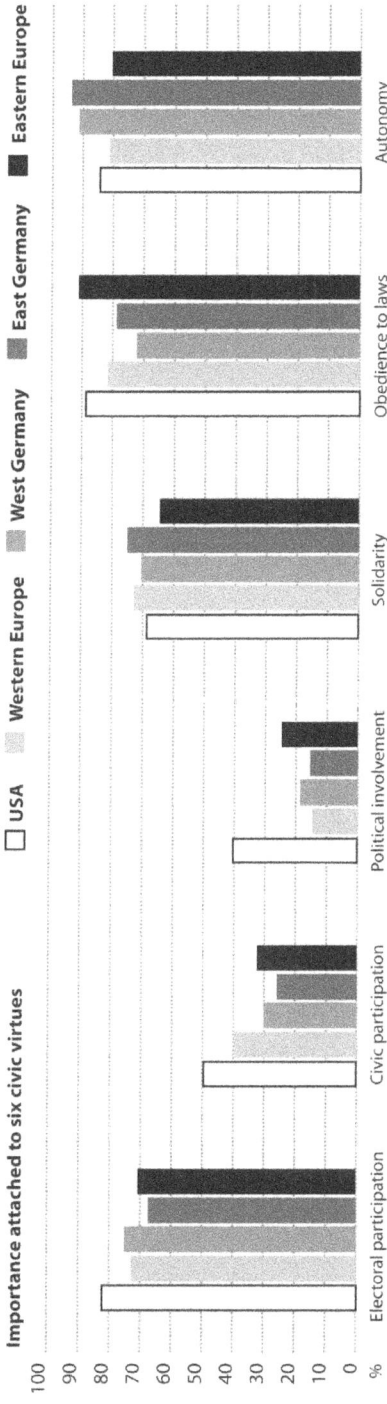

Note: Data from ESS 2002/3 and US Citizen Involvement and Democracy Study 2005 for those aged 18+. The data show percentages giving an importance score of at least 7 out of 10 to each civic virtue. 'Western Europe' in this analysis includes: Austria, Belgium, Denmark, Finland, France, Greece, Ireland, Italy, Luxembourg, the Netherlands, Norway, Portugal Spain, Sweden, Switzerland and the UK. 'Eastern Europe' includes: the Czech Republic, Hungary, Poland and Slovenia.

Source: Based on analysis by S. Roßteutscher in ESS (2008, 17).

protests and movements of the last decades vary widely in their ideological vectors – from religious fundamentalist through nationalist to liberal-democratic – but they also are initially multifaced and vague in their goals and aspirations. There is nothing strange or new in that. Almost all popular movements mobilise against rather than for; they are public contestations rather than affirmations. Their unity is precarious and initially mainly negative because it is based on shared objections against some unfair, corrupt or discriminatory practices. Therefore such movements split and fragment in the process of organisation that typically involves the formation of elites and the formulation, typically by emergent leaders, of positive goals and objectives. Democratisation is often one of these positive goals, but not always the dominant one. In every protest movement there are not only democrats, but also nationalists who support nationalistic Bonapartism, religious zealots, secessionists interested in redrawing boundaries, as well as those who have no clear vision and who would accept any power arrangement that offered hope for improving their lives. Therefore the political outcomes of movement organisation and consolidation are always uncertain; they depend on who prevails politically and who assumes national leadership.

The Uncertain Future of 'Leader Democracy'

If our diagnosis and forecast of a continuous shift toward 'leader democracy' are correct, neither of the scenarios proposed by the 'demo-optimists' and 'demo-pessimists' is plausible, 'democratic malaise' is more imaginary than real, and the participatory therapy suggested by the green paper is not likely to work. This is because the suggested shift toward 'leader democracy' heralds a change in the democratic form, as well as a change in public expectations concerning the character, the quality and the working of democracy. The shift, as argued here, is towards representative democracy with trusted leaders; it is directed toward better representation, a stronger elite–mass linkage that maximises public confidence in leaders and elites. The modern centralistic trends, in other words, do not arrest the progression of mass democratisation, but seem to direct it in a more leader-centric and elite-dependent direction, as anticipated by Weber and Schumpeter. This actual evolution of contemporary democratic practices seems compatible with this anticipate shift.

Are the leader-centric trends likely to continue? In our view, they are, at least in the near future. The main 'drivers' of these trends – the party–voter dealignment, the weakening of the mass parties, the proliferation of the mass media, and the global interdependency and risk – show no signs of abating. The accompanying centralisation of authority is also likely to continue propelled by the spreading public awareness of social change, uncertainty and anxiety about the future, and therefore the need for further 'reforms' and 'adjustments', as well as by growing international competition for best 'positioning' of national governments and businesses in the global stakes. Firm and trusted leaders and strong executives are increasingly seen as a necessary condition of effective adjustments and as the best international champions of national interests. In other words, leadership groups are likely to remain the main drivers of democratic states, public repositories of trust, the key reassurers of anxious publics, and the principal loci of public responsibility.

Furthermore, there are no indications of successful rebuilding of 'party democracy'. Trust in political parties may have levelled off, but public scepticism about the capacity of the bureaucratised parties to transcend their oligarchic-bureaucratic interests and create a viable notion of 'public/national interest' persists. Leaders, rather than parties and party programmes, seem to gain public confidence, and leaders rather than parties or ideologies win mass vote. Perhaps more importantly, parties weaken even further due to the increasing capacities of persuasive leaders and allied opinion shapers to propose innovative responses to the challenges posed by globalisation. The proliferation of 'leader parties' indicates that leaders and leadership groups are capable of taking initiative in electoral contests by capturing the attention of voters, 'shaping the agendas', 'framing' debates and directing 'public opinion' (the latter following leadership appeals). To simplify, parties become more dependent on leaders in shaping public perceptions and securing electoral victories.

This is likely to be facilitated and further reinforced by expanding mass media. The media shape not only the domain traditionally seen as 'public opinion' and 'popular culture', but also dominate 'political communication' and monopolise the organisation of political competitions for leadership. Moreover, the media increase their influence. While election campaigns become 'permanent campaigns', the media arenas become identified with 'public arenas'. Under the pressure of the expanding mass media, and as a result of symbiosis between the news-hungry journalists and publicity-hungry leaders, political competitions are likely to drift further and further in the direction of confrontations of images and oratory-demagogic rivalry – all highly personalised and increasingly mass mediated. In this game, image projection, capacity to inspire trust, skills in persuasion and reassurance are likely to continue as the main conditions of success – and this seems to favour leader-centric politics.

Finally, the nature of political competitions is likely to follow the logics of both advanced modernisation and globalisation. If globalising trends persist and if interdependency between nations and regions further increases, so will the current pressure towards 'global governance', understood as wider international consultation and coordination of leadership action. These pressures, one should note, are also prompting the further centralisation of policy decisions in the hands of leadership teams, and increasing the attention paid to 'world leaders'.

What about the power and influence of business corporations? They are likely to continue, possibly even grow, but within the democratic framework that is under the benevolent, business-friendly and business-supportive control of powerful state apparata. There seems to be a strengthening symbiosis between the two. Private corporations need strong states (strong governments and leaders) and they seem to blossom under the conditions that combine stable social order, open access to global markets and a strong legal and political framework accompanied by governmental control. They need social order – the national and global social order – and most of them benefit from the power of democratic states to impose and stabilise it. They also benefit from market liberalisation, but such liberalisation that does not destabilise the legal frameworks and social-political order. High levels of national regulation and international control are most conducive to successful business operations, especially when crises hit or when foreign operations require protection. The democratic state leaders and elites, in turn, have to harmonise major interests and protect their economies in order to deliver mass prosperity and high employment – the highly valued political outcomes necessary for reelection. States and regimes heavily rely on revenues coming from corporate profits and on employment provided by economically successful business sectors. Such a symbiosis is not new, but it is difficult to cultivate under conditions of rapid globalisation when crises prove contagious and control is limited.

Therefore the initial enthusiasm towards deregulation subsides among political and corporate leaders. Similarly, the attempts to 'roll back the state' have proven very risky, and they lose support even among the corporate leaders. The waves of deregulation pursued in the 1980s and 1990s caused massive disruptions in the economies, undermined social order, and were seen by many as hurting, rather than benefiting, the political and the corporate world alike. The lesson of these failed deregulatory experiments seems to be that economic elites, including corporate businesses, need (wise and moderate) state regulation and protection – and therefore firm leadership – and that the regulative framework maintained by liberal-democratic states (and sustained by good political leadership) is necessary not only for successful business operations but also for protection at the times of crises.

The data on government spending confirm the persisting dependency of private corporations on the political muscle-cum-legitimacy of democratic states. Government spending measured as a proportion of GDP has been increasing in most advanced societies – especially during the time of economic boom – even in those societies and regimes that embraced the neoliberal doctrine of privatisation, deregulation and fiscal austerities (*Economist* 2011b). The average proportion for the OECD countries increased from about 28 per cent in 1960 to 44 per cent in 1980, and to 48 per cent in 2009. The respective figures for the USA alone are 27 per cent (in 1960), 31 per cent (in 1980) and 42 per cent (in 2009). Private corporations may grow in size and influence, but they remain dwarfed by powerful – and growing – state apparata and their executives. Yet, the interventionist states also increase their dependency on corporate taxes and other sources of state revenue, as well as on mass prosperity and employment. This relation of mutual dependence has been clearly demonstrated during the recent fiscal crisis. It is the state executives that bailed out (or in some cases refused to bail out) major financial corporations – especially those on which governments depended in their daily operation and which proved 'too big to fail'. It is also the state executives that protect and sponsor business giants in their international dealings and pave the way for new dealings. The contemporary political elites do it in a more systematic and coordinated manner than their predecessors. Therefore we can predict that the symbiosis is likely to continue. It is accompanied by high-profile leaders' meetings, summits, specialised working forums – the main arenas of political decision making.

Yet, the future of 'leader democracy' is uncertain. This is not because the leader-centric trends reverse, because democracy withers away, or because it takes a direct-participatory turn.

Rather, this is because the ascendant 'leader democracy', like any other type (elite configuration), has its own vulnerabilities. The discussion of these vulnerabilities will resume in the next and final chapter.

Chapter 6

THE DEMOCRATIC CYCLES

The previous chapter critically assessed two 'rival' visions competing with the proposed scenario of expanding 'leader democracy': a sanguine vision of expanding and participatory democracy, and a dark vision of declining democracy. Both these rival visions, as argued above, look implausible. Instead, we suggest a scenario based on theoretical projections of changing forms of democratic representation, as well as our reading of the current trends and the empirical diagnoses of the 'state of democracy'. However, this scenario has to be presented with some cautioning notes about the contingent nature of historical change, especially the 'long-run' change, the nonlinear character of social-political processes, the widening diversity of democratic configurations, and – perhaps most importantly – the vulnerabilities of 'leader democracy' to leadership vacuums and leadership failures.

Before we explore these themes and outline the predicted pattern of democratic change, let us pause and look back at the main argument, if only to remind the reader of the broader context of the proposed scenario. The central tenets of the book, painted with a thick brush, can be summarised as follows:

Over the last 30 to 40 years, we have observed and experienced in almost all advanced Western democracies an ever more pronounced centrality of – and focus on – political leaders. This increasing leader-centeredness is detectable in both parliamentary and presidential systems: it is reflected in the centralisation of authority in leaders' hands (vis-à-vis other segments of the political elite); in more firm, often unilateral, actions taken by leaders (and applauded by the mass publics); in a widening media exposure given to leaders and their personalities, especially in election campaigns; in the proliferation of 'leader parties', and in the mass expectation and approval of 'firm' and 'decisive' leadership', typically contrasted with 'weak leadership', the latter condemned as a serious political affliction. It does not mean that political heads always deliver such expected and applauded firm and decisive leadership. Nor does this mean that decisive leaders, even when emerging in the competition, deliver the desired outcomes: a sense of prosperity, stability, security and dignity-cum-national pride. Even though many leaders have failed to deliver these outcomes, the role of leaders has been enhanced, especially vis-à-vis other segments of political elites, such as party officialdom, factional bosses and the top mandarins. Leaders gain media exposure and public prominence unprecedented in their intensity, and unusual in democratic politics.

All these leader-centric developments reinforce each other and change the physiognomy of contemporary liberal democracies by moving them toward 'leader democracies', that is, toward political elite configurations in which leaders play the prominent role in generating mass trust and confidence of voters. Leaders also integrate political elites, and play the key role in cultivating the link of trust between these elites and the mass voters, the citizenry at large. Their position is gained and sustained through heavily mass-mediated electoral contests for democratic mandate-authorisation. Such contests – which formerly were restricted to electoral campaigns but today become permanent, ongoing, continuous competitions – lie at the very heart of democratic 'coupling' between political leaders and elites on the one hand, and mass publics on the other. Democracy is widely seen and highly valued as a representative system in which political elites are held responsible and accountable to the public through regular, open, free and fair electoral contests for political representation and executive leadership. These contests intensify and extend well beyond election campaigns.

This leader-centricity of contemporary democratic politics is relatively new, and it contrasts with the 'party-centric' elite configurations in most postwar Western democracies. In these 'party democracies', top party officials and factional 'bosses', often allied with the top governmental bureaucrats, played the dominant role. The elite–mass linkage was cultivated through stable 'alignment' between mass parties (and their ideological programmes and platforms) and loyal voters. Therefore the shift towards leader-centric democracy has been accompanied – and partly caused – by a decline of mass ideological parties (*Volksparteien*). It was also aided by the proliferation of the mass media and increasing interdependency or globalisation, the latter increasing the complexity of decisions and the scope of risks associated with their implementation. All these changes should be seen as a part or aspect of general processes of political modernisation and mass democratisation rather than an anomaly or a decline of democracy. Leader-centric democracy belongs to a family of modern representative democracy, the latter seen as most compatible with conditions of social complexity, mass mediation of political communication and progressive globalisation. Under such conditions, democratic leaders ally themselves with citizens by competitively winning mass votes, and through these victories they secure mass confidence in their leadership and the ruling mandate-authorisation.

The theoretical foundations of competitive 'leader democracy' – anticipated and outlined by Max Weber and Joseph Schumpeter about a century ago – need more systematic elaboration and updating. This has been done by identifying the key causes of leader-centric trends, the conditions reinforcing leader-centrism, and by articulating the key dimensions of 'leader democracy' understood as a specific elite configuration and a form of elite– mass alignment. We argue that such an updated model is more consistent, and descriptively more accurate and realistic, than the rival theoretical visions (the 'deliberative-participatory', and 'neoclassical'). 'Leader democracy' also fulfils the key normative criteria and expectations of democracy, though in a way that may differ from typical anticipations of contemporary (apologetic and critical) theorists of democracy, especially the theorists embracing the aggregative-pluralist and the deliberative-participatory models.

The proposed theoretical model of 'leader democracy' depicts political leaders as key democratic actors embedded in broader elites, especially 'core executives' in the modern state. Political action of leaders is motivated by political will, determination and commitment of the actual and aspiring leaders, and it is exercised through mass persuasion that actively shapes (rather than reflects) preferences of mass voters and generates public trust and confidence. The central role of mass persuasion exercised by political leaders gives more 'substance' and meaning to political processes than the formalised bureaucratic procedures associated with the rival models of democracy. Competitive elections – the mass-mediated contests for executive leadership in the state – are the key elements of the contemporary leader-democratic process. They provide not only the opportunity for leaders to generate 'the confidence of the masses' (Weber 1978, 1452) and exercise innovative 'political entrepreneurship' (Schumpeter 1942/1987, 34), but also form the main testing grounds for potential and aspiring leaders, strengthen elite integration, provide an opportunity for broad alliances within elite ranks, and enhance a sense of dignity among voters who gain the status of chief arbiters and 'king makers' in leadership contests. Competitive elections also allow leaders to innovate and to formally discharge what is widely seen as public responsibility-cum-accountability in the sense of making promises and generating expectations that are 'tested' in subsequent electoral cycles. But the main aspect of democratic 'representation' is achieved through active political leadership, as opposed to statistical 'mirroring', aggregation or deliberative self-adjustment of citizens' preferences.

Leader-centrism and leader-democratic configuration should not be confused with creeping autocracy, technocracy, tutelage, bureaucratic domination or 'despotic democracy'. The latter types seldom involve systematic leader–mass 'coupling' and do not rely on the open and fair competition for leadership that lies at the heart of responsible democratic government. By contrast, 'leader democracy' is compatible with democratic elitism understood as representative and competitive elite rule. The proposed theoretical model of 'leader democracy' reconciles democratic principles and practices with elite theory and visions of competitive leadership. It also provides an interpretive lens for current developments, and some guidance for anticipating future developments. Seen through this theoretical lens, neither of the popular scenarios – the 'demo-optimistic' and the 'demo-pessimistic' – looks plausible.

Perhaps the most obvious problem these visions face, as argued in Chapter 5, is a paucity of supportive evidence. The demo-optimists, especially those anticipating participatory or deliberative shifts, must feel disappointed with the current trends. While pro-democratic values and commitments do spread worldwide, it is not clear that this spread involves direct-participatory forms of democracy. The survey of values and attitudes reveal enormous variation in popular understanding of democracy among those who live in democratic polities and those under nondemocratic regimes, but the most popular are invariably the representative images. Moreover, as pointed out by students of social movements and democratisation, participatory civic activism does not seem to increase, but rather oscillate. Popular protest mobilisations serve as means to articulate discontent with policy outcomes rather than policy making. Antiautocratic protest mobilisations and movements come in waves and ebbs, and they vary widely in their ideological (pro- and antidemocratic) vector and fervour.

The sceptical visions of civic atrophy are equally suspect and at odds with empirically backed diagnoses. There are undeniable symptoms of 'democratic deficit' – a gap between public expectations and perceived performance of democratic institutions and regimes – but this deficit, as pointed out by Norris (2011), is the result of rapidly rising expectations (among the educated urban strata), rather than increasing public dissatisfaction with democratic performance. The latter, that is, democratic performance or 'the way democracy works', is assessed positively, though there is increasing dissatisfaction with economic and political outcomes. There is also evidence of a decline in trust granted to politicians, especially parliamentary politicians – a trend recently arrested in Europe. However, as pointed out by Robert Dahl (2000, 35), this is symptomatic not of the decay of democracy, but of a democratic paradox: 'In many of the oldest and most stable democratic countries, citizens possess little confidence in some key democratic institutions. Yet most citizens continue to believe in the desirability of democracy'. If there is a public dissatisfaction, this dissatisfaction is more with political-economic *outcomes* than with democratic *processes* and practices. Similarly, if there is a desire for change in democratic practices – and it is by no means clear that such a desire is widespread – it is a desire for a reconfiguration of democratic governance, and not a rejection of democracy (Blühdorn 2009). There is solid evidence of widespread and persisting *satisfaction with democracy* as evident in a wide endorsement of democratic values and principles, approval of democratic procedures (especially elections), and confidence in democratically elected leaders.

The mistrust in politicians, increasing at the end of the past century, has levelled and even reversed, at least in Europe. There are no signs of desertion of democracy by the mass publics, educated 'political strata' or political elites. Instead, there are growing expectations as to what democracy may deliver in terms of good governance, stability, and (in newly democratised nations) economic security and prosperity. The expectations increase most rapidly among the educated strata and generate a sense of 'democratic deficit', but this sense is socially circumscribed, found only among the highly educated segments of the most established liberal democracies.

Vulnerabilities of 'Leader Democracy'

The conclusion drawn from these diagnoses is that leader-centric trends are likely to continue and that the advanced democracies will approximate the model of 'leader democracy'. However, this is an anticipation and prediction for a near future. Longer term developments can be charted only on the basis of theoretical models and predictions, and the theoretical model suggested by Weber and Schumpeter anticipate not so much a directional trend as dynamic cycles, driven by both the logic of modernisation and the internal dynamics coded into different types/models of democracy. There is no balance or stable equilibrium in social-political arrangements, and this means that each model elite configuration contains internal tensions, and it is vulnerable to destabilisation and change. 'Leader democracy' is no exception to this general rule; like other forms it is tension ridden and vulnerable to failure – or self-destructing outcomes. Perhaps the most important weaknesses and vulnerabilities can be labelled the leadership vacuums and leadership failures.

The main alternative to 'leader democracy', warned Weber a century ago, is a leaderless configuration – a leadership vacuum in which party machines, bureaucrats and politicians without vocation direct and shape national policies. Leadership vacuums occur when leader-dependent polities are unable to generate (select and groom) politicians with leadership qualities. This has disastrous effects resulting in 'directionless' politics, and in a progressive 'alienation' fragmentation and delegitimation of political elites. Public confidence declines and political gridlocks multiply, thus starting dangerous vicious cycles of inaction, chaos and delegitimation. The more the political elite depend on leaders as a source of dynamism and direction, the more dangerous are such states of leadership vacuum. Yet it is seldom appreciated, and very few elites develop good mechanisms for the systematic selection, testing and grooming of not only professional politicians, but also talented and skilled leaders. While Weber attributed this weakness to competitive envy (especially among the parliamentarians and party officials), contemporary analysts point to a number of 'systemic' obstacles: narrow political recruitment, bureaucratic constrains, factional struggles, excessive burdens and stresses producing burnouts, and media overexposure. The democratic-egalitarian ethos is hostile to a notion of leadership 'training or 'grooming' – leaders should emerge spontaneously in an open meritocratic competition. As pointed out by Putnam (1976), modern political recruitment is increasingly open and meritocratic, but this may weaken leadership selection, because such selection falls under the control of local party organisations and other organised political 'selectorates'. Party selectorates are seldom sensitive to leadership talent, and instead of talent spotting, they tend to select complacent or spectacular candidates, those with established name, image and reputation. This results in the negative selection of party 'hacks', dynastic 'scions', local celebrities and political professionals – especially lawyers, who combine oratory skills with professional autonomy. Talented leaders are in short supply. They often rise accidentally, due to serendipity rather than design, through nonroutine recruitment channels: trade union, social movements and civic activism. Even if they progress to parliaments, such talented candidates often fall victims of factional struggles and vendettas. Factions fight to place at the top their loyal patrons and not necessarily the most talented innovative leaders. The 'grooming' process is neglected, and often occurs through informal patronage and mentorship. Moreover, even when successful, the new recruits face a danger of an early burnout – often afflicting the most talented and ambitious leaders. They are easily overwhelmed by extra duties, contradictory expectations, stress, and media overexposure, especially if there is no concerted effort by the colleagues to protect and support them. Very few political systems develop such protection and cultivation strategies. In most cases, talented candidates undergo a political equivalent of 'trial by fire' with few political survivors. A single error, when amplified by the opposition and publicised by the media, may derail a promising political career, regardless of the talent of the unfortunate candidate. Hardly anyone can count on tolerance or on discrete 'burying' of the errors, partly because the climate of intense competition; relentless oppositional scrutiny and continuous media hunt for scandals are most unforgiving. In a nutshell – and one may say paradoxically – contemporary 'leader democracies' fail to develop a reliable system of selecting, grooming and protecting talented leaders, and this failure results in frequent leadership vacuums with all their disastrous consequences.

'Leader democracies' are also vulnerable to leadership failures. Because of the centrality of leaders – as key strategic visionaries, innovators and elite integrators – they are particularly sensitive to a damage that poor or failing leaders may inflict. There are some protections against the rise of poor leaders – leaders who prove mediocre, incompetent, weak, impulsive or afflicted by poor judgement – but these protections seldom work well. Particularly dangerous are such leaders whose weaknesses are well hidden and who can compensate for the lack of leadership qualities by developing an attractive image, seductive media presentation or superficial oratory gloss. In the media-saturated environment, skilful manipulators, opportunistic populists, ruthless demagogues, and narcissistic publicity seekers may easily reach the highest office, especially if propelled by powerful interests, public anxieties and media hype. The enormous advantage of incumbency – another vulnerability of 'leader democracy' – gives them an opportunity to entrench themselves in office. They ultimately fail, but only after the damage is done. The highly publicised examples of such failures are George W. Bush in the United States, and Silvio Berlusconi in Italy. Both rose to the leadership positions as 'outsiders', with the help of powerful sponsors and media campaigns. Both gained wide popularity through media appearances and image manipulation. Both made decisions that weakened the economic and social order of their countries. George W. Bush and his leadership team pursued a hubristic 'faith politics' marked by contradictory moves and ill-considered decisions that resulted in budget imbalance, the near-collapse of financial institutions in the Great Financial Crisis, and the damaging Iraq and Afghanistan imbroglio. Berlusconi, backed by manipulative media, tolerated a systematic mismanagement of the economy, corruption and political polarisation. Under his rule, Italy found itself in the state of a permanent economic, political and moral crisis. Yet both leaders had a superficial 'gloss' that allowed them to win elections and secure, at least initially, high popularity. They were confident speakers and masters of image presentation. Both could stir public emotions, ruthlessly attack the rivals and critics, and both ruled in a populist manner.

The popular defence against poor leadership is through limiting the term of office and/or intensifying elite circulation. However, such intensified mobility may also destabilise the entire political system by making leadership fickle and disposable. While poor leaders may be swiftly deposed, talented leaders are hard to find, and they cannot be retained for longer periods of time. Moreover, the intense elite mobility also lowers the experience of political leaders, elite cohesion, and the attractiveness of the political office. All three increase the danger of negative selection and leadership vacuums. Restrictions placed on leaders' and elites' autonomy does not work either. Leaders who are unable to lead, and elites who cannot rule, are not able to accept public responsibility for their actions.

'Leader democracy', it is worth repeating, is not *the* solution, not an ideal we champion, not an attractive normative proposition we advocate. Rather, it is a type of democracy that we see emerging today in advanced societies out of the crisis of 'party democracy'. Our portrayal of this type highlights its mode of operation and its democratic credentials – but also its vulnerabilities.

Changing Democratic Representation

The picture that emerges from this analysis is that of a dynamic and changing democracy. In line with Weber's and Schumpeter's diagnoses, such democracy is always torn by tensions and contradictions and never stabilises in one form. The long-term pattern of change suggested by their comments combines a directional 'master trend' of modernisation (systematic rationalisation) with a cyclical change reflecting the tensions and vulnerabilities of each elite configuration, historical 'path dependencies' and contingencies – all three strongly influenced by the key actors: leaders and elites.

Let us cast a glance at the big picture of historically changing forms of democratic representation through the Weberian–Schumpeterian lens. Modern mass democracy was born on the national level and in an organised representative form. It developed in Western nation-states as diverse systems of coupling between the 'political society' anchored in the state apparata and party machines on the one hand, and the increasingly complex 'civil society' of diverse social interests (material and ideal) and 'social forces' on the other. The increasing social complexity, and the formation of the modern bureaucratic and interventionist state, had dramatically affected the process of mass democratisation that accompanied political modernisation. The processes of democratic representation took a 'top-down' direction in the sense of political elites dominating politically, that is actively shaping and socially formatting their constituencies of representation – a point noted by most political observers at the turn of the twentieth century. This did not make democratic representation less 'real' or less effective. On the contrary, the strongest linkages – and the most effective elite–mass couplings – were achieved by charismatic leaders and elites seeking mass electoral mandate-authorisation. A disaster struck at the beginning of the twentieth century when a series of elite failures resulted in a disastrous world war followed by worldwide economic crises. Few democracies survived this combination. The political chaos wreaked by these crises spawned autocratic leaders who brutally imposed order through suppression of opposition, elimination of competition and winding down civil liberties. They not only destroyed democratic institutions, but also gave a bad name to strong political leadership. Following the defeat of fascist autocracies in the Second World War, democracy was reconstructed in Europe in a liberal, popular, collegial, ideological and 'leader-shy' form, as 'party democracy'. It relied on party officialdom developing democratic linkages with mass public through party–voter alignment. Party leader-heads and surrounding elites actively shaped the identities and outlooks of voters by transforming them into loyal constituencies: class, regional, ethnoreligious, and so on. They did it through 'social-political formatting': convincing the supporters that they share certain interests, that they form a real community (as a class, a nationality, or a core element of the nation, etc.), and by promoting shared collective identities combined with a specific political outlook – all encapsulated in ideologically based party programmes. Most importantly, the parties and their leaders represented these socially formatted constituencies by generating confidence, party-ideological loyalty and mass consent.

This part of the argument is not new; the less known part concerns the changing forms of representation. In the early stages of democratisation, especially when political leaders emerged from mass movements, representation took a more direct and personal form – or as Cotta and Best (2007, 17) call it, 'representation by peers' in which social background characteristics and overall social and status proximity played an important role in generating public trust. With the emergence of bureaucratised party machines and state apparata, another form of representation proliferated: 'representation by professional agents/politicians' (Cotta and Best 2007, 18–19). This was the central object of Weber's and Schumpeter's study and theoretical attention. Such representation relied not so much on social proximity, as on skills and resources that justified and legitimated claims to representation. Professionalisation of roles and differentiation of political elites reflected this mode of representation. Its proliferation accompanied the transformation of parties into class and cleavage parties, then into 'mass' and 'catch-all' parties (*Volksparteien*), as well as 'cartelization' of parties into state agencies (Katz and Mair 1995) and emergence of some (initially few) 'leader parties'. The 'cartelized' parties developed strong 'machines', and their autonomous party interests – often seen as divorced from the interests of constituencies and 'national interests' (however construed) – became dominant. Interests of their staffs became identified with 'public interests'; party electoral success became the principal goal. Thus in the process of 'cartelization', many mass parties became de facto 'spoils/patronage' parties. Their predominance – and their initial successes in delivering prosperity, stability and dignity to democratised nations – marked a period of 'party democracy'.

It was the crisis of 'party democracy' that initiated a shift towards 'leader democracy'. Is this crisis reversible? Very few observers entertain such a possibility. The importance of major political parties in the electoral competition is still waning and party ranks continue to shrink. In the USA, the electoral alliances, minor parties and protest movement-propelled independents have proliferated, together with Political Action Committees (PACs) – private organisations replacing party organisations in raising money for various political causes – gaining ground. They 'represent' and fund interest groups, associations, movements, and other influence-seeking social forces. Parties are also displaced and replaced by the digital media. The 2008 presidential campaign revealed the potential of the internet to overtake parties as the main source of election funds. Digital campaigning allowed Barack Obama to collect hundreds of millions from small donors and outspend his political rivals. Modern mass media – the daily press, radio and TV, and more recently the internet – also reduce politicians' dependence on party machines in generating mass publicity and support. Gaining an endorsement from a popular press, radio jock or TV anchor is as important as attracting support of local party bosses. Similar problems plague the European mass parties, most of which continue to lose identity and members. The principal roles performed by these parties – formulating electoral platforms, selecting and grooming candidates, mobilising voters, financing and organising campaigns, uniting and disciplining politicians, directing governmental strategies, and monitoring the performance of rival parties, especially those in power – has been gradually taken over by other groups and organisations. This is accompanied by further and steady decline in party membership. Half a century ago, 1 in 8 citizens was a member of a political party. Today it close to 1 in 100. Party identification continues to wane, in line with a declining trust and loyalty. The number of independents – those claiming no party affiliation – has been growing rapidly since the 1970s together with the increasing popularity of single cause movements, civic initiatives and local activism, all typically indifferent or hostile to party 'establishments'. Split-ticket voting is more and more common, and it replaces straight party ticket voting.

As argued in Chapter 3, the new leader-democratic configuration has evolved parallel to the decline of party-centric democracy. National leaders started to circumvent parties and to couple themselves with mass constituencies in a more direct and personalised manner, less dependent on, and less mediated through, party organisations and programmes. Leaders became the main agents generating public trust and the 'confidence of the masses' by presenting an attractive image, compelling vision and promoting a course of action that won mass votes and provided them with a democratic authorisation. Such forms of 'representation through active leadership' – typically accomplished through highly mass-mediated appeals – should be distinguished from both 'representation by peers' (which persists but in a marginal form), and 'representation by professional agents' – the two forms of representation discussed by Cotta and Best (2007). For a start, it has been more direct, though mass mediated. It has also relied, from the very start, on leaders' appeal, conviction, 'charisma of rhetoric' and skilful image projection. The linkage with the mass public may have been more fragile than in the other forms, but it has been easier to build, especially with the assistance of PR machines. This 'representation through leadership' has always coexisted with other forms of representation, but it is developing into a dominant form approximating 'leader democracy'.

Contemporary 'leader democracy' appears in many variations. Perhaps the most conspicuous is the variation in leadership styles. Prominent leaders come in waves of 'leonine' leaders – tough, determined, rigid and loyal – as well as 'vulpine' leaders – intelligent, cunning, compromising and opportunistic. They also differ in their image presentation. Some leaders achieve prominence as decisive visionaries, with a strong will and clear plan of action, and they appeal to those who are anxious and long for reassurance. Others present an image that resembles 'leadership by peers' by presenting themselves as empathetic, ordinary, close to the people, easy to identify with – and therefore deserving trust and confidence. What they share is a high profile and dominant role in building the elite–mass linkages

The shift toward 'leader democracy', as noted earlier, is neither uniform, nor linear. Like all processes of political modernisation and mass democratisation, it is likely to continue in an uneven and patchy manner. Political parties are not disappearing, though their hold on executive power has been weakening and their membership continues to dwindle. Professional politicians, including party politicians (apparatchiks, party hacks, 'faceless men'), are not disappearing either, and their professional-bureaucratic recruitment through party-administrative channels is likely to remain the 'mainstream'. But with the increasing prominence of leaders, the number of top state executives who enter elites through personal patronage, as trusted followers/supporters of prominent leaders, is likely to increase. Similarly, the 'lateral' entries and executive appointments are likely to be more frequent as party-administrative channels open to more 'clientelist' forms of selection.

Does this indicate the declining 'quality' of democracy? Not really, though many observers would see it as tantamount to democratic decay. As argued above, 'leader democracy' is just a different form of democracy showing the basic democratic credentials. One may like it or despise it, but this form fulfils the minimal normative criteria of democracy – and should be recognised as 'sufficiently democratic'. More importantly, leader-democratic regimes are widely seen as success stories, in spite of intense elite circulation and some elite and leadership failures. It is not accidental that the shift toward the leader-democratic configuration also coincides with the spread of democratic values and commitments worldwide, and that the consolidation of leader-centric regimes in the most advanced and established democracies accompanies high levels of public satisfaction with 'the way democracy works'.

The Dynamics of (Leader) Democracy

While any predictions must face the Weberian warning about overpowering contingencies and the inherent unpredictability of charismatic revivals, we lean towards a cyclical view of change in democratic forms, in line with Weber's theoretical hints and the past pattern of change. The hints, as mentioned earlier, point to the dynamic forces that cause the change of democratic forms: internal tensions, social circumstances and a specific 'path dependency'. The tensions are between charisma and bureaucracy. Charismatic leaders are likely to appear periodically at the time of crises and mass anxieties. Such form of leadership is symptomatic of social disruption – and it causally contributes to rapid and often crisis-induced change (the gale 'winds of creative destruction' in Schumpeter's parlance) and the accompanying public uncertainties and anxieties. Under conditions of mass anxieties, leaders are more likely to achieve prominence than under the conditions of relative stability and 'business as usual'. When uncertainty and anxiety reign, public expectations of 'heroic' leadership grow, 'great statespersons' easily gain prominence, and charismatic authority relations are easily established. 'Leadership qualities' – innovativeness, determination, consistency, clarity of vision and a firm policy stand – take precedence over other 'political virtues'. Then, if the expectations of good leadership are not fulfilled, the rulers are condemned as 'failures', 'weaklings', 'weathervanes', or dismissed as populist opportunists – and their political ascendancy proves short. Another leadership rival/candidate may emerge, and if successful, generate another period of trust, enthusiasm and hope.

However, such leadership circulation, leadership ascendancies and failures, do not change the character of democracy. Democratic cycles are longer than leadership cycles. They end not when leaders fail, but when leadership declines in centrality, leaders lose prominence, and when the linkage between elites and the masses is established not by leaders, but another political actor. Such major changes or democratic shifts, as suggested here, accompany major social-political crises – crises of confidence – and changes in power configuration within political elite. The series of social and political crises in the 1970s led to such a major change: a crisis of confidence in party-managed 'neocorporatist' rule, and the accompanied shift in elite structure bringing leaders/reformists and their 'staffs' to prominence.

There seems to be another causal factor behind democratic cycles, namely the centrifugal/centripetal trends. The centripetal trends in power distribution seem to accompany the rise in the prominence of leaders, as if fed by a popular fear of 'power dissipation' or, more accurately, 'power misappropriation'. Democratic publics loath and fear 'power and influence exercised behind the throne', that is, by illegitimate coteries, entrenched interests, anonymous party machines, hidden mandarins or ideological cabals. Therefore the ascendancy of leaders and mass investment of public trust in leadership typically occur in response or backlash to (real or perceived) power dissipation-cum-usurpation. Prominent leaders are expected to prevent such usurpation, recover power to the 'rightful' owner, and to override the power-usurping interests. As Pareto, Weber and Schumpeter observe, there is a democratic impulse and intention behind leader-centric shifts, though such shifts may sometimes degenerate into 'autocratic' rule (Caesarism or 'despotic democracy'). The domination of officialdoms of mass parties, typically allied with the bureaucratic 'mandarinate' – both condemned in the popular ethos as 'faceless men' and 'hidden masters' – was widely seen as an usurpation, a neocorporatist distortion of democracy. It was tolerated when it worked well. But the unravelling of the neocorporatist deals in the form of 'stagflation' and the disruption brought by waves of strikes, protests and demonstrations put the proverbial nail into the coffin of 'party democracy' – and paved the way for a leader-centric backlash.

Conditions that generate high demand for and high expectation of leadership, and that propel leaders to the centre stage seldom last very long. The social and political orders stabilise, and the accompanying crises and public anxieties abate. When that happens, Weber and Schumpeter suggest, the resulting periods of stabilisation and routinisation diminish the prominence and centrality of leaders. Power decentralises and 'transactional' leaders replace prominent 'transformational' reformers. Moreover, 'leader democracy', like the preceding forms, is vulnerable to crises – in this case, to leadership failures. Such failures – the policy errors and biases that are attributed not to inadequacies of individual leaders (leader's failures) but to the elite structure (leadership failures) – may undermine 'leader democracy' and transform it from a solution into a problem. This may pave the way for different elite configurations and, possibly, an alternative 'coupling' or linkage between political elites and mass citizenry. Such variations are historically contingent and therefore hard to predict with any degree of accuracy, but they are inevitable. The Schumpeterian theory of economic development, like Weber's theory of charismatic reforms, highlights the inevitable but also contingent character of change, and it emphasises the anticipated but unpredictable appearance of leaders/innovators.

There is another hint buried in Weber's and Schumpeter's analyses. Historical developments are never one-tracked. At any point in time we encounter different power configurations that coexist – typically in different nation-states. This is due to path dependency of change, relative autonomy of states, and increasing complexity of developmental paths. 'Leader democracy' will always be one of many coexisting forms of democracy. But, as argued throughout this book, it is becoming the most common in Europe and America due to a combination of leader-centric trends and hegemonic influence of the Anglo-American 'models'. Leader-centric democracy seems better established in the presidential systems than in the parliamentary ones, and it seems more conspicuous in the most advanced liberal democracies than in the new democracies. The very fact that the most powerful and hegemonic democracy, the United States, approximates 'leader democracy' most closely makes the spread of such democracy more likely.

Thus, the conclusion should be qualified further. While the short-term future of 'leader democracy' looks bright, it should not be seen as the only form of democracy or an 'end of history'. The dynamic tensions persist, and the vulnerabilities indicate the possible sources of crises. 'Leader democracy', it needs to be stressed again, is one of many possible power and elite configurations that emerged in a 'path dependent' way from the crises of 'party democracy', as well as from the ascendancy of the mass media and cults of celebrities that accompany the spread of popular culture. However, like all preceding forms of democracy, 'leader democracy' will have its heyday – most likely stretching over a few decades – as well as its twilight.

REFERENCES

Aberbach, Joel D., Robert D. Putnam, Bert A. Rockman. 1981. *Bureaucrats and Politicians in Western Democracies*. Cambridge, MA: Harvard University Press.

Almond, Gabriel A. and Sidney Verba. 1963/1989. *The Civic Culture: Political Attitudes and Democracy in Five Nations*. London: Sage.

Archibugi, Danielle and David Held (eds). 1995. *Cosmopolitan Democracy*. Cambridge: Polity.

Arrow, Kenneth. 1951. *Social Choice and Individual Values*. New York: John Wiley & Sons.

Beck, Ulrich. 1999. *World Risk Society*. Cambridge: Polity Press.

_____. 2005. *Power in the Global Age*. Cambridge: Polity.

Beetham, David. 1974. *Max Weber and Theory of Modern Politics*. London: Routledge.

Bellamy, Christine and John Taylor. 1998. *Governing in the Information Age*. Milton Keynes: Open University Press.

Bellamy, Richard. 1991. 'Schumpeter and the Transformation of Capitalism, Liberalism and Democracy'. *Government and Opposition* 26(4): 500–19.

Bendix, Reinhardt. 1962/1977. *Max Weber. An Intellectual Portrait*. Berkeley and Los Angeles: University of California Press.

Bennett, Lance W. and Robert Entman. 2001. *Mediated Politics: Communication in the Future of Politics*. Cambridge: Cambridge University Press.

Berle, Adolf A. and Gardiner C. Means. 1932. *The Modern Corporation and Private Property*. New York: Basic Books.

Best, Heinrich. 2008. 'New Challenges, New Elites? Changes in the Recruitment and Career Patterns of European Representative Elites'. In M. Sasaki (ed.), *Elites: New Comparative Perspectives*, 77–102. Leiden and Boston: Brill.

Best, Heinrich and John Higley. 2009. 'Democratic elitism in transition'. Special issue of *Comparative Sociology*, 8(3).

_____. (eds). 2010. *Democratic Elitism: New Theoretical and Comparative Perspectives*. Leiden and Boston: Brill.

Best, Heinrich and Maurizio Cotta (eds). 2000. *Parliamentary Representatives in Europe 1848–2000*. Oxford: Oxford University Press.

Birch, Anthony H. 1964. *Representative and Responsible Government*. London: Unwin.

Blondel, Jean. 1987. *Political Leadership*. London: Sage.

_____. 2005. 'The links between Western European parties and their supporters. The role of personalisation'. Occasional Paper 16/2005, Centre for the Study of Political Change (CIRCaP), University of Siena.

Blühdorn, Ingolfur. 2006. 'billig will Ich: Post-demokratische Wende und Simulative Demokratie'. *Forschungsjournal Neue Soziale Bewegungen* 19(4): 72–83.

_____. 2009. 'Democracy beyond the Modernist Subject: Complexity and the Late-modern Reconfiguration of Legitimacy'. In Ingolfur Blühdorn (ed.), *In Search of*

Legitimacy. Policy Making in Europe and the Challenge of Societal Complexity, 17–50. Opladen and Farmington Hills, MI: Barbara Budrich.

Bobbio, Norberto. 1987. *The Future of Democracy: A Defence of the Rules of the Game*. Cambridge: Polity Press.

Bohman, James and William Rehg (eds). 1997. *Deliberative Democracy: Essays on Reason and Politics*. Cambridge, MA and London: MIT Press.

Boswell, Terry and Christopher Chase-Dunn. 2006. 'Transnational Social Movements and Democratic Socialist Parties'. In Christopher Chase-Dunn and Salvadore J. Babones (eds), *Global Social Change*, 317–36. Baltimore: Johns Hopkins University Press.

Bottomore, Tom. 1964/1993. *Elites and Society* (2nd ed.) London: Routledge.

Bowman, Karlyn. 2000. 'Polling to Campaign and Govern'. In Norman Ornstein and Thomas Mann (eds), *The Permanent Campaign and Its Future*. Washington DC: AEI.

Brittan, Samuel. 1975. 'The Economic Contradictions of Democracy'. *British Journal of Political Science* 5(2): 129–159.

Brooks, David. 2007. 'How voters vote' *New York Times*. http://topics.nytimes.com/top/opinion/editorialsandoped/oped/columnists/davidbrooks/index.html?inline=nyt-per (accessed March 2011).

Bryce, James. 1921. *Modern Democracies*. London: Macmillan.

Brzezinski, Zbigniew. 2007. *Second Chance*. New York: Basic Books.

Burnham, James. 1942. *The Managerial Revolution*. London and New York: Putnam.

Burns, James MacGregor. 1978. *Leadership*. New York: Harper & Row.

Carroll, William K. and Meindert Fennema. 2002. 'Is There a Transnational Business Community?' *International Sociology* 17(3): 393–419.

———. 2004. 'Problems in the Study of the Transnational Business Community'. *International Sociology* 19(3): 369–78.

Carty, R. Kenneth and Donald E. Blake. 1999. 'The Adoption of Membership Votes for Choosing Party Leaders: The Experience of Canadian Parties'. *Party Politics* 5: 211–24.

Chase-Dunn, Christopher. 1998. *Global Formations* (updated ed.) Lanham, MD: Rowman & Littlefield.

Chemers, Martin M. 2002. 'Cognitive, social, and emotional intelligence of transformational leadership: Efficacy and effectiveness'. In R. E. Riggio, S. E. Murphy and F. J. Pirozzolo (eds), *Multiple Intelligences and Leadership*. Mahwah, NJ: Lawrence Erlbaum Associates.

Chirot, Daniel. 1977. *Social Change in the Twentieth Century*. New York: Harcourt Brace Jovanovich.

Cho, Kisuk. 2004. 'Leadership and Collective Action'. In G. Goethals and G. Sorenson (eds), *Encyclopedia of Leadership*, 218–22. New York: Sage.

Clark, Terry and Seymour M. Lipset. 2001. *The Breakdown of Class Politics*. Baltimore: Johns Hopkins University Press.

Cockerell, Evan. 1988. *Life from Number Ten*. London: Faber & Faber.

Coleman, Stephen. 2001. 'The Online Campaign'. In Pippa Norris (ed.), *Britain Votes, 2001*, 21–43. Oxford: Oxford University Press.

Converse, Philip E. 2011. 'The Nature of Belief Systems in Mass Public', WikiSummary. http://wikisum.com/w/Converse:_The_nature_of_belief_systems_in_mass_publics (accessed 7 October 2011).

Cotta, Maurizio and Heinrich Best. 2007. *Democratic Representation in Europe*. Oxford: Oxford University Press.

Crouch, Colin. 2004. *Post-Democracy*. Cambridge: Polity Press.

_____. 2009. 'Post-Democracy'. A lecture given at the Bruno Kreisky Forum in Vienna, 5 March 2009. http://www.kreisky-forum.org/pdfs/2009/2009_03_05. pdf (accessed 1 March 2011).

Crozier, Michael, E. Freidburg and A. Goldhammer. 1980. *Actors and Systems: The Politics of Collective Action.* Chicago: University of Chicago Press.

Crozier, Michael, Samuel P. Huntington and Joji Watanuki. 1975. *The Crises of Democracy.* New York: New York University Press.

Cunningham, Frank. 2002. *Theories of Democracy: A Critical Introduction.* London: Routledge.

Dahl, Robert. 1961. *Who Governs? Democracy and Power in an American City.* New Haven, CT: Yale University Press.

_____. 1971. *Polyarchy: Participation and Opposition.* New Haven, CT and London: Yale University Press.

_____. 1989. *Democracy and Its Critics.* New Haven, CT and London: Yale University Press.

_____. 1999. 'Can International Organizations be Democratic?' In Ian Shapiro and Casiano Hacker-Cordón (eds), *Democracy's Edges,* 34–61. New York: Cambridge University Press.

_____. 2000. 'A Democratic Paradox?' *Political Science Quarterly* 15(1): 35–40.

Dahrendorf, Ralf. 1959. *Class and Class Conflict in Industrial Society.* Stanford: Stanford University Press.

_____. 1967. *Society and Democracy in Germany.* New York and London: W. W. Norton & Company.

Dalton, Russell J. 2004. *Democratic Challenges, Democratic Choices.* Oxford and New York: Oxford University Press.

Dalton, Russell J., Ian McAllister and Martin P. Wattenberg. 2000. 'The Consequences of Partisan Dealignment'. In Russell J. Dalton and Martin P. Wattenberg (eds), *Parties Without Partisans: Political Change in Advanced Industrial Democracies,* 37–63. New York: Oxford University Press.

Dalton, Russell J. and Manfred Kuechler. 1990. *Challenging the Political Order.* Oxford: Oxford University Press.

Dalton, Russell J. and Martin P. Wattenberg (eds). 2000. *Parties Without Partisans: Political Change in Advanced Industrial Democracies.* New York: Oxford University Press.

Davidson, Roei, Nathaniel Poor and Ann Williams. 2009. 'Stratification and Global Elite Theory: A Cross-cultural and Longitudinal Analysis of Public Opinion'. *International Journal of Public Opinion Research* 21(2): 165–87.

Denemark, David, Ian Ward and Clive Bean. 2007. 'Election Campaigns and Television News Coverage: The Case of the 2001 Australian Election', *Australian Journal of Political Science* 42(1): 89–109.

Dogan, Mattei (ed.) 2003. *Elite Configurations at the Apex of Power.* Leiden: Brill.

_____ (ed.) 2005. *Political Distrust and the Discrediting of Politicians.* Amsterdam: Brill.

Domhoff, William G. 1979. *The Powers That Be: Processes of Ruling Class Domination in America.* New York: Random House.

_____. 2009. *Who Rules America? Challenges to Corporate and Class Dominance.* New York: McGraw Hill.

Downs, Anthony. 1957. *An Economic Theory of Democracy.* New York: Harper & Row.

Dryzek, John S. 2000. *Deliberative Democracy and Beyond: Liberals, Critics, Contestations.* Oxford: Oxford University Press.

_____. 2006. *Deliberative Global Politics: Discourse and Democracy in a Divided World.* Cambridge: Polity Press.

Dryzek, John S., David Downes, Christian Hunold, and David Schlosberg, with Hans-Kristian Hernes. 2003. *Green States and Social Movements: Environmentalism in the United States, United Kingdom, Germany, and Norway.* Oxford: Oxford University Press.

Dryzek, John S. and Patrick Dunleavy. 2009. *Theories of the Democratic State.* Basingstoke: Palgrave Macmillan.

Dryzek, John S., Bonnie Honig, and Anne Phillips (eds). 2006. *The Oxford Handbook of Political Theory.* Oxford: Oxford University Press.

Economist. 2002. 'Present at the creation. A survey of America's world role', 29 June.

_____. 2008. 'The road to e-democracy', 15 February.

_____. 2011a. 'Taming Leviathan. A special report on the future of the state', 19 March.

_____. 2011b. 'Taking stock of the world's plutocrats. A special report on global leaders', 20 January.

Elster, Jon. 1997. 'The Market and the Forum. Three Varieties of Political Theory'. In James Bohman and William Rehg (eds), *Deliberative Democracy: Essays on Reason and Politics,* 3–34. Cambridge, MA and London: MIT Press.

_____ (ed.) 1998. *Deliberative Democracy.* Cambridge University Press.

Etzioni-Halevi, Eva. 1993. *The Elite Connection.* Cambridge: Polity.

Farrell, David M. and Ian McAllister. 2006. *The Australian Electoral System.* Sydney: University of NSW Press.

Femia, Joseph. 2001. *Against the Masses.* Oxford: Oxford University Press.

_____. 2009. 'Elites vs. the Popular Will: A False Dichotomy'. In Joseph Femia, András Körösényi and Gabriella Slomp (eds), *Political Leadership in Liberal and Democratic Theory,* 67–78. Exeter and Charlottesville, VA: Imprint Academic.

Field, G. Lowell and John Higley. 1980. *Elitism.* London: Routledge.

Finer, Samuel E. 1966. *Vilfredo Pareto: Sociological Writings.* New York: Praeger.

Fishkin, James. 1991. *Deliberative Democracy.* New Haven, CT: Yale University Press.

Fishkin, James and Peter Laslett (eds). 2003. *Debating Deliberative Democracy.* Oxford: Blackwell.

Franklin, Bob. 1997. *Newszak and News Media.* London: Arnold.

Freedom House. 2011. *Freedom in the World 2011: The Authoritarian Challenge to Democracy.* Washington DC: Freedom House.

Friedrich, Carl J. 1963. *Man and His Government: An Empirical Theory of Politics.* New York: McGraw-Hill Books.

Fukuyama, Francis. 1992. *The End of History and the Last Man.* London: Penguin.

_____. 2006. *America at the Crossroads.* New Haven, CT: Yale University Press.

Gallop, Geoff. 2007. 'Leaders the life of the party' *The Australian,* 30 May, 28.

Giddens, Anthony. 1994. *Beyond Left and Right.* Cambridge: Polity.

_____. 1998. *The Third Way.* Cambridge: Polity

Goodin, Robert. 2000. 'Democratic Deliberation Within'. *Philosophy & Public Affairs* 29(1): 79–107.

Guttsman, William L. 1958. *The British Political Elite.* London: Macgibbon & Kee.

Habermas, Jürgen. 1989. *Structural Transformation of the Public Sphere: An Inquiry into a Category of Bourgeois Society.* Cambridge, MA: MIT Press.

_____. 1990. 'Discourse ethics: Notes on a program of philosophical justification'. In Jürgen Habermas, *Moral Consciousness and Communicative Action,* 43–115. Cambridge, MA: MIT Press.

_____. 2001. *The Post-National Constellation.* Cambridge, MA: MIT Press.

Haerpfer, Christian W., Patrick Bernhagen, Ronald Inglehart, and Christian Welzel (eds). 2009. *Democratization*. Oxford: Oxford University Press.

Hay, Collin. 2007. *Why We Hate Politics*. Cambridge: Polity Press.

Hazan, Robert. 1996. 'Presidential Parliamentarism'. *Electoral Studies* 15: 21–38.

Held, David. 1995. *Democracy and the Global Order*. Cambridge: Polity Press.

_____. 1987/1996/2006. *Models of Democracy*. Cambridge: Polity Press. (1st ed. 1987, revised 2nd ed. 1996, 3rd ed. 2006.)

Helms, Ludger. 2005. *Presidents, Prime Ministers and Chancellors*. Basingstoke: Palgrave Macmillan.

Hennessy, Peter. 2000. *The Prime Minister: The Office and Its Holders Since 1945*. London: Penguin.

Hermet, Guy. 2007. *L'Hiver de la Democratie*. Paris: Armand Colin.

Higley, John and Michael Burton. 2006. *Elite Foundations of Liberal Democracy*. New York and Oxford: Rowman & Littlefield.

Higley, John, Desley Deacon and Don Smart. 1979. *Elites in Australia*. London and Sydney: Routledge.

Higley, John and Jan Pakulski. 2007. 'Elite and Leadership Change in Liberal Democracies'. *Comparative Sociology* 6(1–2): 6–26.

Higley John, Jan Pakulski and Wlodzimierz Wesolowski (eds). 1998. *Postcommunist Elites and Democracy in Eastern Europe*. Houndmills: Macmillan.

Hindmoor, Andrew. 2008. 'Policy Innovation and the Dynamics of the Party Competition: A Schumpeterian Account of British Electoral Politics, 1950–2005'. *The British Journal of Politics & International Relations* 10(3): 492–508.

Hindmoor, Andrew. 2004. *New Labour at the Centre: Constructing Political Space*. Oxford and New York: Oxford University Press.

Hobolt, Sarah Binzelt and Robert Klemmemsen. 2005. 'Responsive Government? Public Opinion and Government Policy Preferences in Britain and Denmark'. *Political Studies* 53: 379–402.

Horton, John. 2009. 'Political Leadership and Contemporary Liberal Political Theory'. In Joseph Femia, András Körösényi and Gabriella Slomp (eds), *Political Leadership in Liberal and Democratic Theory*, 11–30. Exeter and Charlottesville, VA: Imprint Academic.

Huntington, Samuel P. 1991. *The Third Wave*. Norman, OK and London: University of Oklahoma Press.

Inglehart, Ronald. 1977. *The Silent Revolution*. Princeton: Princeton University Press.

Jacobs, Lawrence R. and Robert Y. Shapiro 1994. 'Studying Substantive Democracy'. *Political Science and Politics* 27(1): 9–17.

Jones, Christopher. 2010. 'Newspaper coverage of leaders in Australian federal election campaigns 2001-10'. Paper presented at the 4th Annual Public Leadership Workshop, Hobart, 25–26 November 2010.

Judge, David. 1999. *Representation*. London and New York: Routledge.

Judt, Tony. 2005. *Postwar: A History of Europe Since 1945*. New York: Penguin.

Kagan, Robert. 2006. *Dangerous Nation: America's Place in the World from Its Earliest Days to the Dawn of the Twentieth Century*. New York: Alfred Knopf.

Kane, John and Haig Patapan. 2008. 'The Neglected Problem of Democratic leadership'. In Paul t'Hart and John Uhr (eds), *Public Leadership: Perspectives and Practices*, 25–37. Canberra: Australia National University E Press.

Kane, John, Haig Patapan and Paul t'Hart (eds). 2009. *Dispersed Democratic Leadership*. Oxford: Oxford University Press.

Kapstein, Ethan B. and Nathan Converse. 2008. 'Why democracies fail?' *Journal of Democracy* 19(4): 57–68.

Karvonen, Lauri. 2009. *The Personalisation of Politics: A Study of Parliamentary Democracies.* Colchester: ECPR Press.

Katz, Robert and Peter Mair. 1995. 'Changing Modes of Party Organization and Party Democracy'. *Party Politics* 1: 5–28.

Keane, John. 2009. *The Life and Death of Democracy.* New York: W. W. Norton.

Keller, Susan. 1962. *Beyond the Ruling Class.* New York: Random House.

Kennedy, Paul. 1987. *The Rise and Fall of the Great Powers.* New York: Vintage.

Körösényi, András. 2005. 'Political Representation in Leader Democracy'. *Government and Opposition* 40(3): 358–78.

_____. 2009a. 'Beyond the Happy Consensus about Democratic Elitism'. *Comparative Sociology* 8: 364–82.

_____. 2009b. 'Political Leadership: Classical vs. Leader Democracy'. In Joseph Femia, András Körösényi and Gabriella Slomp (eds), *Political Leadership in Liberal and Democratic Theory*, 79–100. Exeter and Charlottesville, VA: Imprint Academic.

_____. 2010. 'Stuck in Escher's staircase: Leadership, manipulation and democracy'. *Österreichische Zeitschrift für Politikwissenschaft* (ÖZP) 39: 289–302. http://www.oezp.at/pdfs/2010-3-3-Korosenyi.pdf (accessed March 2011).

Kuyper, Jonathan and Matthew Laing. 2010. 'Deliberative Democracy and the Neglected Dimension of Leadership'. Paper prepared for the 4th Annual Public Leadership Workshop, Hobart, 25–26 November 2010.

Lasswell, Harold D. and Abraham Kaplan. 1950. *Power and Society.* New Haven, CT: Yale University Press.

Lasswell, Harold D., Daniel Lerner and C. Easton Rothwell. 1952. *The Comparative Study of Elites.* Stanford CA: Stanford University Press.

Lipset, Seymour M. 1960/1981 *Political Man* (2nd ed.) London: Heineman.

Lipset Seymour M. and Stein Rokkan. 1967/2006. 'Cleavage Structure, Party Systems and Voter Alignments'. In Martin Gallagher, M. Laver, and P. Mair, *Representative Government in Modern Europe*, 268–9. New York: McGraw-Hill.

Lippmann, Walter. 1922. *Public Opinion.* New York: Free Press.

_____. 1925. *Phantom Public.* New York: Free Press.

Loasby, Brian J. 1984. 'Entrepreneurs and Organisation'. *Journal of Economic Studies* 11(2): 75–88.

Mackie, Gerry. 2009. 'Schumpeter's Leadership Democracy'. *Political Theory* 37(1): 128–53.

Mair, Peter. 1990. *The West European Party Systems.* Oxford: Oxford University Press.

Mair, Peter and Ingrid van Biezen. 2001. 'Party Membership in Twenty European Democracies'. *Party Politics* 7(1): 5–21.

Manin, Bernard. 1997. *The Principles of Representative Government.* Cambridge: Cambridge University Press.

Manin, Bernard, Adam Przeworski and Susan C. Stokes. 1999. 'Elections and Representation'. In Bernard Manin, Adam Przeworski and Susan C. Stokes (eds), *Democracy, Accountability, and Representation*, 29 –54. Cambridge: Cambridge University Press.

May, John. D. 1978. 'Defining Democracy: A Bid for Coherence and Consensus'. *Political Studies* 26(1): 1–14.

McAllister, Ian. 1996. 'Leader'. In Lawrence LeDuc, Richard G. Niemi and Pippa Norris (eds), *Comparing Democracies.* Thousand Oaks, CA: Sage.

———. 2003. 'Prime Ministers, Opposition leaders and Government Popularity in Australia' *Australian Journal of Political Science* 38(2): 259–77.

———. 2007. 'Personalisation of Politics'. In R. J. Dalton (ed.), *The Oxford Handbook of Political Behaviour*, 571–88. Oxford: Oxford University Press. http://politicsir.cass.anu.edu.au/staff/mcallister/pubs/personal.pdf (accessed January 2011).

McChesney, Robert W. 1999. *Rich Media, Poor Democracy*. New York: The New Press.

Medearis, John. 2001. *Joseph Schumpeter's Two Theories of Democracy*. Cambridge, MA: Harvard University Press.

Meyer, Thomas with Lew Hinchman. 2004. *Media Democracy: How the Media Colonize Politics*. Cambridge: Polity.

Michels, Robert. 1911/1958. *Political Parties*. Glencoe, IL: Free Press.

Mill, John Stuart. 2007. *Considerations on Representative Government*. Charleston, SC: Biblio Bazaar.

Miller, David. 1983. 'The competitive model of democracy'. In G. Duncan (ed.), *Democratic Theory and Practice*. Cambridge: Cambridge University Press: 133–55.

Mills, C. Wright. 1956. *The Power Elite*. Oxford: Oxford University Press.

Mitchell, George J. 1997. *Not For America Alone: The Triumph of Democracy and the Fall of Communism*. Washington DC: Kodansha America.

Mitzman, Arthur. 1970. *The Iron Cage*. New York: Oxford University Press.

Mommsen, Wolfgang J. 1974. *The Age of Bureaucracy: Perspectives on the Political Sociology of Max Weber*. Oxford: Oxford University Press.

Mosca, Gaetano. 1939. *The Ruling Class*. New York: McGraw-Hill.

Mughan, Anthony. 1993. 'Party leaders and presidentialism in the 1992 British election'. In David Broughton, David Denver, Pippa Norris and Colin Rallings (eds), *British Elections and Party Yearbook, 1993*. London: Harvester.

———. 2000. *Media and the Presidentialization of Parliamentary Elections*. London: Palgrave.

Nicholson, Brendan. 2010. 'The faceless men return'. *Australian*, 9 November, 7.

Nieuwbeerta, Paul. 1997. *The Democratic Class Struggle in Twenty-five Countries, 1945–1990*. Leiden: Brill.

Norris, Pippa. 1997. *Electoral Change Since 1945*. London: Sage.

——— (ed.) 1999. *Critical Citizens*. New York: Oxford University Press.

———. 2001. *Digital Divide: Civic Engagement, Information Poverty, and the Internet Worldwide*. Cambridge: Cambridge University Press.

———. 2011. *Democratic Deficit*. Cambridge: Cambridge University Press.

Norris, Pippa, John Curtice, David Sanders, Margaret Scammell and Holli A. Semetko. 1999. *On MesSAGE: Communicating the Campaign*. London: Sage.

Nye, Joseph S. 1990. *Bound to Lead: The Challenging Nature of American Power*. New York: Basic Books.

———. 2004. 'The Decline of America's Soft Power'. *Foreign Affairs* 83(3): 7–29.

Nye, Joseph S., Philip Zelikow and David King (eds). 1997. *Why People Do Not Trust Government*. Cambridge, MA: Harvard University Press.

Olson, Mancur. 1965. *The Logic of Collective Action*. Cambridge, MA: Harvard University Press.

Page, Benjamin I. and Robert Y. Shapiro. 1983. 'Effects of public opinion on policy'. *American Political Science Review* 77(1): 175–90.

Pakulski, Jan. 2007. 'Elite(s)'. In Bryan S. Turner (ed.), *The Cambridge Dictionary of Sociology*, 162–3. Cambridge: Cambridge University Press.

———. 2010. 'Leader Democracy. Weber's Theory of Mass Democratization'. Paper presented at the 4th Annual Public Leadership Workshop, Hobart, 25–26 November.

Pakulski, Jan and John Higley. 2008. 'Towards Leader Democracy?' In Paul t'Hart and John Uhr (eds), *Public Leadership: Perspectives and Practices*. Canberra: ANU E-Press. http://epress. anu.edu.au/anzsog/public_leadership/mobile_devices/ch04.html (accessed March 2011).

Pakulski, Jan, Bruce Tranter and Christopher Jones. 2011. 'Political Leaders and Voting Behaviour in Australia'. Mimeo, School of Sociology and Social Work, University of Tasmania.

Pakulski, Jan and Malcolm Waters. 1996. *The Death of Class*. London: Sage.

Paterson, Thomas. 1993. *Out of Order*. New York: Alfred Knopf.

Pareto, Vilfredo. 1916/1935. *The Mind and Society*. New York: Dover.

Parkinson, John. 2003. 'Legitimacy Problems in Deliberative Democracy'. *Political Studies* 51: 180–96.

Parry, Geraint. 1969/2005. *Political Elites* (new ed.) Colchester: ECPR Classics.

Pennings, Paul and Reuven Hazan. 2001. 'Democratizing Candidate Selection: Causes and Consequences'. *Party Politics* 7: 267–75.

Pharr, Susan and Robert Putnam (eds). 2000. *Disaffected Democracies*. Princeton: Princeton University Press.

Pitkin, Hanna. 1967. *The Concept of Representation*. Berkeley: University of California Press.

Plamenatz, John. 1973. *Democracy and Illusion*. London: Longman.

Poggi, Gianfranco. 1991. *The State: Its Nature, Development and Prospects*. Cambridge: Polity.

_____. 2001. *Forms of Power*. Cambridge: Polity.

Poguntke, Thomas and Paul Webb (eds). 2005. *The Presidentialisation of Politics in Democratic Societies*. Oxford: Oxford University Press.

Przeworski, Adam. 1998. 'Deliberation and Ideological Domination'. In J. Elster (ed.), *Deliberative Democracy*, 140–60. Cambridge: Cambridge University Press.

_____. 1999. 'Minimalist conception of democracy: A defence'. In Ian Shapiro and Casiano Hacker-Cordón (eds), *Democracy's Value*, 23–55. Cambridge: Cambridge University Press.

Putnam, Robert. 1976. *Comparative Study of Political Elites*. Englewood Cliffs, NJ: Prentice-Hall.

_____. 2000. *Bowling Alone*. New York: Simon & Schuster.

Radkau, Joachim. 2009. *Max Weber: A Biography*. Cambridge: Polity.

Rawls, John. 1971. *A Theory of Justice*. Cambridge, MA: Harvard University Press.

_____. 1993. *Political Liberalism*. New York: Columbia University Press.

Rhodes, Rod A. W. 1995. 'Introducing the Core Executive'. In Rod A. W. Rhodes and Patrick Dunleavy (eds), *Prime Minister, Cabinet and Core Executive*. London: Macmillan.

_____. 2005. 'Executives in Parliamentary Government'. In Rod A. W. Rhodes, S. A. Binder and B. A. Rockman (eds), *The Oxford Handbook of Political Institutions*, 323–44. Oxford: Oxford University Press.

Rhodes, Rod A. W. and Patrick Weller (eds). 2001. *The Changing World of Top Officials*. Buckingham: Open University Press.

Riker, H. William. 1982. *Liberalism Against Populism*. San Francisco: W. H. Freeman and Company.

_____. 1983. 'Political Theory and the Art of Heresthetics'. In Ada W. Finifter (ed.), *Political Science: The State of the Discipline*, 47–67. Washington DC: American Political Science Association.

_____. 1986. *The Art of Political Manipulation*. New Haven, CT and London: Yale University Press.

Ritzi, Claudia and Gary S. Schaal. 2010. Politische Führung in der "Postdemokratie"'. *Aus Politik und Zeitgeschichte* 2–3. http://www.bundestag.de/dasparlament/2010/02-03/Beilage/002.html (accessed 1 March 2011).

Robinson, William. 2004. *A Theory of Global Capitalism*. Baltimore: Johns Hopkins University Press.

Robinson, William and Jerry Harris. 2000. 'Towards a Global Ruling Class?' *Science and Technology* 64(1): 11–54.

Rose, Richard and E. Suleiman. 1980. *Presidents and Prime Ministers*. Washington DC: American Enterprise Institute.

Rothkopf, David. 2008. *Superclass: The Global Power Elite and the World They are Making*. New York: Farrar, Straus and Giroux.

Ruscio, Kenneth. 2004. *The Leadership Dilemma in Modern Democracy*. Cheltenham and Northampton, MA: Edward Elgar.

Sanders, Lynn M. 1997. 'Against Deliberation'. *Political Theory* 25(3): 347–76.

Santoro, Emilio. 1993. 'Democratic theory and individual autonomy: An interpretation of Schumpeter's doctrine of democracy'. *European Journal of Political Research* 23: 121–43.

Sartori, Giovanni. 1962. *Democratic Theory*. Detroit: Wayne State University Press.

_____. 1970. 'Concept Misformation in Comparative Politics'. *American Political Science Review* 64(4): 1033–53.

_____. 1981/1987. *The Theory of Democracy Revisited, Part I: The Contemporary Debate*. Chatham, NJ: Chatham House Publishers.

Sassen, Saskia. 2008. *A Sociology of Globalization*. New York and London: W. W. Norton.

Savoie, Donald J. 2007. *Court Government and the Collapse of Accountability in Canada and the United Kingdom*. Toronto: IPAC Series in Public Management and Governance.

_____. 2010. *Power, Where Is It?* Montreal and London: McGill-Queens University Press.

Saward, Michael. 2000. 'Less than meets the eye: Democratic legitimacy and deliberative democracy'. In Michael Saward, *Democratic Innovation*, 66–77. London: Routledge/ECPR.

Sawer, Marian and Barry Hindess (eds). 2004. *Us and Them: Anti-Elitism in Australia*. Perth: API Network.

Scarrow, Susan E. and Burcu Gezgor. 2010. 'Declining memberships, changing members? European political party members in a new era'. *Party Politics* 16(6): 823–43.

Schickel Richard. 2000. *Intimate Strangers: The Culture of Celebrity in America*. Chicago: Ivan R. Dee.

Schlessinger, Arthur M. 1973. *The Imperial Presidency*. Boston: Houghton Mifflin Company.

Schlosstein, Steven. 1989. *The End of the American Century*. New York: Congdon & Weed.

Schmitt, Carl. 1928. *Die Diktatur*. Berlin: Duncker & Humblot.

Schmitter, Philippe C. 2002a. 'The Future of "Real–Existing" Democracy'. European University Institute seminar paper. http://web.ceu.hu/polsci/teaching/seminarpapers/Schmitter11.pdf (accessed 1 March 2011).

_____. 2002b. 'A Sketch of What a "Post-Liberal" Democracy Might Look Like'. Unpublished manuscript, European University Institute.

Schmitter, Philippe C. and Gerhard Lehmbruch (eds). 1979. *Trends towards Corporatist Intermediation*. London and Beverly Hills: Sage.

Schmitter, Philippe C. and Alexander H. Trechsel. 2004. 'The Future of Democracy in Europe. Trends, Analyses and Reforms. A Green Paper for the Council of Europe'. Strasbourg: Council of Europe Publishing. http://www.eui.eu/Documents/DepartmentsCentres/SPS/Profiles/Schmitter/FutureOfDemocracy.pdf (accessed March 2011)

Schumpeter, Joseph. 1911/1959. *The Theory of Economic Development*. Cambridge, MA: Harvard University Press. (First English translation of 1934.)

————. 1942/1987. *Capitalism, Socialism and Democracy*. New York: Harper.

————. 1989. *Essays: On Entrepreneurs, Innovations, Business Cycles, and the Evolution of Capitalism*, ed. Richard V. Clemence. New Brunswick and London: Transaction Publishers.

Scott, John (ed.) 1990. *The Sociology of Elites*. London: Edward Elgar.

Shapiro, Ian. 2003. *The State of Democratic Theory*. Princeton: Princeton University Press.

Sklair, Leslie. 1995. *Sociology of the Global System* (2nd rev. ed.) London: Prentice Hall, Harvester Wheatsheaf.

————. 2001. *The Transnational Capitalist Class*. Oxford: Blackwell.

Skowronek, Stephen. 1997. *The Politics Presidents Make*. Cambridge, MA: Belknap.

————. 2008. *Presidential Leadership in Political Time*. Lawrence: University Press of Kansas.

Slomp, Gabriella. 2009. 'The Janus Face of Leadership: The Demands of Normality and Exception'. In Joseph Femia, András Körösényi and Gabriella Slomp (eds), *Political Leadership in Liberal and Democratic Theory*, 49–66. Exeter and Charlottesville, VA: Imprint Academic.

Stanyer, James. 2008. *Modern Political Communication*. Cambridge: Polity.

Stiglitz, Joseph. 2008. *The Three Trillion Dollar War*. New York: W. W. Norton.

Sykes, Patricia L. 2000. *Presidents and Prime Ministers*. Lawrence: University Press of Kansas.

Tarrow, Sidney G. 1994. *Power in Movement: Social Movements, Collective Action, and Politics*. Cambridge: Cambridge University Press.

t'Hart, Paul and John Uhr (eds). 2011. *How Power Changes Hands*. Basingstoke: Palgrave Macmillan.

Thompson, John B. 1995. *The Media and Modernity*. Stanford: Stanford University Press.

Thompson, David. 1999. 'Democratic theory and global society'. *Journal of Political Philosophy* 7(2): 111–25.

Tocqueville, Alexis de. 1835/1969. *Democracy in America*, vol. 1. New York: Harper.

Torcal, Mariano and Jose R. Montero. 2006. *Political Disaffection in Contemporary Democracies*. London: Routledge.

Tucker, Robert C. 1995. *Politics as Leadership*. Columbia: University of Missouri Press.

Uhr, John. 2008. 'Distributed Authority in a Democracy: The Lattice of Leadership Revisited'. In Paul t'Hart and John Uhr (eds), *Public Leadership: Perspectives and Practices*, 37–45. Canberra: ANU E-Press.

————. 2009. 'Parliamentary Oppositional Leadership'. In John Kane, Haig Patapan and Paul t'Hart (eds), *Dispersed Leadership*, 59–82. Oxford: Oxford University Press.

Useem, Michael. 1986. *The Inner Circle: Large Corporations and the Rise of Business Political Activity in the US and UK*. Princeton: Princeton University Press.

Volkens, Andrea and Hans-Dieter Klingemann. 2002. 'Parties, Ideologies, and Issues: Stability and Change in Fifteen European Party systems 1945–1998'. In Kurt Richard Luther and Ferdinand Müller-Rommel (eds), 143–67. *Political Parties in the New Europe: Political and Analytical Challenges*. Oxford: Oxford University Press.

Wallerstein, Immanuel. 1974. *The Modern World-System*. New York: Academic Press.

Wattenberg, Martin P. 1998. *The Decline of American Political Parties*. Cambridge, MA: Harvard University Press.

Weber, Max. 1919/1972. 'Politics as a Vocation'. In H. H. Gerth and C. W. Mills (eds), *From Max Weber*. New York: Oxford University Press. http://www.ne.jp/asahi/moriyuki/abukuma/weber/lecture/politics_vocation.html (accessed March 2010 – July 2011).

————. 1919/1978. 'Politics as a Vocation'. In W. G. Runciman (ed.), *Max Weber, Selections in Translation*, 212–16. Cambridge: Cambridge University Press.

_____. 1930. *The Protestant Ethic and the Spirit of Capitalism*. New York: HarperCollins.

_____. 1978. *Economy and Society*. Berkeley: University of California Press.

_____. 1994. *Political Writings*, ed. Peter Lassman and Ronald Speirs. Cambridge: Cambridge University Press.

Welsh, William. 1979. *Leaders and Elites*. New York: Holt, Rinehart and Winston.

Wolin, S. Sheldon. 2008. *Democracy Incorporated: Managed Democracy and the Specter of Inverted Totalitarianism*. Princeton and Oxford: Princeton University Press.

Zakaria, Fareed. 2008. *The Post-American World*. New York and London: W. W. Norton.

Zolo, Danilo. 1992. *Complexity and Democracy*. Cambridge: Polity Press.

INDEX

Weber, Max 4–10, 10n4, 12–13, 13n5,
    14, 15–17, 16n1, 16–21, 21n3, 22–6,
    26n8, 29–33, 30nn11–12, 31n13,
    32n14, 33nn15–17, 37, 39–40,
    47–9, 51, 55, 63, 65, 72, 74, 77–9,
    82, 84, 88, 93–5, 98, 98n14, 101,
    103–6, 103n16, 105–6nn17–18, 116,
    119, 138, 142, 149, 151–2, 154–5,
    158–60

will: democratic 95; of the governed
    14, 23; of the leader 30, 33, 94,
    96, 157; political 29, 48, 97–8,
    149; popular 3, 89, 90–2, 96–7,
    98, 105
Wilson, Harold 57, 67–8
Wilson, Woodrow 22

Xiaoping, Deng 6n2

www.ingramcontent.com/pod-product-compliance
Lightning Source LLC
Chambersburg PA
CBHW020000290326
41935CB00007B/248